Paths to Democracy

How do countries manage to establish democracy after revolution, totalitarianism or defeat in war? What can the comparative study of France, Germany and Russia tell about paths to democracy?

Rosemary H. T. O'Kane investigates paths to democracy through the comparative historical analysis of three countries – France, Germany and Russia – whose histories are intertwined in war and peace and whose paths have been broken by one or both of revolution and totalitarianism. The book is divided into five parts. Part I discusses theories and method, arguing for the importance of theories from the discipline of politics as well as those from historical sociology. Parts II, III and IV focus on the principal case studies while Part V concludes that democracy is not only achieved through a struggle against dictatorship, pluralist democracy is also achieved through a struggle against ideas, institutions and supporters of kinds of democracy that are not modern.

How and why countries become democracies remain intriguing questions. This innovative volume provides a theoretically informed comparative investigation of the links between revolutions, totalitarianism and democracy. It will appeal to those interested in the relationship between history and democracy and the implications for the understanding of democracy today.

Rosemary H. T. O'Kane is Professor of Comparative Political Theory at Keele University, UK. Her research focuses on social and political disorder, political change and the building of both legitimate and illegitimate governments.

(not in W.)

Paths to Democracy

Revolution and totalitarianism

Rosemary H. T. O'Kane

Routledge
Taylor & Francis Group

LONDON AND NEW YORK

First published 2004
by Routledge
11 New Fetter Lane, London EC4P 4EE

Simultaneously published in the USA and Canada
by Routledge
29 West 35th Street, New York, NY 10001

Routledge is an imprint of the Taylor & Francis Group

British Library Cataloguing in Publication Data
A catalogue record for this book is available from the
British Library

Library of Congress Cataloging in Publication Data
O'Kane, Rosemary H. T.
  Paths to democracy : revolution and totalitarianism / Rosemary H. T.
O'Kane.
    p. cm.
Includes bibliographical references and index.
  1. Democracy–History. 2. Revolution–History. 3.
Totalitarianism–History. I. Title
  JC421.O43 2004
  321.8'094–dc22

                                        2003020217

ISBN 0–415–31473–9 (hbk)
ISBN 0–415–31474–7 (pbk)

To Harriet

Contents

Preface

The idea for this book began with appreciation of the method of comparative historical analysis and a view that, in practice, application of the method has been strong on sociology but weak on politics, even though political phenomena, such as democracy, revolution, dictatorship and the state have featured centrally. By putting politics back in, the new insights gained might challenge existing theories and new lessons might be learnt. The idea for this book also grew from a realization that comparison over time between three cases – France, Germany and Russia – with their varied and intertwined histories, constituted almost a natural experiment for investigating general questions about democracy.

This realization that the histories of France, Germany and Russia constituted natural controls for comparative historical analysis grew not from specialism in the modern politics of these countries, or even any one of them, but from a quite opposite direction, my own research into terror regimes and revolutions. Questions about the similarities and differences between the three cases kept arising and the roughness of the paths to democracy taken by these cases was evident. The possibility that more could be learnt about democracy from the investigation of rough and broken paths to democracy than from smoother ones proved inviting and this was encouraged through another area of my research, military regimes that give way to the adoption of institutions of democracy. The attraction of investigating the development of a few democracies over centuries rather than lots over decades seemed attractive and especially so as it would mean that I would be entering unknown terrain.

For reasons explained in Chapter 1, comparative historical analysis of a small number of cases cannot be used to generate a theory of democracy. The experiment, rather, is ideal for exploring ideas and investigating hypotheses whether derived from existing theories or suggested by the process of comparison itself. In this way tentative lessons may be drawn and understanding of democracy may be furthered. In Chapters 1, 2 and 3, therefore, hypotheses are generated to guide, but not determine, investigation through comparisons for similarities and differences. These hypotheses are drawn, in Chapter 1, from works of historical sociology and, in Chapter 2, from empirical political theories, that is works of political science and political sociology. In Chapter 3, normative political theories are also considered but not as a dry academic debate about the nature of democracy. Such considerations of problems of definition and comparative historical research are covered in Chapters 1 and 2, where a working definition is proposed. In Chapter 3, rather, debates about what democracy ought to be are put within their historical context of revolution and the theorizing and practice of post-revolutionary government. In this chapter the cases of England/Britain and America serve as valuable additional controls to be used in the chapters that follow. In so far as some may wish more hypotheses had been included I plead not lack of space, though space is a problem, but that of being a human being, not value free, who arrives at present research armed with a selection of hypotheses and ideas gathered from past study and research. The advantage is that here, at least, prior positions are laid bare for anyone to see.

The claimed novelty of the approach, offered here, however, lies not in setting out the hypotheses derived from existing theories that guide the comparative analysis, even though perhaps done differently than before. Rather the claim for novelty lies in the approach to the cases as paths to democracy. History is viewed not simply as a case description of past events and social, economic, cultural and international conditions that have impressed themselves on the present such as to open or to limit possibilities. History, rather, is also viewed as something lived through, where choices are made within the setting of the time which may then independently affect the future and not only for the case in question. Each case sits within the setting made not only by its own past but also by the histories of other countries that touch on events at home. For example, ideas of democracy grown from and through events in one situation may be taken to another country and applied in another situation with a very different outcome. The expectations and pressures of other democracies may also impact on decisions made at home.

Paths to democracy are not the histories of the growth of democratic institutions. Not only may the paths be rough and broken, but the knowledge that they are paths to democracy is known only through the benefit of hindsight. The book is designed to convey this through itself being broken into parts. The three cases, France, Germany and Russia, are compared, whether as different from or similar to each other, in three situations. The first of those situations, with which Chapters 4 and 5 are concerned, is that of attempting to establish ideas of democracy after a revolution. The second, with which Chapters 6 to 8 are concerned, is the failure of democracy and the development of a totalitarian regime, the very antithesis of democracy. Understanding of democracy benefits a good deal, it is argued, from detailed consideration of what democracy is not. In Chapter 6 existing hypotheses are considered and examined through the comparative method with Italy also brought in for additional control. These chapters on totalitarian regimes draw on *Terror, Force and States* (1996) and serve not only to address the questions of when and why democracies fail but also to convey the sheer desolation and destruction, the ashes, from which democracy may arise. The third situation, covered in Chapters 9 and 10, is that of democracy as synthesis, in Russia's case a synthesis that also proves synthetic. Constructed in this way, the aim is that the inter-relationships between the cases are drawn out at critical times, the timing of each case being placed into the changing history of democracy and democracies and against the backgrounds of turmoil in which they may be set.

Tentative lessons about democracy are drawn from comparative analysis wherever possible, throughout. In the conclusion (Chapter 11), while respecting the limitations imposed by the method of comparative historical analysis and resisting the temptation of a general theory of democracy, general lessons are considered and tentatively supported or questioned. In this concluding chapter, final, though still tentative, additional lessons are also drawn. One of these is that there is no simple explanation for democracy. Another is that democracy is not only achieved through a struggle against dictatorship; pluralist democracy is achieved through a struggle against ideas, institutions and supporters of kinds of democracy that are not modern.

Acknowledgements

This book, even when pressed against other demands has been a work of enjoyment, the pleasure that comes from finding things out and discovering yet more things to learn. I have benefited from the kindness of my colleagues here at Keele, especially in directing me to invaluable sources. I also wish to thank the unknown referee of my original proposal for arguing the case for the importance of including America. Not only the right advice, it has proved a stimulation and helped me to focus more clearly on democracy. I also wish to thank Routledge for their willingness to publish the book and for their sympathetic approach. As always my thanks go to my family, Les and Harriet Rosenthal. They make it all worthwhile.

Rosemary H. T. O'Kane

Part I

Democracy

Method and theses

1 On method

Comparative historical analysis and politics

To move beyond description, the narrative of the path taken by a country to democracy, and to engage with general questions about democracy it is necessary to make comparisons. As C. Wright Mills (1970: 163) has it, 'Comparisons are required in order to understand what may be the essential conditions of whatever we are trying to understand.' As Sartori (1994a: 15) explains, 'comparisons control – they control (verify or falsify) whether generalizations hold across the cases to which they apply'. Comparing for similarity and difference against controls is the comparative method and its purpose is to judge significance. For a subject such as democracy, how precise that judgement can be is limited, in practice, by a number of problems. The most widely recognized are those neatly put by Lijphart (1971: 685): 'many variables, small number of cases'. The chances of a study of democracy escaping these problems are slim. It is, clearly, reasonable to expect paths to democracy to be complex and though in recent times democracies have grown greatly in number, established democracies remain few.

In addition to the problems of few cases and large numbers of variables the study of democracy is also constrained by conceptual logic. The extent to which general explanations can be claimed is limited both by the number of things to which the concept can apply (for example, the list of democracies) and by the capacity of the concept to drop properties and be defined not only in terms of what it is but also in terms of what it is not.[1] As Collier and Levitsky's (1997) consideration of 'democracy with adjectives' has shown, in practice the properties of democracy, rather than being pared down, tend to be heaped up to incorporate more identifying characteristics. The consequent 'conceptual stretching' (Sartori 1970) thereby allows in cases that are not democracy. Employed in statistical analysis in search of general explanations stretched concepts run the very real risk of producing messy and even misleading research.[2] It follows, therefore, that for the study of democracy it is necessary to move down Sartori's 'ladder of abstraction', away from global explanations towards more 'country-by-country' studies seeking descriptions of similarities and differences and comparing cases within an area (Sartori 1970: 1042).

In country-by-country studies the comparative method is still employed, similarities and differences are examined against controls in search of regularities and investigation of hypotheses. Country-by-country studies have the benefit that the concept of democracy employed in them is not required to have the scientific precision of an empirical universal concept. The loss is that lessons produced cannot make claims to be general explanations, theories. They remain lessons about situations favourable or unfavourable to democracy, concerned with necessary but not sufficient conditions. So long, however, as the claim for general theory is resisted, there is much to be said for studying small numbers of cases and particularly so where a comparative historical approach is adopted.

Comparative historical analysis

Skocpol (1984) has delineated three comparative historical approaches. The first is the application of a general model to one or more historical cases; the second is the use of concepts to interpret history, the 'interpretive' approach; the third is the analysis of causal regularities in history, the search for a 'pattern' of history.[3] The second approach, the 'interpretive' approach, constructs a concept to aid understanding, in the sense of how things work, independently or together, to produce effects in history. Though concerned to understand occurrences in history this approach is not directed at highlighting generalities but at bringing understanding to particularities through comparison. Both the first and the third approaches seek causal explanations. The first approach is deductive, hypotheses to be tested are deduced from a theory or model and applied to a historical case or cases. Within this category comes Lakatos's (1978) methodology of scientific research programme. The third approach is inductive; the explanation is generated from examination of the cases and alternative hypotheses are tested arising from consideration of those cases. In contrast to the interpretive approach, both the deductive and the inductive methods are concerned with sequences, that is they seek out conditions, events, situations which, logically, precede the event that they are intended to explain.

As a method of comparative historical analysis, Skocpol argues for the superiority of the third approach, the analysis of causal regularities. This inductive method, employed by Skocpol (1979) in *States and Social Revolutions*, is also the method employed by Moore (1969) in *Social Origins of Dictatorship and Democracy*. In arguing for the inductive method, Skocpol (1984: 365–8) stresses the problems of the other two methods: the interpretive method frustratingly stops short of investigating causal regularities; the deductive approach requires the availability of a model that has not been generated from the cases to which it is to be applied. If available, the application of such a pre-existing model may lead the researcher to overlook important contrary evidence and to squash evidence into shape to make it fit. With concentration on a few cases, cases may also be selected for their fit while other less supportive cases may be ignored. Skocpol's broad concern is that restriction to one model or theory acts like a straitjacket around the research, preventing the study of the cases opening up new ideas.

In elaboration of her preferred method, the search for causal regularities in history, Skocpol (1984) argues as follows:

> Neither the logic of a single overarching model nor the meaningful exploration of the complex particularities of each singular time and place takes priority. Instead, the investigator assumes that causal regularities – at least regularities of limited scope – may be found in history. He or she moves back and forth between aspects of historical cases and *alternative hypotheses* that may help to account for those regularities.
>
> Ideas about causal regularities may come from two or more preexisting theories that are brought into confrontation with the historical evidence. Or they may be generated more inductively from the discovery of what Arthur Stinchcombe[4] calls 'causally significant analogies between instances' during the course of a historical investigation.
>
> (Skocpol 1984: 374–5)

As Skocpol (1984: 378–9) makes clear, in this approach to comparative historical analysis J. S. Mill's methods of agreement and disagreement are applied, as outlined in his *A System of Logic*. In the method of agreement, comparisons are made between cases in the search for similarities and causal significance is ascribed to the factors that agree across the cases. In the method of disagreement, comparisons between cases are made on the basis of contrast. Differences are sought to explain why something happened in one case but not the other and it is the presence of the disagreed factor that is given causal significance.

Mill's methods, however, are open to criticism and they are particularly vulnerable to criticism when applied to a small number of cases (Lieberson 1992). The major problem is that, limited to a small number of cases, the methods are unable to examine probabilistic relationships and must assume that relationships between variables are deterministic. Yet, in the real world, most hypotheses are probabilistic, which relates to a second problem. The methods are also unsuited to revealing the interaction between variables and the assumption that each variable is independent of each other goes against the nature of hypotheses involving many variables reacting on each other.

Furthermore, such complex hypotheses are the type most usual in the study of subjects such as democracy or revolution. Single cause hypotheses, to which the methods of agreement and disagreement are suited, are rare in such research areas.[5] Because of the small number of cases, the methods of agreement and disagreement also run the risk of associations being found and given causal significance when, in fact, they are due entirely to chance (Lieberson 1992: 113).

In *A System of Logic*, first published in 1724, Mill (1967: 253) identifies not just two but 'four methods of experimental inquiry'. In addition to the method of agreement and the method of disagreement, he also identifies the 'method of residues', which is a joint method of agreement and disagreement, and the 'method of concomitant variations', which is concerned with cases where a phenomenon is inseparably present for all cases but where variations occur. Mill (ibid.: 285–91) is aware of the limitations of his methods and is particularly concerned with cases where causes are plural, where causes are not independent of each other and where the number of cases is small. It is because of his concerns that he generally recommends his joint method, the method of residues, which combines use of both the methods of agreement and disagreement. Importantly, offering all four as purely inductive methods, he accepts that deciding on what to compare may be shaped by hypotheses deduced from existing theories (laws) (ibid.: 287).

Though Mill is aware of some, at least, of the limitations of his methods, even where there are sufficient cases and hypotheses are simple the crucial problem remains that the choice of cases for the methods of agreement and disagreement will differ and the combination of the two approaches to seeking regularities may therefore produce misleading findings. As illustration, in *States and Social Revolutions*, Skocpol offers France, Russia and China as cases of 'social revolution' and also of 'bourgeois revolution' (France) and of 'communist revolution' (Russia and China). The hypothesis under consideration determines whether a case is to be used for contrast (bourgeois or communist) or compared for similarity (social revolution). Clearly, if France and China are compared as communist revolutions then it is doubtful that much will be learnt of value about communist revolutions. Less obviously, comparison of France and China as social revolutions may also mislead understanding. For example, the Communist Party and the guerrilla army played crucial roles in one of the cases (China) but not in the other (France) and as a consequence their relevance will be downplayed, even ignored, in the explanation for social revolutions.[6]

Selectivity bias, the selection of cases because they are most likely to confirm the hypothesis or support the theory being induced also presents problems (King, Keohane and Verba 1994: 128–9). This criticism has been levelled at Moore's *Social Origins* for excluding small countries: the argument is discussed below in more detail. Selection bias is especially problematic when cases chosen are only those of examples of the phenomenon to be studied (selection on the dependent variable) because, lacking variation, the controls essential for the comparative method are absent. This is a criticism levelled at Skocpol (1979) for her choice of three social revolutions, France, Russia and China. In contrast, Moore (1969) has cases not only of revolution leading to democracy (England, America and France) and of revolutions leading to communist regimes (China with Russia as a lesser control case) but also countries that avoided revolutions and had fascist regimes (Japan with Germany and Italy as lesser control cases). Skocpol modifies her dependent variable selection bias through consideration of the lesser control cases of England, Germany and Japan.

The combined methods of agreement and disagreement do not, then, escape the problem that Skocpol attributes to the deductive method of, potentially, misleading understanding through downplaying or ignoring crucial factors, while wrongly highlighting the importance of others. While it may be true that the deductive approach, in viewing everything through a preconceived theory or model, may portray the evidence in a biased light, in the inductive method it is the overarching explanation that may be concealed. In the inductive approach, the underlying conditions that cause the variables under analysis to behave as they do may never be investigated. It is this that is of greatest concern to Burawoy (1989).

In opposition to Skocpol, Burawoy (1989) has argued strongly for the advantages of the deductive method over the application of Mill's inductive methods employed in the search for causal patterns in history. More specifically, Burawoy makes a detailed case for the superiority of the methodology of scientific research programme, as proposed by Lakatos (1978). The methodology involves not simply the application of a theory but incorporates the dynamic of developing new adaptations to the theory in 'a progressive defense of the hard core (theory)' that 'takes the form of an expanding belt of theories that increase the corroborated empirical content and solve successive puzzles' (Burawoy 1989: 761). New hypotheses may be developed, but they remain adaptations of the core theory; cases are not used for refutation of the theory but, through appreciation of its shortcomings, for its strengthening and refinement.

Burawoy demonstrates and defends his position through comparison of Skocpol's *States and Social Revolutions*, as an example of the inductive approach, with Trotsky's application of Marx's theory in the analysis of the Russian Revolution, as an example of the deductive research programme approach. Burawoy (1989: 762) argues, first, that the methodology of research programme has the greater chance of expanding our knowledge because, in moving beyond simply accounting for what happened to producing new lessons, it has the capacity for generating predictions that may, in some instances, be later corroborated. Second, Burawoy (ibid.: 769–70) argues that while the application of Mill's logic rules out the possibility that one case (of revolution) affects another, a research programme can build in, as he puts it, 'historical emulation, borrowings or breakthroughs' (ibid.: 770). These are exactly the kinds of complexities for which the methods of agreement and disagreement are poorly designed.

In sum, Burawoy's argument is that, on balance, it is the application of a general theory to a historical case or cases that is the more scientific approach than is the search for regularities through the application of Mill's system of logic. A research programme seeks out problem cases and engages in problem-solving and stresses falsification and prediction over verification. Furthermore, Burawoy (1989: 777–8) contends that, in practice, Skocpol succeeds in producing a stimulating new idea on the causes of revolutions not because she slavishly follows Mill's inductive approach but because she drops the application of his methods at crucial points and introduces hypotheses derived from existing theories (Moore's and Marx's) along with insights brought to the analysis through her own experiences of the present. As explained above, however, the inductive method as proposed by Skocpol and explicit in her statement that 'ideas about causal regularities may come from two or more preexisting theories that are brought into confrontation with the historical evidence' (Skocpol 1984: 374–5), does not rule out pre-existing theoretical hypotheses. As also explained, in allowing that ideas about causal regularities may come not only from the cases but also from pre-existing theories, Mill's 'laws', Skocpol is not deviating from Mill.

Generating hypotheses

The importance of hypotheses deduced from pre-existing theories is common to both Burawoy's and Skocpol's approaches. The difference between their methods is not simply that the former is structured through the application of one core theory while the latter involves hypotheses deduced from several models or theories together with hypotheses induced from the cases. Burawoy's defence of Trotsky's approach lies also in its value for practice. Trotsky wanted revolution of a particular kind, one that produced a communist society, and his exploration of the Russian case through Marx's theory, focusing on anomalies, produced hypotheses about future practice. In this lies an important lesson about the kinds of hypotheses that need to be investigated in a comparative historical study of democracy. Just as Trotsky wanted Marx's theory to come true and so applied Marx's theory analytically to Russia not simply to gain deeper theoretical understanding of revolution but also to draw practical lessons for making revolution, so those involved in making democracy want it to happen.

Their whole purpose is to devise schemes, structures, means, procedures and constitutions in order to make democracy a reality.

In seeking to understand how and why paths have been taken to democracy and how and why democracies have adopted their particular form, it is necessary to consider not only social scientific hypotheses concerned with the underlying conditions of democracy. It is also necessary to include consideration of the fact that the actors were trying to create democracy and that their ideas and decisions were likely to impact on the choices made about political institutions and procedures. It follows that ideas about democracy may, for example, be affected by the works of political philosophers being discussed at the time when the new political system is being set up[7] or by ideas being debated about the attractions or otherwise of earlier or contemporary democracies elsewhere. It follows also that the constitutional design chosen and the ideas behind its choice need to be considered in analysis.

The idea that the ideas and practicalities of democracy debated at the time at which the institutions and processes of democracy are chosen may have significant and independent effects on political outcomes raises questions not only about the importance of actors and ideas but also about the nature of history as explanation. History is not a narrative from which social scientists glean evidence to be employed as data for the testing of hypotheses. There is not one history but many approaches to a particular phenomenon or era. There is social history, economic history, political history, the history of ideas, international history and so on. Added to this, there is the difficulty of knowing when historical explanation is appropriate. As C. Wright Mills has it:

> The relevance of history, in short, is itself subject to the principle of historical specificity. Everything, to be sure, may be said always to have 'come out of the past', but the meaning of that phrase – 'to come out of the past' – is what is at issue. Sometimes there are quite new things in the world, which is to say that 'history' does and 'history' does not 'repeat itself'.
>
> (Mills 1970: 173)

Such an argument about democracy is made by Bermeo (1992), theorizing on democratization. Rather than the beliefs and behaviours of the past being viewed as a source of continuity, a view common in political cultural explanations, Bermeo stresses that sometimes experiences of regimes can lead to a severance from old ways of thinking and doing:

> Old regimes can be the sort of nightmare that is simply so horrifying that it never leaves our consciousness. These old regimes are not a

source of continuity but of discontinuity. They give rise to the feelings 'Nunca Mas!' – 'Never Again!' They are the lessons learned and the past mistakes to be avoided.

(Bermeo 1992: 281)

It follows that not only the experience of dictatorship but also episodes of violence or, simply, of prolonged instability may have this effect of discontinuity. While paths to democracy may not be understandable in separation from historical experiences, it does not follow that the past necessarily provides a direct link, whether politically, socially, economically or culturally, with the present. Rejection of the past may be more important. In the balance of explanation for the politics of today, the present, therefore, may weigh far more heavily than the past. Indeed, that historical analysis is important is itself a hypothesis and its importance has been challenged.

Femia (1972) has specifically challenged the importance of historical explanation to democracy in respect of Moore's *Social Origins*, arguing as follows:

The notion of necessity in historical causation, always questionable, becomes less tenable in direct proportion to the time span involved. If the allegedly necessary event had not taken place, certain long-run consequences caused by it might still have come about by other means at other times. No one can really say what the future configurations of men, ideas, and events would have been. Insofar as social development is affected by combinations of these factors, it becomes unpredictable.

(Femia 1972: 37)

Femia's reference to 'men' which shows no intimations of the sexual revolution in the process of having significant effects at the time, including on the use of language, illustrates the problem of prediction, which he rightly highlights. Nevertheless, Femia's criticism of Moore in respect of necessity and historical causation is open to question. More detailed consideration of Moore's *Social Origins*, particularly in respect of his arguments about democracy, proves valuable in highlighting both the benefits and the potential pitfalls of comparative history and also in suggesting the way to proceed in this new study of paths to democracy.

Moore: democracy and alternative outcomes

To claim something to be necessary for an outcome is not to predict that the outcome will happen. Necessary is not the same as sufficient. Moore's argument in *Social Origins* is that for bourgeois liberal democracy to become a possibility the non-commercializing landlords (and monarch) had to be ousted from power in violent revolution and the bourgeoisie had to be installed in power. Taking the case of France, he argues that, in practice, the only way this democratic route could be achieved was through the revolution of 1789. For Moore, as for Marx, revolution was necessary in order that the landlords and king representing the old feudal order should be defeated and a new order put in place, which supported the interests of the bourgeoisie. Though for Moore the term 'bourgeoisie' refers not narrowly to the owners of capital, as for Marx, but, more broadly, to town-dwellers of all kinds and especially to those interested in new methods of production, commercialization. Also in contrast with the Marxist pattern of class conflict, for Moore it is alliances between classes (the town-dwellers together with the commercial farmers against the uncommercializing landowners, the lords) which are crucial for the path to democracy.

Moore also differs from Marx in that the democracy with which he is concerned is not Marx's 'bourgeois democracy' which serves only the interests of the owners of capital but the kind of representative democracy which seeks to serve and protect the interests of all. In Moore's view:

> Key elements in the liberal and bourgeois order of society are the right to vote, representation in a legislature that makes the laws and hence is more than a rubber stamp for the executive, an objective system of law that at least in theory confers no special privileges on account of birth or inherited status, security for the rights of property and the elimination of barriers inherited from the past on its use, religious toleration, freedom of speech, and the right to peaceful assembly.
>
> (Moore 1969: 429)

Again in contrast with Marx's view, Moore's arguments is not that democracy was the inevitable outcome of the French Revolution of 1789 due to a feudal mode of production being replaced by a bourgeois one. For Moore, democracy is not the only way in which the feudal epoch could end. It is crucial to Moore's argument that feudalism in Germany and Japan ended differently from the case of France. Moore's claim is that history has demonstrated three different routes taken to the modern world: the democratic, the fascist and the communist. His quest was to discover, therefore, not only why the particular one of the three routes had been taken by each country studied but also why the other paths had been avoided. To this extent, though employing an inductive comparative historical method, Moore embarked on a kind of research programme. Though there was no core theory, there was a central conviction that a focus on the nature and timing of commercialization of agriculture together with a social structural approach was the right one. General lessons were derived through comparative analysis of the case studies but each of the detailed cases were developed through critical appraisal of alternative hypotheses, including non social structural ones, with his social structural analysis thereby developed, strengthened and refined.

Moore views communist revolutions as twentieth-century phenomena, occurring in countries where the lords had failed to commercialize and where, therefore, the bourgeoisie were too weak to lead a revolution. In the nineteenth century (and also the previous two centuries, to include the English Civil War), he argues that the democratic route vied with the fascist (or 'reactionary', or 'conservative') route. In the American Civil War, the reactionary route was avoided because the North Western farmers aligned with the Northern industrialists and not with the Southern plantation owners. The Southern plantation owners are viewed as equivalent to the non-commercializing landowners, the lords, in England and France. On the fascist route, revolutionary overthrow is avoided and 'revolution from above' engineered with the bourgeoisie allying with rather than against the monarch.

In the case of the French Revolution, Moore makes a strong argument that France came close to taking the reactionary route, an argument which he uses to good effect in explaining the extreme violence of the case. In his analysis, because the revolution succeeded in overthrowing the king and with him the old order supported by those landlords opposed to commercialization, and because the new order was won in the interests of the commercializing landlords and urban-dwellers, the way was opened for liberal democracy to develop in France. Japan and Germany, Moore argues, took the militarist, reactionary path to fascism; there the bourgeoisie aligned with, not against, the monarch. In Russia and China, lacking the commercialization that would lead to the development of a sizeable bourgeoisie and, so, retaining a large peasantry into the twentieth century, peasant revolution led to communism.

As is to be expected for such a wide-ranging and challenging theory Moore's thesis has provoked much debate and criticism, particularly in respect of the relationship between causes and outcomes. For example, Black (1967: 1338) pointed out straightaway that the reactionary route did not 'culminate' in fascist dictatorship. Both West Germany and Japan turned to democracy from 1945 and, oddly little mentioned in criticisms made at the time, East Germany became communist. As we now know, following the events of 1989 and 1991, communism proved permanent in neither East Germany nor Russia. Looking back, the deduction for the longer term lesson seems to be that paths to the modern world, however twisted and contorted they may be, are likely to turn out to be paths to democracy.

Also on 'outcome', Lowenthal (1968), making both general and specific claims for the importance of the role of ideas in history, questions the sense in which liberalism and parliamentary democracy could be said to follow naturally from Moore's class structural analysis of England, France and America. The ideas of liberalism, he stresses, are concerned with Lockean principles about the rights of the citizen to own property, to representation if paying taxes, to religious toleration and freedom of speech. Lowenthal points out that the Civil War which Moore views as critical for the path taken by England is conceived by Moore only in terms of its relevance to what will 'eventually' happen.[8] Accepting that the Puritan Revolution did not immediately install the bourgeoisie in power, Moore (1969: 19) argues that 'the outcome of the struggle was an enormous if still incomplete victory for an alliance between parliamentary democracy and capitalism'. His emphasis is on the ending of the divine right of kings, signalled in England by the execution of King Charles I. Moore's contention is that without the king's execution the development of constitutional monarchy after the Interregnum would not have been possible.

Recognizing that Moore's interest is not simply why something – democracy – happened but also why something else – dictatorship – did not, Smith (1983) also expresses concern about the nature of 'outcome'. We know parliamentary democracy to be the outcome in modern France but Smith asks whether, given the wartime Vichy Republic, had Germany not been defeated in the Second World War we would be explaining France in terms of its taking the reactionary path to the modern world. Similarly, with the benefit of hindsight we can now ask whether Moore would have arrived at a different theory, that is one which highlights different variables, if the 'outcome' of the route taken by Russia had been democracy.

These counterfactual examples of Vichy France and non-communist Russia today serve as reminders that, as discussed above, a major problem for comparative historical analysis as the search for regularities is that the generalizations produced are likely to fit only the cases included in the study at the time and therefore to lack predictive power. Had Moore been writing in the early 1940s when French politics was reactionary and not democratic, in contrast to France in the 1960s when he was actually writing, then either the theory itself would have been different or France would have been dropped as a case. From the German occupation of 1940 France would have ceased to fulfil the requirement of being included as a case, for along with the small countries omitted by Moore, politics in France from 1940 to 1944, was characterized by 'the spread and reception of institutions that have been hammered out elsewhere' (Moore 1969: x). Had Moore been writing later, say in 1992, given that on his analysis the 'outcomes' in Japan, Germany and Italy were eventually democracy (following military defeat, in 1945) then knowledge of the end of communism in Russia might, similarly, have led Moore to add another variable.

Consideration of these counterfactual examples highlights the process of theory building when comparative analysis moves beyond the search for regularities. Had the Vichy Republic become permanent, it would not necessarily follow that the theory itself would have needed to be changed. The clearest comparative lesson to be drawn would be that where foreign invasion results in the permanent imposition of a new political system it would be pointless to examine the defeated political system for causal links with the imposed one. Essentially, of course, this is Moore's justification for excluding countries for which political institutions 'have been hammered out elsewhere', cases where 'the decisive causes of their politics lie outside their own boundaries' (Moore 1969: x). Implicitly, therefore, Moore accepts the importance of external factors in shaping political outcomes in some cases, but for the cases that he chooses to include it is internal factors which are stressed. This, however, illustrates a further problem of the method employed. By explicitly comparing only for factors internal to a political system and selecting cases specifically to highlight the importance of internal factors, Moore introduces a selectivity bias and it is not surprising that the accusation will be raised that important external factors are missed.

Skocpol and international factors

The challenge to the importance of the internal factors stressed by Moore – feudal contracts between lords and peasants, the speed of commercialization of agriculture, strengths of classes and class alignments – has been raised by Skocpol (1979), who offers not simply criticism but a new theory of revolution and post-revolutionary state building. Skocpol challenges Moore's claim that social structural differences before the revolutions in France, Russia and China explain the differences in their outcomes, democracy in France and communism in Russia and China. She argues that the causes of each of these three revolutions were crucially similar (each of the three countries' agrarian bureaucracies suffering the consequences of state bankruptcy and collapse through fighting foreign wars and peasant rebellions) and that events occurring after the revolutionary overthrows made the difference to their outcomes. These crucial post-revolutionary factors she identifies, primarily, as the international factors of foreign trade and war.

Skocpol (1979) argues that state centralization, so crucial to post-revolutionary state building, developed in the mobilization for fighting the foreign wars that broke out after the outbreak of revolution in France, Russia and China. At the time of the French Revolution communism as an outcome, she argues, was not possible because the level of industrial development was inadequate for central control to be achieved over the economy. Skocpol (1979: 192–3) argues, 'A French economy consisting almost entirely of small-scale agricultural and commercial units (and some non-mechanized industrial enterprises) simply could not be directed from above by a political party.' In France in 1789, she explains, 'There were no "commanding heights" for the state to manage; and even foreign models of large-scale industry were entirely lacking at that point of world history' (ibid.: 193). So France developed what Skocpol (ibid.: 162) terms a 'professional-bureaucratic state' with 'national markets and private property' while Russia with its 'party of the proletariat', 'ideological self-justification' and the 'realistic organizational basis' of 'large-scale, modern industries' developed in the twentieth century, as did China, a 'development-oriented party-state'.

Concerned with post-revolutionary state building, Skocpol does not go on to develop the links between capitalism and the longer term development of democracy in France. Clearly, however, the link between the presence of a free market, private property and the absence of a single (ideological) party system bent on development is implicit. These are common themes for democracy. There are two additional common themes, however, which are noticeable for their absence from Skocpol's argument. One is the claim for the importance of the bourgeoisie, the class theme crucial to Moore and Marx. The other is the importance of ideas other than those relating to profit and property rights, such as the rights to representation if paying taxes, to religious toleration and to freedom of expression; that is, to the Lockean principles highlighted by Lowenthal (1968) in criticism of Moore, as noted above.

There is also a further theme absent from Skocpol's *States and Social Revolutions*, a political system structured positively for competing political parties. This is important because the simple negative absence of a single party includes a political system without political parties at all and such was the case in France after the revolution.[9] As will be shown in Chapter 4, there was no easy jump from 1789 to modern democracy in France. Clearly, however, the lesson stands that in investigation of democracy hypotheses about external factors, such as war and interaction between countries in respect of both trade and philosophical ideas, need to be considered along with hypotheses concerned with internal factors such as classes, economy, parties and political ideas.

Democracies and controls

As the above discussion has shown, the notion of 'democracy' is conceived differently by different theorists. Just taking the examples so far, there is the bourgeois democracy of Marx, structured to reflect and benefit the interests of the owners of capital in which protection of private property is crucial. There is liberal democracy, linked to the liberalism of Locke, which is based on the rights of the individual; and there is the democracy of Moore, which combines Lockean principles with Marx's concern for social equality while also stressing the universal right to vote. And these by no means exhaust the list of 'democracies'. There is, for example, also social democracy, to which social and economic welfare is intrinsic. Leaving aside whether any one of these conceptions is to be preferred, a discussion which will be left to Chapter 2, the point here is that in seeking explanations or understanding for each of these conceptions of democracy, investigation would be directed to different factors. For Marx and Moore a revolution to overthrow the old privileged order would be essential. For liberal democracy, based on individual rights, investigation would concentrate, rather, on things such as the enactment of laws and the writing of a constitution.

Moore's view of democracy as bourgeois-liberal democracy points him to the necessity of revolution and also directs his attention to social classes. In pursuit of good comparative method, he not only examines cases where the alternative reactionary and communist routes were taken but also investigates India where democracy developed but revolution was avoided. Moore's solution to the conundrum of India is to predict (on the basis, among other things, of so many peasants in society) that India may take a route to the modern world that is different from those taken by the other cases. An obvious deduction to draw, one rejected by Moore, is that experience of British colonialism played a significant part in developing modern democratic political structures in India.[10] As Smith (1983: 105) argues, 'Moore's crucial omission is his failure to pay more attention to the consequences for India's political institutions of the ideological assumptions and related practices transmitted from the British colonial rulers to the native Indian intelligentsia'. If it is the case that the influence of British colonialism was so strong on India's choice of democracy, an example therefore of democracy being 'hammered out elsewhere', then it becomes inappropriate to seek explanation for Indian democratic institutions in terms of internal factors such as social structures and levels of commercialization. It is an observation that may also be relevant to the case of America, once the thirteen colonies of Britain. Importantly, however, even if colonialism has played a significant part, Moore's social structural explanation may, nevertheless, remain highly appropriate for explaining where and why political structures, once introduced, take hold and survive.

Moore's problem in satisfying his critics lies in his failure to include the necessary cases as controls. He may not have wished to concern himself with 'the spread and reception of institutions that have been hammered out elsewhere' (Moore 1969: x) but in including the case of India, once a colony of Britain, as a democracy, it becomes crucial for his argument to prove that Indian democracy had not been 'hammered out elsewhere'. To do this it is not sufficient to demonstrate the value of his preferred explanation, it is necessary to seek out critical controls. The case of China, though also in Asia, is inadequate for Moore's purpose. He also needs a case which, like India, was once a British colony but which, unlike

India, did not sustain political democracy. For example, comparison between India and Pakistan, with the history of the two countries shared for so long, holds potential for developing understanding of India's democracy. In contradiction of Moore's social structural argument, however, comparison for difference between these two cases clearly invites consideration of religion and related cultural ideas.

Religion and cultural ideas are not the only variables that Moore has been accused of neglecting. For example, Femia (1972: 40) argues, 'No theory purporting to understand democracy can neglect the world-wide diffusion of techniques and ideas which has resulted from rapidly improving communications, cultural exchanges, imperialism, expanding trade, neo-colonialism and supra-national organization.' Nevertheless, to argue that additional factors should be considered in analysis is not the same as proof that they are important in explanation of democracy in either the particular or the general case. They are testable hypotheses, no more and no less than that; they may be disproved or, more probably, may run into the problems of too many variables and too few cases. This is exactly why Sartori (1970: 1035) stresses the need for inclusion of 'as many cases as possible' in the 'systematic testing' of 'hypotheses, generalization and laws of the "if–then" type' in the search for general explanation. When cases are few, it is essential that Ockham's razor be applied to any explanation offered, otherwise we end up with what Moore (1969: 135) terms 'intellectual chaos', the failure to investigate the nature and significance of the relationships between explanatory factors.

Femia (1972: 40) then asks, 'In an increasingly interdependent world, might not the "preconditions" of liberal democracy change?' Again, the answer is not self-evident. If democracy once institutionalized is later adopted as a form elsewhere, the origins of democracy remain the same. Rather, as discussion of India above has suggested, for cases where democracy is adopted as a practising political form the line of enquiry should be concerned with the conditions which enable that adoption to be successful rather than fail.

Meaningful comparison

This contrast between independently developed democracy and democracy essentially adopted from elsewhere highlights the need to make only meaningful comparisons. The requirement for meaningful comparisons relates to the issue, discussed above, of the limitations imposed by conceptual logic. To consider these two types of democracy, for brevity 'natural' and 'adopted', as the same and then to compare factors, whether in respect of social structural or economic variables, ideas, international factors or whatever, would be likely to produce findings which rather than enhancing understanding could mislead. For example, the two types, 'natural' and 'adopted', compared for similarity would be likely to conceal the relevance of both structural difference and colonialism because the former could apply only to 'natural' democracies, the latter only to 'adopted' democracies. Contrasted for difference, however, the relevance of time and the effects of the earlier case on the latter might be revealed with the relevance highlighted, perhaps, of differences in social structural factors between the natural and adopted democracies with the presence or absence of colonialism also relevant for the adopted ones. This highlights that comparative historical analysis must not concentrate independently on each case but recognize the interdependence of histories and the relevance of the sequence of events that this implies. Most obviously the arrival of democracy in one place before another and the effect this may have on a later case, indeed in a chain of reactions, needs to be built into the analysis.

The issue of meaningful comparisons relates to Sartori's concerns with 'conceptual stretching'. Sartori (1991: 247) illustrates the problem of conceptual stretching with the example of the 'cat-dog'. Both are mammals (just as natural and adopted democracies are both democracies) but if cats and dogs are pooled together as the conceptually stretched (and non-existent) cat-dog, hypotheses about meowing and barking will both be rejected, each in turn misleading our understanding of real dogs and real cats. Similarly, the pooling together of both natural and adopted democracy will not constitute 'democracy' but a conceptually stretched, non-existent variety of political system, as impossible as the cat-dog – a natural democracy developed from within but at the same time a political system adopted from without. This is not to rule out that democracy may be constructed in practice on past experiences in combination with present impositions but it does mean that origins should not be confused with choices.

Moore's concept of democracy fits with the requirements of conceptual logic for global generalization in so far as it is defined through the logic of negation: democracy is not dictatorship of either the fascist or the communist kind. Conceptually, this is a strength in Moore's analysis but his capacity to produce generalizations is limited by the inclusion of insufficient cases to justify even the tentative level of general explanation to which he aspires.

Fertile cases

Concerned with the origins of democracy and dictatorship in both their reactionary and communist forms, Moore draws wide comparisons: democracies in England, France, America and India; Japan and China the two full case studies of fascist and communist dictatorships, respectively. In his concluding section Germany and Italy are referred to for comparison with Japan for the fascist route and Russia with China for the communist route. These are global comparisons. In adopting the comparative pattern of hypothesis testing and then choosing the particular cases for comparison, Moore is pushed, whether intentionally or not, towards the testing of predominantly Marxist hypotheses. Before Moore, it was Marx and Engels who compared the western feudal and capitalist with the Asiatic mode of production, identified Japan as different from other Asian countries in being feudal not Asiatic, stressed class structures, emphasized revolution and was concerned with (bourgeois) democracy and communism (see Melotti 1977). Had Moore's interests been more narrowly democracy and had he focused more directly on European history and compared, say, France (and England) with Germany (and Italy) and Russia, the area restriction could have been liberating in inviting a wider set of hypotheses.

Walton (1992) brings the relationship between cases and hypotheses sharply into focus:

> Cases come wrapped in theories. They are cases because they embody causal processes operating in microcosm. ... In the logic of research we endeavour to find fertile cases, measure their fundamental aspects, demonstrate causal connections among those elements, and suggest something about the potential generality of the results. ... Cases are always hypotheses.
>
> (Walton 1992: 122)

Critical consideration of Moore on democracy has pointed to three such 'fertile cases'. Democracy for Moore is western democracy and it is in Europe, North America and the antipodes that the oldest continue to thrive. Long-lived democracies provide the richest soil for comparative historical analysis of democracy because the heritage of western history, including the history of ideas, wraps the cases in theory and provides, in effect, a set of controls. The advantage of concentrating on western democracies is also that the history of the West has been shaken by a number of far-reaching historical events. Most strikingly, these are: the French Revolution; the First World War; the Bolshevik Revolution; totalitarianism in Germany and the Soviet Union; the Second World War; the division of Europe between East and West; and the fall of communism in Eastern Europe.[11] Of the countries central to these events, three stand out as particularly fertile cases – France, Germany and Russia. For comparative analysis their importance lies not simply in their prominent historical roles but in the very changing and contrasting nature of their political systems, which offer such rich soil for testing hypotheses through comparison for difference and similarity against controls. In essence, for political science, these cases constitute natural sets of controls, which enable the problem of selection on the dependent variable to be avoided and provide, in their paths to democracy, a large number of cases and sets of hypotheses and theories of the 'if–then' type.

During their histories, France, Germany and Russia were each involved in both world wars, and each compared for similarity with one of the other cases but difference from the remaining case in respect, in turn, of revolution, totalitarianism and democracy. While France and Russia underwent violent revolutions in 1789 and 1917 respectively, in Germany, between 1918 and 1920, violent revolution failed. While Russia and Germany in the 1930s and 1940s developed totalitarian regimes, in France totalitarianism was avoided. While liberal democracy failed to take hold in Russia, re-emerging as a possibility only after the collapse of communism in Eastern Europe, in France the path to democracy can be traced back for more than a century, and Germany with its split into West and East after 1945 compares at times closely with the experience of democratization and democracy in Russia and France, in turns.

In making claims for the particular value of drawing comparisons between France, Germany and Russia over time it is the claim for the richness of the variety of hypotheses represented which is being made; that they are Walton's 'fertile cases'. They come wrapped in hypotheses about democracy. Comparative historical analysis of the three cases permits investigation not only of the relationship between democracy and revolution but also into the effects of the experience of totalitarian regimes on the building or re-building of democracy and into the role played by war and the history of democracy itself in providing theories and examples for adaptation or adoption. Furthermore, these cases interrelate and invite investigation of democracy as a phenomenon within the sphere of politics, a sphere in which choices count and Mills's 'quite new things in the world' play their part and may follow from rejection of the past.

Guiding hypotheses

The aim of this study is to gain understanding of the paths taken to democracy by France, Germany and Russia with the objective of generating lessons with more general relevance on democracy and on the necessary conditions of democratic political systems. The approach to be adopted in this investigation of paths to democracy is that of comparative historical analysis; to be more precise, it is the comparative historical analysis of fertile cases, guided by hypotheses so to put politics back in. For short, it can be described as historical comparative political analysis. The comparative analysis will be structured around the three fertile cases, France, Germany and Russia, each at times similar and at other times contrasting with each other on their historical journeys through their experiences of revolution, totalitarianism and democracy – their paths to democracy. As will become clear, lesser controls, where judged appropriate in the light of theoretical and historical relevance, will also be drawn from other cases, notably Britain, America and, also, Italy.

As discussed, hypotheses derived from theories must inform investigation, but they must not restrict it; they must remain guiding hypotheses. As argued above, sometimes hypotheses suggest themselves directly through the comparison of cases in the search for regularities. Comparative analysis of history may also be restricted by the availability of evidence, sometimes prohibitively so. It is important, therefore, that hypotheses are employed as a source for stimulating investigation, working with what is available but not thereby excluding interest in the less accessible. This fits, in any case, with the acceptance that the small number of cases prevents scientific analysis of the significance of variables. In line with the discussion above of the method chosen, claims for general theory will be resisted.

Guiding hypotheses for the comparative analysis of paths to democracy have already been generated in this chapter through consideration of existing works of historical sociology, in particular, those of Moore and Skocpol. They connect democracy with revolution, with social structure and alignments between classes to include the bourgeoisie. They also relate democracy to the economy, whether in respect of commercialization of agriculture or industrialization or capitalism or international economic conditions. A relationship with foreign war is also suggested. Importantly, too, the historical sociologists draw attention to the pressures of alternatives; democracy is under threat from anti-democratic forces, whether reactionary or communist. Consideration of the criticisms of these theories has also highlighted that theoretically informed investigation should not be limited to social and economic hypotheses and that it is important to put politics back in. In particular, discussion has highlighted the roles both of political ideas and of political actors in the making of decisions about the construction of new political systems using knowledge of political systems elsewhere.

The broad claim of this study of the paths to democracy in France, Germany and Russia, its research programme if you will, is that democracy is within the sphere of politics and guidance by hypotheses from the discipline of politics must not be neglected. It is necessary, therefore, to generate guiding hypotheses from the works of both empirical and normative political theory. It is to this that Chapters 2 and 3 turn before the historical analysis of the cases in the chapters that follow; conclusions are finally drawn in Chapter 11.

2 Democracy and empirical political theory

From the present to the past

Conceptualising democracy

To be guided towards understanding of democracy through comparative analysis of paths taken to democracy it is necessary to have, at least, a clear notion of what democracy is, a working definition. As noted in Chapter 1, however, there are competing conceptions of democracy and views of what counts as democracy have also changed over time. This is not simply a matter of suffrage being first restricted to men owning property, then extended to all men and finally becoming universal with women given the vote. As will become clear as the cases unfold, past political systems have been counted as democracy where, for example, severe property restraints have been imposed on those eligible to stand for office, when votes have been indirect rather than direct, and where ballots have not been secret. The institutions and structures of democracy have varied greatly and this continues to be so today. Constitutional monarchies, presidential systems, federal systems and so on may all be kinds of democracy in practice and, in theory, democracies may be classified as 'liberal' or 'social' or 'consociational' and so on. On their paths to democracy countries may move from liberal to social, introduce federalism, remove constitutional monarchs and, of course, extend suffrage and make all kinds of significant changes to constitutions and electoral laws. Because of the changing nature of democracy in practice, and because of competing ideas on what the best kind of democracy is, historical analysis of democracy is problematic. It is no less so in political science.

One way around these problems of defining democracy, taken in political science, has been to suggest a set of minimum conditions. For example, Hewitt (1977: 456–7) who is concerned to operationalize the concept for comparison of a wide array of countries, defines democracy as having the following minimum requirements: an elected executive responsible to an elected parliament; universal manhood suffrage; and fair elections by secret ballot. For those living in western democracies today, especially females, there are obvious objections to this minimum definition.

Another way of approaching a measurable definition has been to view democracy as having gradations. As Bollen (1991: 9) argues: 'For instance, the fairness of elections is a matter of degree. Is a country with widespread fraud the same as one with minor irregularities?' He continues, 'Even ignoring the questionable practice of restricting the franchise criterion only to men, suffrage is a continuous variable. Is there no difference in the degree of political democracy if 95 per cent of men are eligible in one country versus 20 per cent in another?' Bollen (ibid.: 10) therefore proposes a measurable definition of democracy in terms of the level of 'political liberties' and 'political rights' which incorporate the ideas of freedom (such as of the press and to form parties) and fairness (of the elections and in the effectiveness and level of the 'elective nature' of the national legislature).

In turn, however, the question can be raised as to whether or not democracy can be measured as a 'matter of degree'. As Gasiorowski (1991: 119, fn 10) argues, 'distinctions of the "degree" of democracy can be made only among partial democracies and *not* among full democracies'. In other words, either something is a democracy or it is not and this, therefore, returns consideration to what counts as democracy. The debate continues over whether there is a minimum set of criteria on which all can agree and, if so, whether the criteria should, as in the example of Hewitt's definition, be a list of institutions, or, as in Bollen's, be concerned with principles.

In the practice of political science, the failure to agree on an accepted definition of democracy in combination with the wide variety of political institutions found in political systems most widely viewed as democratic has led to a burgeoning of conceptualized sub-types of democracy, Collier and Levitsky's (1997) 'democracy with adjectives'. In their work on democracy with adjectives Collier and Levitsky (1997: 433) quote from W. B. Gallie's famous *Essentially Contested Concepts* the view that democracy is '*the* appraisive political concept *par excellence*' (Gallie 1956: 184). Collier and Levitsky also note that this proliferation of democracy 'with adjectives' has occurred 'despite the efforts by leading analysts to standardize usage of the term democracy on the basis of procedural definitions in the tradition of Joseph Schumpeter and Robert A. Dahl' (1997: 431). In line with similar definitions employed in political science,[1] Collier and Levitsky choose to

> focus on a 'procedural minimum' definition of democracy that presumes fully contested elections with full suffrage and the absence of massive fraud, combined with effective guarantees of civil liberties, including freedom of speech, assembly and association.
>
> Collier and Levitsky (1997: 434)

This 'procedural minimum' definition is strikingly similar to that offered by Moore in *Social Origins*, as discussed in Chapter 1.

In seeking, as Collier and Levitsky (1997: 431) put it, to 'standardize usage of the term democracy', Schumpeter and Dahl do not proceed from the view of democracy as an 'essentially contested concept'. Schumpeter's (1952: 269) definition of democracy as 'that institutional arrangement for arriving at political decisions in which individuals acquire the power to decide by means of a competitive struggle for the people's vote' is too narrowly focused on elite competition at election time. It is a definition, highly influenced by the American and British political systems, which serves as a kind of summary of developments up to around the end of the first half of the twentieth century but which is itself now part of history. Dahl's definition of democracy, or rather 'polyarchy', however, continues to be influential and as part of a body of work on democracy it provides a good springboard for the search for guiding hypotheses on democracy from political science.

Democracy and polyarchy

It is not democracy but 'polyarchy' that Dahl defines in terms of procedural definitions. His definition is constructed through consideration of the 'institutional guarantees' which ensure citizens equal and 'unimpaired' opportunities to 'formulate' and 'signify' their preferences and have them 'weighted equally in the conduct of government' (Dahl 1971: 3). In *Polyarchy* he proposes eight of these institutional guarantees, as follows:

1   Freedom to form and join organizations
2   Freedom of expression
3   Right to vote
4   Eligibility for public office
5   Right of political leaders to compete for support and for votes
6   Alternative sources of information
7   Free and fair elections
8   Institutions for making government policies depend on votes and other expressions of preference.

(Dahl 1971: 3)

Dahl offers these eight guarantees as necessary (though not necessarily sufficient) conditions for the workings of democracy. They are later reduced to seven 'institutions of polyarchy' with guarantees 5 and 8 combined under 'elected officials' (Dahl 1989: 221). Dahl (ibid.: 222) holds the institutions of polyarchy, in various combinations, to be necessary to guarantee the democratic process, defined as the satisfaction of five

criteria: voting equality, effective participation, enlightened understanding, control of the agenda, and inclusion.

Importantly, Dahl does not simply list the institutional guarantees but
also defines polyarchy in terms of what it is not. What polyarchy is not is
a 'hegemony', a regime which lacks either 'liberalization (public
contestation)' or 'inclusiveness (participation)' or both (Dahl 1971: 7).
These 'nonpolyarchies' include totalitarian, authoritarian, despotic,
autocratic and absolutist regimes (ibid.: 9).[2] Dahl also distinguishes
polyarchy from 'near polyarchy'. He argues that the 'electoral
restrictions' in Chile (where there was a literacy restriction on voting),
Switzerland (which lacked universal female suffrage) and the United
States (where there was discriminatory exclusion of black votes in the
South until after the 1964 Civil Rights Act and by the summer of 1968
still significant lack of voter registration) were, at the time, 'special cases'
of polyarchy, lacking fully inclusive polyarchy (ibid.: 246–8). In respect of
the United States before 1964/1968 he comments in parenthesis: 'It
would not be entirely unreasonable to define polyarchy as requiring a
degree of inclusiveness greater than that met by the United States, in
which case this country would have to be classified as a near polyarchy'
(ibid.: 29). He also makes it clear that the liberal democracies of the
nineteenth century were near-polyarchies only (ibid.: 10).

The core meaning of democracy

The term 'polyarchy' is useful for steering round the problem of cases,
whether in the past or the present, which do not match ideas of what
democracy should entail. Differentiating polyarchy from democracy,
Dahl argues as follows:

> I should like to reserve the term 'democracy' for a political system
> one of the characteristics of which is the quality of being completely
> or almost completely responsive to all citizens. Whether such a
> system actually exists, has existed, or can exist need not concern us
> for the moment. Surely one can conceive a hypothetical system of this
> kind: such a conception has served as an ideal, or part of an ideal, for
> many people. As a hypothetical system, one end of a scale, or a
> limiting state of affairs, it can (like a perfect vacuum) serve as a basis
> for estimating the degree to which various systems approach this
> theoretical limit.
>
> (Dahl 1971: 2)

For Dahl democracies in practice (polyarchies) can differ in degrees, but
importantly they differ as measured against the theoretical construct of

the ideal democracy in which the polyarchical characteristics achieve the goal 'of being completely or almost completely responsive to all citizens'.

Dahl's definition of democracy is wrongly dismissed, as it mostly is by normative political theorists, as simply a list of institutional devices for he clearly and importantly emphasizes the separation between the 'institutional guarantees' (of polyarchy) and democracy as an ideal towards which these guarantees aim in their practice. Democracy as an ideal is central to normative political theory and Beetham (1999: 29) argues that the view of democracy as an essentially contestable concept, a view which he challenges, has been encouraged by, among other things, the split between normative and empirical political theory. Summarizing the perspective of normative political theory, Arblaster (1994) argues,

> At the root of all definitions of democracy, however refined or complex, lies the idea of popular power, of a situation in which power, and perhaps authority too, rests with the people.
>
> (Arblaster 1994: 9)

Similarly, Held (1996) argues,

> Democracy means a form of government in which, in contradiction to monarchies and aristocracies, the people rule.
>
> (Held 1996: 10)

As Held (1996: 1) explains, the roots of the word democracy are Greek, *demos* (people) and *kratos* (rule), though, as he also explains, the word did not enter the English language until the sixteenth century, adapted from the French. Arblaster (1994: 9), however, goes on to point out that 'Democracy is not always taken to signify only a form of government, or of choosing a government: it may be applied to a whole society.' He cites Alexis de Tocqueville's *Democracy in America*, the two parts written in 1835 and 1840 (see de Tocqueville 1862), as being 'primarily about American society, not its governmental or political system'. Held (1996: 1), too, adds, 'Democracy entails a political community in which there is some form of *political equality* among the people.' Equality is central to de Tocqueville's theory of democracy.

Rather than approaching the question of the essential meaning of democracy either in terms of the common ingredient or ingredients of all normative definitions or in terms of the word's etymology, Beetham (1999) approaches the definition of the concept in terms of its 'core principles'. He starts by considering 'the relevant sphere of democracy', which he identifies as 'the sphere of collectively binding decisions, or decisions for a collectivity' (ibid.: 4). In contrast to individual decisions and personal choices, which are not binding on others, collective decision-making is inherently political. As Beetham explains,

> A society in which there is maximum room for individual choice may be described as a free society, but is not thereby democratic which is a matter of how collective decisions are arrived at.
>
> If democracy, then, belongs to the sphere of the political, of decision-making for an association or collectivity, then a system of collective decision-making can be said to be democratic to the extent that it is subject to control by all members of the relevant association, or all those under its authority, considered as equals.
>
> (Beetham 1999: 4–5)

It follows, therefore, that the core principles of democracy are 'popular control' and 'political equality' (ibid.: 5).

Beetham's conclusions are consistent with Arblaster's and Held's general summary statements and he stresses that the two core principles of democracy apply just as much to direct democracy, possible for small groups, as to representative democracy, appropriate for large groups, arguing:

> They (the two principles) are most fully realized in small groups or associations where everyone has an equal and effective right to speak and to vote on policy in person. In larger associations, and especially at the level of a whole society, whose members have decided for reasons of time and space to entrust decisions to elected representatives, democracy is realized to the extent that they exercise control, not over the decision-making itself, but over the decision-makers who act in their place: control is mediated rather than immediate.
>
> (Beetham 1999: 5)

Both Dahl's claim for the importance of the list of institutional guarantees for representative democracy in practice (polyarchy) and his claim for the value of comparing the practice of representative democracies in terms of the capacities of their institutions actually to achieve citizens' political control over their representatives fit with the logic of Beetham's argument. The lack of universal suffrage stressed by Dahl is an indication of considerable distance from achieving Beetham's core principles of democracy.

The task for the association or collectivity will be to devise rules and construct procedures to achieve the two principles of popular control and political equality. Where the government is the collectivity, the task is at its most complex. This is so not only because the numbers of people involved will be so large, nor simply because the scope of government is so wide. The task of government as a democracy is so complex because a democratic government is one which rules through a society of associations which themselves make collective decisions, democratically. This is why the notion of 'political equality' means far more than everyone having the vote. It extends to collective decision-making in the widest political sphere, not only having the opportunity to collect together to form associations but having the will to do so, the aspect which so intrigued de Tocqueville in his study of democracy in America. Certainly, democracy, as an ideal, is more than a list of institutions but, as Dahl argues, for large collectivities those institutions are necessary if the ideal of democracy is to be guaranteed.

Democratization

Countries in the process of democratization, those moving towards polyarchy, do so, Dahl (1971) argues, through expanding participation – inclusiveness – and through increasing 'public contestation' – liberalization. It is essential that both occur because liberalization involves the introduction of the means for competition (for example, parties and elections) and inclusiveness involves increasing participation (essentially through expanding suffrage). It follows that increasing quantities of polyarchical characteristics will signify that the process of democratization is occurring if and only if both dimensions are adequately satisfied; movement along either the inclusiveness or the liberalization dimension alone will not lead to polyarchy (Dahl 1971: 6–7). He perceives democratization as consisting of first the move from hegemonic regimes and competitive oligarchies to near-polyarchies, then from near-polyarchies to full polyarchies, full polyarchies then moving further towards the ideal of democracy.

In reaching these views, Dahl considers the ways in which such moves to democratization took place in the western world in the nineteenth century through to the present. How these democratizations took place varied, both polyarchies and near-polyarchies having begun in a variety of ways. In Britain, Belgium, Denmark, Norway and Sweden, inauguration occurred through an evolutionary process (Dahl 1971: 41–2). Elsewhere in Europe, he identifies democracies as having been installed either in response to a 'collapse or revolutionary displacement' (ibid.: 42), as in France (1789–92, 1848, 1870), Germany (1919), Austria (1918), and Spain (1931), or following military conquest, as at the end of the Second World War in Austria, Germany (The Federal Republic) and Italy.

Dahl (1971: 42–3) observes that 'in the three most notable cases (of abrupt collapse or revolutionary overthrow) – the French Revolution,

Weimar Germany, and the Spanish Republic – revolution or collapse was followed by an unstable regime that soon regressed to hegemony'. The likely explanation that Dahl offers for these cases of regression to hegemony is the lack of a 'legacy of legitimacy' (ibid.: 43) in the early years following revolution or civil war. He contrasts the situation with wars of independence, where the old colonial power leaves. After revolutions and civil wars, he argues, opposition loyal to the old order remains around, as citizens. This observation that revolutions and civil wars lead to reversals of democratization to hegemony prompts Dahl to take issue with Moore's *Social Origins*, arguing as follows:

> Moore's emphasis on the vital importance of the violent revolution as a stage along the road to democracy is, I believe, misleading, particularly if it is applied to the process of inauguration. Moore stresses heavily the English Civil War, the French Revolution, and – a very doubtful case – the American Civil War.
>
> (Dahl 1971: 45, fn 8)

The problem potentially posed by those opposed to democratic institutions is very real and this is why it is so central to Moore's argument that the reactionaries, those supportive of the old order, but not of the new, are defeated. For Moore, these reactionaries are the non-commercializing landowners, who in the American case are the Southern plantation owners. If not defeated, then, indeed, in Moore's argument, not democracy but dictatorship will result. It is important, however, to appreciate that Moore classifies Germany, along with Japan, as not having had a revolution that successfully defeated the landowners, viewing Germany as having taken the 'conservative' or 'fascist' route of 'revolution from above', in which commercial classes join with the landowners rather than fighting against them. This is why the American Civil War is chosen by Moore rather than the American War of Independence. After the War of Independence, which defeated the outside colonial power, the Southern plantation owners, within the country, remained as a force of reaction sharing power.[3]

It is certainly reasonable to view the American Civil War, as Dahl does, as a 'very doubtful case', but not because it undermines Moore's general claim for the importance of violent revolution but because of the absence of lords and peasants as normally defined. Moore's case of the American Civil War, nevertheless, valuably draws attention to two important considerations. First, it offers a timely reminder about the centrality to Moore's argument of alliances between classes and the potential for reaction and not only for democracy. His argument is that had the Western farmers aligned not with the Northern industrialists but with the Southern plantation owners then America would have taken not the democratic but the reactionary route, to fascism. Secondly, and therefore, the case draws attention to the problem with American 'democracy' after the War of Independence – the continuation of slavery.

As Dahl's (1971) questioning of America as a democracy, before 1968, because of the suffrage denied to Southern African-Americans attests, he too is concerned about slavery and civil rights. For Dahl, full inclusiveness is essential to count as a polyarchy but the process of democratization begins with less than full inclusiveness, and, indeed, far from perfect liberalization. Dahl's criticism of Moore is, therefore, important. Democracy is a political form; it involves the setting up of institutions and structures. As such the existence of such institutions and structures is identifiable though they may later be destroyed (as in Dahl's example of Germany, 1919, and the setting up of the Weimar Republic) and democracy may be constructed through outside insistence and help (as in Germany in 1945). The American War of Independence, resulting as it did in an early form of presidential democracy and a republican constitution, was no less an event for democracy, therefore, than the American Civil War, the English Civil War or the French Revolution. So, too, the Weimar Republic, which was for a time a notable example of working democracy. Dahl's point, also, is that neither Britain nor France jumped straight to democracy and, in France's case 'collapses or revolutionary displacement' occurred in 1848 and 1870, with the first attempt at democracy, in 1789, collapsing in 1792. In this light, it does, indeed, seem odd that analysis is made of America in the Civil War, passing over the War of Independence and that so much attention is given to France in 1789 without continuing on to consideration of 1848 and 1870.

Developing stable polyarchy

Though not concerned with class structural analysis, Dahl (1989) shares Moore's concern with the relationship between society and democracy. Dahl's focus is on the type of society which sustains democracy and which enables that move from near-polyarchy to full polyarchy and on towards the ideal of democracy in which the system is fully responsive to all citizens. In addition to his 'institutions of polyarchy', which are inherently pluralistic, Dahl identifies a set of conditions, three positive and one negative, which he views as conducive to the development of stable polyarchy. His negative condition, which acts as an obstacle to polyarchy, is the role of a more powerful foreign country acting to prevent polyarchy (Dahl 1989: 263–4). This clearly highlights the problem that Moore recognized of needing to distinguish between countries that have control over their systems from those that do not, and which led him to concentrate on the larger countries. Dahl, like Moore, needs also to consider the possibility that the role of a foreign country, or countries, may be positive not negative, enabling not disabling democracy.

The three positive conditions that Dahl proposes for polyarchy are: 'civilian control of violent coercion'; the presence of a 'modern dynamic pluralist society' (MDP society); and beliefs in the legitimacy of polyarchy shared, most importantly, by political activists and by the wider population. In respect of 'violent coercion' being under 'civilian control', his worry is that the instruments of coercion might be used by leaders for non-democratic ends. His concern for democratic government, therefore, is that the military and police and also the civilians who control them must 'be subject to the democratic process' (Dahl 1989: 245). He links the development of civilian control over the military and police with the history of mobilization of large numbers of foot-soldiers, with Switzerland offered as a recent and particularly good example of the 'citizen militia' (ibid.: 245–6). The situation that poses the greatest threat to the chances for democracy, Dahl argues (ibid.: 247–8), is that where elite troops with heavy armaments are concentrated in a few hands.[4] This clearly fits with his view of what a polyarchy is not, a system of government through violent coercion.

Dahl's other two conditions, the MDP society and beliefs, address the nature of working democracies and serve, therefore, as gateways to debate in political science about the conditions which make democracy possible in the senses both of being prerequisites and in being involved in an interactive process of sustenance for democracy.

Economy and society

The MDP society, the 'modern dynamic pluralist society', is 'modern' in the senses that it is urban, with people having relatively high levels of wealth and education and with the economy competitive and geared to markets – capitalist. It is 'dynamic' in that it benefits from economic growth and rising standards of living. It is 'pluralist' in the sense that it has 'numerous relatively autonomous groups and organizations, particularly in the economy' (Dahl 1989: 251). Though convinced of the importance of the MDP society, Dahl offers it neither as a sufficient nor as a necessary condition for democracy. It is not a sufficient condition because there are examples of MDP societies that have not produced polyarchy, such as in Yugoslavia, South Korea and Taiwan. It is not a necessary condition because, in the past, democracy has developed in agricultural societies, as in America, Norway and Sweden, and polyarchy is also to be found today in essentially agricultural societies, such as India. For Dahl, therefore, the primary attribute of MDP society is 'that it disperses power and fosters attitudes favourable to democracy' (ibid.: 254). These are the attributes that he argues to be essential to the stability of polyarchy in the long run.

As discussed in Chapter 1, the relationship between capitalist society and (bourgeois) democracy is a theme which has its roots in Marx's work and can be traced through the works of historical sociologists, such as Moore and Skocpol. More recently, it is to be found in the work of Rueschemeyer, Huber Stephens and Stephens (1992). The stress on the importance of capitalism, or more narrowly industrialization, is also to be found in the social science literature, such as that of Lipset (1963) and Vanhanen (1997). While for most theorists it is the bourgeoisie or middle class that is credited with instituting democracy, Rueschemeyer *et al.* stress the importance of the working class rather than the bourgeois class for democracy as we know it today. Though not agreeing with his conclusions on communism, Rueschemeyer *et al.* follow Marx in stressing the role played by trade unions and workers' parties and other political and social organizations with which workers are connected. Berins Collier (1999) argues for the importance of such organizations along with others, to include bourgeois organizations.

Autonomous economic organizations, along with social and political organizations, are crucial to Dahl's pluralist society. They are also crucial to Weber who argues that in order to ensure freedom it is essential that economic organizations exist which are independent of political control.[5] Such economic organizations include firms, banks and corporations of all kinds and also trade unions, indeed any organizations which have control over their own finances. This can include all sorts of social organizations such as clubs as well as political organizations such as pressure groups and parties. These independent organizations are critical to democracy, Weber argues, because of the state bureaucracy's inherent tendency to grow.

For countering state domination, Weber offers two means, one political, the other economic. His political solution is charismatic politicians who are leaders of mass political parties competing for votes, based on universal suffrage, and in a parliament structured such that the opposition is a government-in-waiting. He contends that such politicians, who possess strength of personality and are practised in the art of oratory within parliament, are able to stand up to bureaucrats. Crucially, he also argues that, through the need to seek election, such politicians also take personal responsibility and keep policies within the realm of the possible, the important characteristics of *Sachlichkeit*. He stresses the importance of opposition as a government-in-waiting because it strengthens the capacity of government to be above the state bureaucracy rather than vice versa for bureaucrats have the advantage over elected politicians of being in permanent posts. Strong opposition, he emphasizes, also gives politicians an apprenticeship in oratory. In viewing the electorate as passive, being appealed to by politicians for support, Weber's plebiscitary democracy comes rather closer to Schumpeter's definition of democracy than to Dahl's.[6]

Weber's economic counter to the dangers of bureaucracy for democracy involves the presence of a money economy, independent entrepreneurs and independent economic organizations, in sum modern rational capitalism. The presence of independent entrepreneurs in modern rational capitalism is crucial to Weber's position. Like politicians in plebiscitary democracies these entrepreneurs, he argues, possess that same capacity for taking responsibility, that same matter-of-fact realism, that same independence of thought to counteract the stifling tedium of bureaucratic routine. Independent economic organizations, whether firms, trade unions or businesses of any kind also have their own independent bureaucracies which, again, act as a counterbalance to state bureaucracy. Crucially, he argues, a free market economy, based on competition for goods and labour with a proper banking system, ensures that the economy would be more efficiently run than a centrally planned economy ('substantive rationality' as under socialism) where bureaucracy would grow apace. In a modern capitalist system, where monetary calculations are based on real costs and real prices, Weber holds that not only would individuals, especially entrepreneurs, take responsibility for their actions but competition would ensure that jobs would be filled by the best people. Incentives for all would be brought through monetary reward and job suitability. Modern capitalist society with firms, banks, trade unions and, indeed, a whole host of social and economic and political organizations independent of the state is, in Weber's view, the lifeline of liberal democracy.[7]

Pluralism and pluralistic society

In Dahl's argument, with democracy viewed in far more active terms than Weber's, this 'pluralist' aspect of the MDP society is emphasized because the freedom of participation within these independent organizations plays such an important part in the dispersal of power and the fostering of attitudes compatible with democracy. Through the same logic with which he views pluralism as conducive to polyarchy, Dahl (1989: 254–5) argues that 'subcultural pluralism' is a poor basis for polyarchy. Subcultural pluralism exists where cleavages are reinforcing and based on ethnic, racial, linguistic, regional or religious differences. It is a society where cleavages are cross-cutting, not reinforcing, that presents the conditions conducive to stable polyarchy and the least conducive of all is just two subcultures, each with their interests reinforced to the exclusion of the other's interests. Political activists who seek to moderate intense cleavages (whether by consociational means or not), he argues, may succeed in achieving stable polyarchy but, crucially, only where the other conditions (modern and dynamic) are favourable.[8]

Dahl's distinction between pluralism (as found in MDP societies) and 'subcultural pluralism', is also made by Sartori (1976). For Sartori, however, democracy exists not in the presence of plural institutions (polyarchy), which in Dahl's view guarantees responsiveness to citizens, but in the underlying conditions which give rise to the possibility that voluntary associations (including parties) can compete with each other towards a democratic outcome. He offers two such conditions: the basic condition of the cultural beliefs in diversity and the structural condition of pluralism. In respect of the structural condition he argues as follows:

> Pluralism does not simply consist of multiple associations. These must be, in the first place, *voluntary* (not ascriptive) and, in the second place, non-exclusive, i.e., based on *multiple affiliations* – the latter being the crucial distinguishing trait of a pluralistic structuring. The presence of a large number of identifiable groups by no means testifies to the existence of pluralism but only to a developed state of articulation and/or fragmentation. Multigroup societies are 'pluralistic' if, and only if, the groups are associational (not customary or institutional) and, moreover, only where it can be found that associations have developed naturally, that they are not 'imposed'.
>
> (Sartori 1976: 18)

Societies organized, primarily, on the basis of tribe, race, region, religion and caste are not pluralistic. When societies are so organized as to restrict members of groups only to associations that reinforce outlooks and close opportunities for meeting those of different persuasions then they offer no basis for sustainable pluralistic democracy. A pluralistic society is one where social cleavages are cross-cutting, where membership of groups and associations is voluntary and affiliations are multiple and not reinforcing.

Sartori's arguments, like Dahl's, have significant bearing on the claims for the importance of civil society to democracy.

Civil society and civic community

In his study of democracy in America de Tocqueville differentiated between the political institutions of suffrage, such as elections, and the social condition of equality which combined with the capacity of people to form voluntary associations in support of their interests. The equality of American society which struck him was not a simple observation about the relative distribution and level of wealth or what today is operationalized by GNP per capita and related socio-economic indicators. For de Tocqueville, the notion of equality involved the importance of meritocracy, the equality of inheritance within families, the need for everyone to earn a living, a basic standard of education for all and, naturally, the absence of an aristocracy with the status and privilege which its presence entailed. (See de Tocqueville 1862, First Part: 47–56.) Impressed by this social condition of equality, de Tocqueville was most struck by the capacity of Americans to form voluntary associations in support of their interests:

> As soon as several of the inhabitants of the United States have taken up an opinion or a feeling which they wish to promote in the world, they look out for mutual assistance; and as soon as they have found each other out, they combine.
>
> (de Tocqueville 1862, Second Part: 117–18)

In contrast, in his analysis of the French Revolution, which was fought for both freedom and equality, de Tocqueville comments:

> When the revolution started, it would have been impossible to find, in most parts of France, even ten men used to acting in concert and defending their interests without appealing to the central power for aid.
>
> (de Tocqueville 1966: 223)

It is to this lack not simply of the existence of associations but of the capacity of people to form together to achieve their own common interests rather than looking to the central power to do something for them that he ascribes the failure of representative government, the 'irresponsible sovereign assemblies' (ibid.) and the predictable move to authoritarianism after the French Revolution. It is to this incapacity and the political centralization that followed that he attributes the chequered and uncertain path to democracy taken by France.

De Tocqueville failed, however, to draw adequate attention to slavery in America and to the lack of equality and democratic freedoms which slavery embodies. Both Dahl's and Sartori's arguments, in stressing the threat to democracy which exclusionary, ascribed or reinforced cleavages pose, offer an important correction to the claims made for the importance of civil society. In their arguments it is overlapping memberships of voluntary associations that are crucial to democracy.

In rather more recent times, Putnam (1993) has extended the idea of civil society, arguing that there is a strong association between memberships of groups, such as choral societies, clubs and so on, and what he terms 'civic community', the support of democratic government based on trust built through reciprocity and cooperation. Putnam's study is of Italy, but rather than reflecting on democracy in one country through the controls of another, as de Tocqueville does in respect of America and France, Putnam employs the comparative method through investigating similarities and differences between the regions of Italy, in his quest to explain the differences between the institutional performances of the various regional governments. Putnam's (1993: 167) analysis reveals the importance of 'social capital', which he defines as 'norms of reciprocity and networks of civic engagement', norms built on trust, proven through the benefits of working together. He argues that social capital enables the spontaneous cooperation on which efficient democracy depends. The weaker social capital is, the weaker civic community will be and the less efficient, therefore, the operation of democracy. In Putnam's view, trust, norms and networks of social organizations are crucial to thriving democracy.

Finding civic community stronger in the north than in the south of Italy and having investigated a number of possible explanations, including that of the effects of industrialization, Putnam turns to a historical explanation. In the north a strong feudal state began to diffuse power and 'associational life' began to develop. In sympathy with de Tocqueville, status is seen as unhealthy for democracy, political equality as healthy, and following consideration of the Vatican City, Putnam (1993: 103) adds, 'the civic community is a secular community'. Though Putnam (ibid.: 89) discusses cross-cutting groups, he, like de Tocqueville but unlike Dahl and Sartori, does not delve into the effects of ascriptive, exclusionary, reinforcing groups. Why the civic community is secular may relate, in some regions at least, to the effect of the Catholic Church. As both Dahl and Sartori argue, some cleavages (and religion is one of them) are more likely to undermine democracy.

In a detailed historical analysis of civil society in Germany, Berman (1997) has produced evidence which suggests a refinement of Putnam's argument, which is in line with Sartori's lesson that exclusionary associations are not a support of democracy. Though Berman finds vibrant civil societies in both Wilhelmine and Weimar Germany, German society was not integrated but fragmented. Rather than membership of clubs (choral societies, bird-watching groups, and so on) drawing diverse people together, there tended to be separate associations (for singing, ornithology, etc.) for socialists, for Catholics and also for 'bourgeois Protestants'. This situation, she argues, was exploited by the Nazis who infiltrated existing voluntary groups and were able to turn the segmented nature of German society to their advantage. Berman (1997: 427) concludes that the case of the Weimar Republic and its destruction highlights the need to interpret the likely consequences of civil society activity through consideration of political reality, to include the strength of political institutions and whether they have support and legitimacy.

She also reminds political scientists that de Tocqueville's analysis was as concerned with political associations as with the non-political, narrowly 'civil', organizations.

Democracy and beliefs

The strength of political institutions and whether they have support and legitimacy relates to Dahl's third positive condition for democracy: beliefs in the legitimacy of polyarchy. For Dahl (1989: 261), these beliefs are most important for political activists but he offers the beliefs condition only as a 'plausible hypothesis' because of the importance of the role played by the decisions of leaders in the perpetuation (and sometimes destruction) of polyarchy and also because of the inadequacy of the necessary evidence. He argues, however, that the evidence is stronger in respect of the importance of the beliefs of political activists, for the very reason that such activists have played important roles in setting up polyarchical institutions in some cases. The evidence is weaker, he concedes, in respect of the importance of wider beliefs in the political culture but he holds the view, in any case, that political culture is likely to develop from the MDP society rather than prior to it (ibid.: 260–3).

Arguments for the importance of beliefs or values are found widely in the literature on democracy. As Diamond (1994) comments,

> Prominent theories of democracy, both classical and modern, have asserted that democracy requires a distinctive set of political values and orientations from its citizens: moderation, tolerance, civility, efficacy, knowledge, participation.
>
> (Diamond 1994: 1)

In political science, such arguments are made in terms of political culture. For example, Almond and Verba (1965: 29) contend that the 'civic culture' plays a crucial role in the 'maintenance of a democratic political system'.[9] The civic culture is a participant political culture in which people not only engage in political activities but are also, as they explain, 'oriented positively to the input structures and the input process' (ibid.: 30). Whether the values of the civic culture lead to democracy or the practice of democracy leads to the development of supportive political values is open to question (Barry 1970: 89–98). Dahl's argument that political culture is likely to develop from the MDP society, rather than vice versa, weighs towards the latter. Political culture is not, in any case, a static thing. As Diamond (1994: 9) points out, political culture can be 'shaped and reshaped' by factors such as 'historical experience' and 'institutional change' and, over time, may also be affected by a variety of other developments including the effects of changes in the social and economic structures and in the international situation.

Importantly, Almond and Verba (1965: 30) argue that participant attitudes combine in the civic culture with 'such nonpolitical attitudes as trust in other people and social participation in general'. Indeed, they stress, in ways quite similar to Putnam on the civic community, 'The role of social trust and cooperativeness as a component of the civic culture cannot be overemphasized' (ibid.: 256–7). Unlike Putnam, however, in practice Almond and Verba investigate trust and cooperativeness largely in relation to the political system itself and, in contrast to Putnam's arguments about the civic community, they argue for the need for a balance between participation and deference. They conclude that 'the sense of trust in the political elite – the belief that they are not alien and extractive forces, but part of the same political community – makes citizens willing to turn power over to them' (ibid.: 357).

Inglehart (1988) has pursued Almond and Verba's theme of the importance of 'nonpolitical attitudes' and engaged in a comparative investigation of democracy and its relationship to trust in other people and feelings of satisfaction with life overall. Inglehart demonstrates that stable democracies, those which have existed since before 1900 – Belgium, Britain, the United States, Luxembourg, Canada, Ireland, the Netherlands, Norway, Australia, Switzerland, Sweden, Denmark, plus Finland (a democracy since 1918) – differ from present-day democracies, with shorter histories – Japan, Italy, Austria, West Germany, France, Greece, Portugal, Spain, Argentina, South Africa and Hungary. The first group differs from the latter, he argues, both in respect of the levels of feelings of satisfaction with life overall and also in respect of feelings of trust in other people. He discounts examples of breakdowns in democracy imposed by external factors such as Norway under Nazi occupation but counts France as having been stable only from 1958 because of the military uprising which ended the Fourth Republic. Inglehart's evidence shows that the longer the duration of democracy the higher the levels of life satisfaction and trust in others. While recognizing that the relationship between stable democracy and life satisfaction (and trust) may be a two-way process, Inglehart takes the view that political culture plays an important independent role in explaining democracy.

Inglehart's (1988: 1219) position has the advantage that the democratic political culture is not defined in terms of beliefs in democracy, as in Almond and Verba's rather circular way, but he admits that 'we do not yet have sufficient data to sort out the causal linkages between political culture, economic development, and democracy in any conclusive fashion'. He also argues for the need for 'further historical analysis', tentatively suggesting that 'the cultural component of these cross-national differences reflects the distinctive historical experience of the respective nationalities' (ibid.: 1207) and suggests the importance of childhood socialization in this.[10] His finding of marked differences in mass life satisfaction, in 1981, between countries with democracies lasting from before 1900 (plus Finland) as compared with those which became democracies after 1945, equally suggests, however, a more direct historical explanation. It would be at least as appropriate to draw special attention to the hiatus caused by the Second World War. Inglehart's assessment of France, which is crucial to the support for his view, is, in any case, controversial and confirms the need for historical analysis.[11] The need for a stronger historical perspective is further reinforced by the fact that the Nazis destroyed the earlier democratic experience of the Weimar Republic in Germany. As Diamond (1994: 10) points out, 'the evidence of Germany, Japan, Spain and Italy – that were once written off as infertile soil for democracy' demonstrates that political culture must be 'somewhat "plastic"'.

Diversity and modern democracy

Like both the political culture theorists and Dahl, Sartori too highlights the importance of beliefs but he develops his arguments not from political science but from political theory. In addition to his arguments about pluralistic society as the underlying condition of democracy, Sartori distinguishes a basic condition on which the structural condition rests. This basic condition is the cultural belief in the value of diversity: 'The belief that difference and not likeness, dissent and not unanimity, change and not immutability make for the good life' (Sartori 1994b: 7). A culture, that is, in which toleration of beliefs different from one's own is valued and where dissensus and diversity is cherished, 'the principle that difference, not uniformity, is the leaven and the nourishment of states' (Sartori 1987: 289).

It is this belief in difference, dissensus over consensus, which, Sartori contends, underlies the capacity for the bargaining, compromise and give-and-take that is so crucial to modern democracy. He argues,

> Above all, modern democracies are related to and conditioned by the discovery that dissent, diversity and 'parts' (the parts which became parties) are not incompatible with social order and the well-being of the body politic.
>
> (Sartori 1987: 289)

Modern democracy is different from ancient Greek democracy. Ancient democracy is based not on 'dissent and diversity' but on 'unity and uniformity'. The crucial break between ancient and modern democracy, he argues, came with the Reformation and the gradual acceptance of toleration.

Sartori recognizes that dissent, compatible with ancient democracy but so essential to a modern democratic system, runs the risk of turning into conflict damaging to democracy. With modern pluralistic democracy based on belief in diversity and not uniformity, consensus on basic values cannot be essential, though it may be a facilitating condition for democracy. He argues, therefore, that there is one area in which consensus is necessary, namely, agreement on the rules for resolving disagreements (Sartori 1987: 90). For Sartori procedural consensus is the necessary condition of modern democracy. Procedural consensus, agreement on the rules, especially for changing governments, is crucial because competitions between factions which seek to reject the system are competitions for alternative positions on unanimity. The notion that the parts (parties) compete within the agreed procedures and allow the possibility that other parts (parties) may form governments in the future is crucial to modern democracy. Without agreement on procedure, however carefully the political system is designed, however strong and entrepreneurial the economy, however pluralistic the society, however supportive of democracy are beliefs in democracy in principle, democracy may become unstable and collapse.

Tentative lessons and further guiding hypotheses

Democracy, it has been argued, is an ideal for which institutional guarantees are designed for the achievement of its two core principles of popular control and political equality. It follows that, at best, those institutional designs will be practical approximations of the ideal and as such imperfect; at worst, the chosen design will fail completely. Paths to democracy are not necessarily, therefore, the same as a process of democratization, in which liberalization and inclusiveness are both increasing, because the histories begin with merely indicative elements of the future democracy they may become and reversals may occur at any time.

With paths to democracy not necessarily the same as a process of democratization, it follows that hypotheses derived from empirical political theory should not be applied to history in a rigorous way but be used simply to inform analysis, to offer guiding hypotheses. Though the hypotheses discussed have neither been found equally convincing nor been necessarily compatible with each other, nevertheless they provide a valuable array of ideas for investigation, wherever evidence can be found. In particular, the political hypotheses suggest the importance of considering the collapses, reversals and adaptations on paths to democracy. They also suggest the need to be guided by investigations into suffrage, the development and nature of competitive political parties, the role of governments-in-waiting (loyal oppositions), the capacity of politicians to take personal responsibility, the strength of governments in relation to the state bureaucracy, and the achievement of constitutions with procedural consensus.

With regard to the economic hypotheses, which are in many ways similar to those suggested by works of historical sociology discussed in Chapter 1, the existence of a capitalist economy, the general wealth of society and the distribution of that wealth need to be considered. The importance of the independence of economic organizations and of entrepreneurship also stands out, with emphasis both on the presence of employers' and workers' organizations. Concerning society, a pluralistic society with large numbers of independently formed voluntary associations with cross-cutting memberships seems to be important.

In respect of beliefs, the valuing of diversity appears crucial as too does trust both in government and more widely in society. In addition, both the political leaders and the coercive forces having beliefs in democracy seem relevant and in respect of the wider population their belief in the value of participation and their capacity to take concerted action seem significant. The strength of a democracy may also be increased by the length of its survival. In addition to these hypotheses about factors and conditions within each country, the effect of outside forces, foreign countries exerting pressure not only against but also towards democracy needs to be kept in mind.

3 Revolutions and ideas of democracy

From the past towards the present

Democracy as a working political system does not happen; it is made. There are limits, therefore, to the benefits of being guided by hypotheses from empirical political theory and historical sociology, which draw on hindsight, in gaining understanding of paths to democracy. Paths to democracy emerge, at least in part, from the political ideas and debates shaped by experiences of the time: ideas which draw on knowledge of past and contemporary political systems, both at home and abroad, and in reaction to the political events and actions of the day. In a well regarded text on democracy Arblaster (1994) stresses the importance of popular action to the history of democracy, arguing:

> It was not primarily *ideas* ... but popular action, and above all the eruption of the French people into politics in the years of the Revolution, that transformed the modern history of democracy. At a stroke, we might say, political ideas which had only been aspirations or dreams in the minds of *philosophes* or popular radicals, were placed on the agenda of real politics, not only in France, or even Europe, but globally.
>
> (Arblaster 1994: 36)

As will become clear, in Chapter 4, the importance of the French Revolution in transforming the modern history of democracy is open to question. Importantly, too, as will also become clear in chapters to follow, action for government by popular consent has led to communism and not only to democracy. There is no denying, however, that revolution has played a crucial role on paths to democracy, but it is a role not limited to that of popular action. Revolutions are forcing-houses for new ideas of government and, crucially, they produce the opportunity to put new ideas into practice.

England: revolution and constitutional monarchy

In respect of their impact on the history of modern democracy the most notable of Arblaster's 'popular radicals' were the Levellers of the English Civil War. The Levellers demanded that government should have the consent of those who were governed by it and that those so governed should include not just rich freeholders but all 'freeborn Englishmen' (see Hill 1969: 119). In addition to the franchise being given to free men and elections to be held on a regular basis, the Levellers also wanted the monarchy and the House of Lords to be abolished; sheriffs and Justices of the Peace to be elected; law reform and full equality before the law; the opening of enclosed lands; the abolition of a state church and tithes; and the end of subscription and privileges (ibid.: 118–19).

In October 1647, the Levellers' draft constitution, the Agreement of the People, was debated at Putney. Debates focused mainly on the franchise and the interpretation of 'freeborn Englishmen'. The Leveller, Colonel Rainsborough famously argued,

> The poorest he that is in England has a life to live as the greatest he, and therefore ... every man that is to live under a government ought first by his own consent to put himself under that government.
>
> (Hill 1969: 119)

The general view was that all those who were independent should have the vote and not, therefore, women, children, paupers and servants (a category which included apprentices and labourers, not only domestic servants, indeed wage labourers of all kinds).[1] Biennial elections for Members of Parliament were proposed as the means for this consent (ibid.).

In practice, in respect of the franchise, it was Cromwell's not the Levellers' view that prevailed and property (propriety), rather than the absence of being dependent on someone else, as the Levellers proposed, remained a condition of political rights. The existing 40 shillings a year freehold franchise was replaced by ownership of estate worth £200 or more. This enfranchised rich merchants and the like but did little to widen suffrage (Hill 1969: 123). Though the Levellers' chosen outcome of the Civil War was not the one that was adopted, later publications on the Levellers ensured that 'the ideas of the Levellers passed into the radical tradition of the seventeen-sixties, and played their part in preparing the American and French revolutions' (ibid.: 168).

The English Civil War of 1642–48 led to the execution of a king, God's appointed on earth under divine right, and to the setting up, under

Cromwell, of the Commonwealth, 1649–53. The Commonwealth was followed by the Protectorates, 1653–58 and 1658–59, unprecedented republics. The restoration of the monarchy, in 1660, two years after Cromwell's death, again ended in the overthrow of a king. The Glorious Revolution of 1688–89 inaugurated a constitutional monarchy, a system without precedent.

The Declaration of Rights, also known as the Bill of Rights, resolved in 1689 by the House of Commons before the appointment of William and Mary as joint monarchs, set down, formally, the conditions of a constitutional monarchy.[2] The aims of the Declaration were to balance the executive and the legislative to ensure the importance of parliament. Under the Bill of Rights, the monarch could no longer suspend laws, impose or levy revenues without parliament's consent, or dispense power.

Crucially, the establishment of constitutional monarchy also ended what had stood in the way of the development of a constitutional opposition. Organized opposition had been a feature of the English parliament since the seventeenth century and records suggest that its origins are earlier (Foord 1964: 8). However, as Foord argues, 'as long as the sovereign exercised the right to punish critics in Parliament, and ultimately to call out an army against them, a constitutional Opposition in the modern sense could not develop' (ibid.). When it is appreciated that such punishment of critics could involve torture, the view that this pre-dates modern opposition is made the more convincing. A constitutional monarch could not only no longer remove parliamentary opposition and impose 'cruel and unusual punishments', but also no longer exact 'excessive bail or fines'. Politically, under the constitutional monarchy, there were to be freedom of elections to parliament and freedom of speech within it, and there were to be 'frequent parliaments'. The franchise returned to 'the traditional ruling class, the shire gentry, and town merchants' (Hill 1969: 237).

Religious toleration for Protestant dissenters, which had featured under Cromwell but had been ended by the Restoration, was partly reinstated in 1689[3] and 'relative freedom of the press' (Hill 1969: 223) was established in 1694. The Triennial Act of 1694 set down that parliaments should meet every three years and not last longer than three years. The Act of Settlement, 1701, ended the possibility of royal pardon of impeachment and so completed control by parliament (ibid.: 239). The Act also transferred the right to dismiss judges from the monarch to parliament (ibid.: 223). In 1707, the Act of Union between England and Scotland established Scottish representation in both houses of parliament (Foord 1964: 9).

Loyal opposition and parties

The Hanoverian succession, in 1714, marks the date by which the development of 'His Majesty's Opposition' was fully on a 'stable political foundation' (Foord 1964: 8). Crucially, from 1714 there ceased to be any question about the loyalty of the monarch to the constitution (ibid.: 10). Foord sets the date by which constitutional opposition 'had reached maturity' (ibid.) as 1830. By this time a system had evolved with 'the rudiments of national parties' (ibid.: 466).

The earliest indication of the Whigs and Tories behaving as the parties that they were later to become was in 1681 when during the recess of parliament the Whigs organized petitions in opposition to the dissolution (prorogation) of parliament and the Tories grouped together in opposition to the petitions. At the time, they became known as the Petitioners and Abhorrers, respectively. (See Foord 1964: 73–4.) In 1714, Whigs and Tories were groups to which Members of Parliament were broadly labelled on the basis of their policy positions. Generally, by 1714, the label 'Tory' was attached to those who supported landed interests, the Church of England and the monarch's prerogatives; the term 'Whig' was given to those who favoured commercial interests, toleration of dissenters, and 'the rights and liberties of the subject' (ibid.: 20).

In 1714, the Tories had accepted King George I's removing them from office and replacing them with what was, in effect, the Opposition. From 1714 to 1830 the two groups evolved as parties through the practice of politics, firming their positions in opposition to each other in order to court public opinion (Foord 1964: 346). To this end organizations outside parliament were developed, pamphlets were distributed (ibid.: 406–7) and efforts were put into influencing newspapers. These organizations, in 1830, did not compare with the modern parties of today with their large mass memberships and countrywide networks. In explanation of the differences between now and then McKenzie (1963) argues as follows,

> The explanation of course is simple. An electorate (in 1830) of 465,000, or about 2 per cent of the adult population, has expanded on the basis of universal adult suffrage to one of almost 35 million. While each M.P. in 1830 represented on average about 330 voters (and a few represented none at all), by 1959 the average M. P. represented 56,000 electors. To win and maintain support among that number of people is of course an expensive process, far beyond the resources of all but the well-to-do.
>
> (McKenzie 1963: 4)

On McKenzie's analysis, then, it is the representation for a large electorate that requires the resources of organized political parties.

In 1830, the new industrial towns of Manchester, Birmingham, Leeds, Sheffield, Wolverhampton, Huddersfield and Gateshead had no representatives in parliament, though these urban areas had expanded rapidly under the growth of industrialization. The population of Manchester in 1830 was 180,000. Of the 656 Members of Parliament elected to the House of Commons only six represented the millions of people who lived in London while, notoriously, Old Sarum which had slipped into the sea and therefore had no population to represent at all, had two MPs. The 1832 Reform Act changed these anomalies and, in consequence, the number of those eligible to vote went up, by around 250,000. (See McKenzie 1963: 3.)

In the Reform Act of 1867, the electorate was increased to around 2 million. It is from this date that the Conservative Party (its name changed from Tory Party in 1832) decided to set up a mass party organization, the National Union. The purpose of the National Union was to win the newly enfranchised urban voters (McKenzie 1963: 146).

Theorizing government

The turbulent times of revolution, civil war, republics, restoration, and constitutional monarchy spawned new theories of government. Of particular note was that of John Locke. Locke's *Two Treatises of Government* (1988), published in 1690 but written in the early 1680s, was not a theory of democracy. However, as Arblaster (1994: 32) comments, 'Locke is rightly identified with the development of liberal political thought, and so by a common mode of thinking, his name is also linked to the idea of democracy'. Held (1996: 74) summarizes liberalism as 'the attempt to uphold the values of freedom of choice, reason and toleration in the face of tyranny, the absolutist system and religious intolerance'. This fits with the change from Whig Party to Liberal Party in Britain after the 1832 Reform Act. Toleration, it will be recalled from Chapter 2, is the critical value which Sartori argues to be the necessary underlying belief of modern democracy.

Locke's concern was with government by consent and such government could include governments that were not democracies. The attraction of Locke's arguments for radicals lay in his justification for resistance against governments that lacked consent. As a man of his times, and not one of the poorest at that, Locke's view was that the consent in question was the prerogative of men of property. Locke's ideas which viewed this consent in terms of a contract between government and enfranchised propertied men were important ideas in the protest years leading to the American War of Independence.

The American Revolution: federal republic

The American War of Independence, 1776–83, was a revolution fought against the injustice of taxes, imposed from Britain by 'the tyrant' George III with the revolutionary slogan, 'no taxation without representation' (Nicholas 1950: 42–5). The Declaration of Independence was published on 4 July 1776 but the publication having the most direct impact on the outbreak of the war was Thomas Paine's *Common Sense*, published in January of that year; it sold 100,000 copies in four months (ibid.: 53). In *Common Sense* Paine berates the English system of government and the rule of (constitutional) monarchy and aristocracy. Much as the Levellers had, Paine argued that men were created equal and, like the Protestant dissenters, Paine supported his argument with Biblical texts (Paine 1989: 9–11). Paine then developed the argument for the thirteen colonies' independence from Britain, as an American republic, and for the time to be ripe for a 'declaration of independence' (ibid.: 37). Paine also proposed a 'continental charter' (drawing parallels with Magna Carta) as a 'bond of solemn obligation' 'to support the right of every separate part, whether of religion, professional freedom or property' and made the case for 'the necessity of a large and equal representation' to the Continental Congress (ibid.: 36).

The charter was to set down the rules of government (the size of the congress, its duration and so on) and was to secure 'freedom and property to all men, and above all things the free exercise of religion, according to the dictates of conscience' (Paine 1989: 28). In the Declaration of Independence, composed principally by Jefferson, these sentiments are elegantly expressed as:

> We hold these truths to be self-evident: That all men are created equal; that they are endowed by their Creator with certain unalienable rights; that among these are life, liberty, and the pursuit of happiness; that, to secure these rights, governments are instituted among men, deriving their just powers from the consent of the governed; that whenever any form of government becomes destructive of these ends, it is right of the people to alter or to abolish it, and to institute new government, laying its foundation on such principles, and organizing its powers in such forms, as to them shall seem most likely to effect their safety and happiness.
>
> (*Declaration of Independence*, 1776 (1997: 379))

Independence from Britain was gained in 1783, the American Constitution not written until 1787. Nicholas (1950: 79) argues, 'It is not too much to say that as Paine's *Common Sense* projected America into the war so *The Federalist* argued America into the Constitution.' *The Federalist* was a series of papers published in a selection of New York journals by

James Madison and Alexander Hamilton, two of the fifty-five delegates to the Convention, which framed the Constitution. The papers were published between 1787 and 1788. Madison, viewed as the 'father of the constitution' (Wilson: 1997: 12) informed his thought through reading works of political philosophy. The most influential of these works were those of the French philosopher, Montesquieu, who, in turn, had been influenced by Locke.

Living under the absolute French monarchy, Montesquieu was an admirer of the English constitutional monarchy and, as Held (1996: 82) explains, 'an advocate of what he took to be the distinctively "English" notions of freedom, toleration and moderation which, he claimed, were admirably expressed (after 1688) by the English constitution itself: "the mirror of liberty".' As he had made clear in *Common Sense*, Paine held the quite contrary view of the English monarchy but, for Madison, what was stimulating was Montesquieu's idea, expressed in *The Spirit of the Laws* (1748), that the institutions of government should be constructed so as to separate and balance powers (see Book X1.6). Those powers Montesquieu (1949: 152) identified as 'that of enacting laws, that of executing the public resolutions, and of trying the causes of individuals' (ibid.: 152): legislative, executive and judiciary.

The idea of the separation and balance of powers rested on Montesquieu's concern with the problem of the threat of tyranny that lay in any group given power over others using that power for their own ends. In addition to the separation of the executive, legislative and judiciary, he also advocated, in line with his interpretation of the 'Constitution of England', a division of the legislative into two chambers. One chamber was to consist of the regularly elected, representatives of 'the common people', to initiate legislation; the other chamber, to consist of hereditary nobles, would have the right to reject legislation (Montesquieu 1949: 154–6).

Though promoting ideas useful to the development of modern democracy Montesquieu's ideas, like Locke's, do not constitute a theory of democracy. It is Madison, the major architect and theorist of the American Constitution who made that crucial discovery about the importance of diversity, that crucial move that Sartori identifies as the discovery of 'how to build a political system on a *concordia discors*, on a dissenting consensus' (Sartori 1987: 290). Madison built on Montesquieu's idea of the separation and balance of powers, proposing a balance and separation of executive, legislative and judiciary, but substituting for Montesquieu's constitutional monarch a president as the executive.

While both Locke's and Montesquieu's thinking remained sympathetic to ancient democracy, in the sense of seeking a non-dissenting consensus, Madison was highly critical. In Madison's view, expressed in *The Federalist, No. 10*, published in November 1787, 'pure Democracy', that is classical, direct democracy, as 'a Society, consisting of a small number of citizens who assemble and administer the government in person', has 'nothing to check the inducements to sacrifice the weaker party or the obnoxious individual' (Madison 1997a: 406). Madison advocated not a (pure) democracy but a republic, 'by which I mean a government in which the scheme of representation takes place' (ibid.). He goes on to explain what he held to be the two crucial differences between pure democracy and a republic: 'first, the delegation of government, in the latter (a republic), to a small number of citizens, elected by the rest; secondly the greater number of citizens, and greater sphere of country, over which the latter (a republic) may be extended' (ibid.).

The advantages of the first point, Madison argued, would be that the elected group, while being in touch with the views of the public, would be able to stand above short-term and self-interested 'considerations' (Madison 1997a: 406) and further the longer and more general interests of the country. Nevertheless, he was aware that corrupt individuals might get themselves elected (ibid.: 407). In defence of a republic, he argued, therefore, first, that the larger number of citizens would provide a richer pool of able representatives. Second, Madison reasoned that the electoral process in combination with a large suffrage would both guard against the 'vicious arts' used in obtaining votes from electors where there are only small numbers of them and would be more likely to lead to the election of good candidates (those who possess 'the most attractive merit, and the most diffusive and established characters') (ibid.). For Madison strength derives from difference.

Madison's argument for his second point for the advantages of a republic over a 'pure democracy', namely that of the larger size of the area and of the number of citizens that can be governed, is concerned with factions. He argues that factious groups in small societies pose the greater threat because one faction may form a majority and oppress opposition (Madison 1997a: 407–8). In a larger society, such differences of view and interests are likely to be the greater and the chances of one faction gaining a majority to act in an oppressive way is, thereby, reduced. If present, then the chances that the group could act together would also be reduced (ibid.: 407–8). Madison's argument amounts to a classic pluralist position. In *The Federalist, No. 51*, published in February 1788, Madison airs his pluralist stance in the clearest terms: 'Different interests necessarily exist in different classes of citizens. If a majority be united by a common interest, the rights of the minority will be insecure' (Madison 1997b: 411). He argues that there are two possible solutions: the one, which he rejects, is the creation of a (general) will; the other, which he advocates, is 'by comprehending in the society so many separate descriptions of citizens, as will render an unjust combination of a majority of the whole, very improbable, if not impractical' (ibid.: 411). This argument amounts, in Dahl's and Sartori's terms, to a society structured to cross-cut cleavages.

Madison expands on this pluralist theme,

> While all authority in (the federal republic of the United States) will be derived from and dependent on the society, the society itself will be broken into so many parts, interests and classes of citizens, that the rights of individuals or of the minority, will be in little danger from interested combinations of the majority. In a free government, the security for civil rights must be the same as for religious rights. It consists in the one case in the multiplicity of interests, and in the other, in the multiplicity of sects.
>
> (Madison 1997b: 411)

Madison goes on to stress the advantages of as large as possible numbers of interests and religious sects, advantages which would be found in a large country with lots of people (ibid.: 411–12). His arguments are consistent with cleavages within states to be cross-cut by the federal system with its strong central government, in order to achieve the protection of minorities.

For Madison, uniformity was an impossible goal because dissent, that is diversity of opinion, and interests in competition with each other were inherent. Factions, active groups united by common interests or passions in opposition to others, were inherent because, as Madison (1997a: 404) explained, 'the latent causes of faction are sown in the nature of man'. People, he argued, have a 'zeal for different opinions' on all sorts of things, especially religion, politics and public figures, and he stressed that such issues can lead to violence. The 'most common and durable source of factions', he argued, 'has been the various and unequal distribution of property': those with it and those without it, those in debt and their creditors, the landed versus those in manufacturing, class interests of all sorts (ibid.: 404–5). In essence, his position is that uniformity is impossible because individuals are inherently diverse.

Madison's solution was to run with, not against, the problem of violent factions for in his view their causes could not be removed. He argued, rather, for the creation of a political system designed to accommodate factions, 'for relief is only to be sought in the means of controlling its effects' (Madison 1997a: 405). It followed, he contended, from his arguments about the advantages of a large system – a republic – over a small system of government that a strong central government, the Union, – a federal system – was to be preferred to the existing confederal system, in which power resided in the thirteen states. A federal system, based on a diverse society, with community factions (as within each state) diluted through the size and structure of a federalist system, would ensure, he argued, that a majority could not achieve the effect of suppression of minority interests (ibid.: 408).

Madison's practical approach, the controlling of effects, was crucial. The immediate outcome of the American Revolution had been the writing of constitutions for each of the thirteen states. Unsurprisingly, given their varied histories, these differed widely and not least in respect of who had the right to vote and hold office (Nicholas 1950: 62). In Pennsylvania, suffrage was wide with only a very small state tax for qualification. In South Carolina, in contrast, suffrage was highly restricted, ownership of fifty acres of land needed to qualify. Views on slavery also clashed, with the Northern states freeing slaves. Each of the states, however, retained in common the division between the legislative assembly and a governor, now to be elected and not, as in the past, appointed by the king.

The downturn in the economy, which followed the end of the revolution, aggravated the problem that Congress had faced during the war, namely that of lacking the legal right to raise taxes (see O'Kane 1991: 121–2). The printing of money which had been the solution at the time continued, and with it a further rise in inflation. Violent conflicts broke out, the most serious of these the Shay's rebellion in Massachusetts (Nicholas 1950: 68). Tariff wars developed between the states and disputes over boundaries between states also grew with Vermont even being prepared to secede to Canada in defiance of New York and New Hampshire claims on their territory (ibid.: 69).

These events are the context to Madison's concerns about the inevitability of conflict and disagreement and the primacy of property distribution as a source for such problems. They also put in context his concern to find a political solution to the effects of differences between states, community factions, and the outbreaks of violent conflicts. Madison, a delegate of Virginia, was one of the fifty-five delegates from all the states, Rhode Island excepted, who met together for the Convention, in early 1787. The Convention went beyond its brief to draft amendments to the existing Confederation and produced the Constitution for a new national government, largely as a consequence of the plan for a new national government drawn up by Madison and the Virginia delegation (Nicholas 1950: 73).

The Constitution

The Convention, under Washington's chairmanship, wrestled with the problems of competing interests, differences between delegates from large as opposed to small states being the most pronounced. In sum, delegates from large states favoured strong central government – the federalists – (the most notable being Madison and Hamilton) and those from small states favoured weak central government – the anti-federalists – (the most notable being Jefferson but also, with the exception of Hamilton, the delegates from the large state of New York) (Nicholas 1950: 73). The resolution of these conflicting interests in respect of the two chambers of the Congress of the United States was that each state should have the same number of senators (two) in the upper chamber – the Senate – but in the lower house – the House of Representatives – the representatives should be in proportion to the size of the population of each state (*The Constitution of the United States*, Article I, Sections 2 and 3). The largest was Virginia with ten representatives, the smallest Rhode Island and Providence Plantations with one. The House of Representatives was to be popularly elected every two years, the Senate chosen by the legislature of each state every six years, with one-third of the seats up for election every two years (*The Constitution of the United States*, Article I, Sections 2 and 3; Wilson 1997: 383). The federal structure enabled separation between issues of general concern and those specific to each state and to the central federal government. The Congress had the new right to raise taxes in accordance with the direct votes that it received and to raise armies (Article I, Section 8).

To avoid the centralization of power that would have potential to override the interests of minority factions the Constitution also stipulated that the president was neither to be a member of Congress nor chosen by it (so avoiding dependence on Congress) but was to be appointed through election, the votes to be filtered through electoral colleges in each state (Article II).[4] In turn, the president could neither appoint nor remove members of Congress and members of the Supreme Court were to be appointed by the president, their independence to be guaranteed by their being irremovable once in office, other than by impeachment. In addition to the division of powers a variety of checks and balances on the powers were included. For example, both Houses had to agree legislation before it could be signed by the president and though the president had a veto over legislation, a bill could be re-passed by a two-thirds majority of Congress. The president was to be elected every four years and to be head of the army, navy and of the (state) militias when in service of the United States. Eligibility to vote was limited to taxpayers and property owners, but as property was widely distributed, among white men that is, this meant that a large proportion of men had the vote.[5]

The Constitution of 1787 was for a 'Republican form of government' guaranteed to 'every State in this Union' (Article IV, Section 4); there is no reference to democracy, the term being reserved for the 'pure' form of direct democracy. Along with its many notable features, including that congressmen, senators, president and Supreme Court judges were to be given payment ('compensation'), was the fact that the Constitution was to be ratified by the electorate of each state and that its agreement was required by a minimum of nine of the thirteen states (Wilson 1997: 79). Achieving that ratification of the Constitution by a minimum of nine states soon showed that an error had been made in not including a bill of rights. In several cases, as for example in Massachusetts, support was won for the Constitution only by promising such a bill (ibid.: 25). In the first session of the First Congress, Madison, therefore, introduced proposals, in sympathy with the Virginia bill of rights, which when ratified in 1791 as the first ten amendments to the Constitution, became known as the Bill of Rights (ibid.). The Bill of Rights prohibited a state religion and guaranteed religious toleration, freedom of speech, of the press, of assembly and of petition (Amendment I). The Bill of Rights also set down the right to keep and bear arms. The rule of law and the right to trial by jury were also guaranteed (Amendments IV–VIII).[6]

Parties

Though now with a Bill of Rights, the 'Republican form of government' had no organized political parties. Parties were perceived as self-interested factions that would threaten the Union. In 1788 and again in 1792, Washington was chosen as president without opposition. When he stood down in 1796 rival factions, the Republicans and Federalists, each put forward their own candidate, Jefferson and Adams, respectively. These factions were the anti-federalist and federalist positions that had emerged in the debates over the Constitution, power to reside with the independent states versus power to reside in a strong central government, respectively. The Electors, rather than mediating as envisaged in the design of the Constitution (Article II, Section 1), reinforced the two factional views (Nicholas 1950: 90). Adams was elected in this first presidential campaign; Jefferson was elected, in 1800, in the second. The year 1800 is taken as the date at which organized political parties began, with the Federalists retaining their factional name and the anti-federalists, the Republicans, becoming the Democratic-Republicans (Wilson 1997: 10).[7] Under Jefferson, property became more widely distributed and education more widely accessible (Nicholas 1950: 94–6). Under President Jackson, 1829–37, the franchise was expanded to incorporate nearly all men, in all but some southern states; to freemen that is (Wilson 1997: 143).

France: revolution and 'The One and Indivisible Republic'

In the French Revolution of 1789, Montesquieu's ideas on the separation and balance of powers which, through Madison, had contributed to the steering of post-revolutionary America towards political consolidation, found competition with the ideas of Rousseau. Rousseau's ideas were in the frame of ancient democracy, a political system based on unity and uniformity – the 'General Will', a position opposed to organized factions (Held 1996: 59) and epitomizing the system so strongly argued against by Madison as 'pure democracy'. Though incompatible, Montesquieu's and Rousseau's writings were those to which the revolutionaries 'continually referred' (Hampson 1986: 49). But, crucially, Hampson explains, the revolutionaries 'quarried the sacred texts for what suited their political convenience and ignored what did not' (ibid.).

Followers of Montesquieu emphasized the importance of dividing and balancing powers, using Britain as their idealized example of practice. Followers of Rousseau stressed the importance of government standing for the general will, defined (by the government) as what was best for society (Hampson 1986: 50). Crucially, the general will was 'one and indivisible'. As such, followers of Montesquieu and those of Rousseau had contrasting ideas of post-revolutionary government. Rather than the idealized British model, with its constitutional monarch, and two houses of parliament, the Rousseauists looked to the classical democracies of Rome and Sparta and sought Rousseau's 'legislator' in the image of a highly moral man, such as Moses. In conflict though these models of government were, as Hampson comments, 'Almost without exception, the men of 1789 tried to have the best of both worlds, to achieve Rousseau's regenerative ends by Montesquieu's libertarian means' (ibid.: 51) and he adds, 'All of them disregarded Rousseau's warning that the general will could not be represented' (ibid.). Their heads viewed the separation of powers as necessary, their hearts followed Rousseau. The general will, as the will of the people, was given expression through elected representatives. The consequence, however, was that opposition within the newly created Assembly was viewed as counter-revolutionary, opposed to the new political system itself.

The practical lessons on party democracy to be drawn from the American Revolution, from 1800, arrived too late to aid the French Revolution. Such lessons, viewed from a Rousseauist position, would in any case have been likely to be ignored. There were, however, some lessons from the American case that were taken up. The arguments against constitutional monarchy, so clearly put by Paine, were not lost on those opposed to the monarchy and Jefferson's Declaration of Independence inspired the French Declaration of the Rights of Man and of Citizens (Nicholas 1950: 87).

The Declaration of the Rights of Man and of Citizens, one of the first acts of the French post-revolutionary National Assembly in 1789, contained clauses similar to the American Declaration of Independence: Clause I, 'Men are born free and equal in respect of their rights'; Clause

II, the 'rights (of man) are liberty, property, security, and resistance of oppression'; Clause XI, 'every man being presumed innocent till he has been convicted'; Clause X, 'No man ought to be molested on account of his opinions, not even on account of his religious opinions'; Clause XI, 'The unrestrained communication of thoughts and opinions being one of the most precious rights of man, every citizen may speak, write and publish freely'; Clause XVII, 'the right to property being inviolable and sacred'.[8]

There are also, however, great differences between the two documents. Whereas the American Declaration of Independence speaks of the 'rights of the people' 'to institute new government', the French Declaration has: Clause III, 'The nation is essentially the source of sovereignty' and, Clause IV, 'The law is an expression of the will of the community'. As Arendt argues,

> The American version actually proclaims no more than the necessity of civilised government for all mankind; the French version, however, proclaims the existence of rights, independent of and outside the body politic, and then goes on to equate these so-called rights, namely the rights of man *qua* man, with the rights of citizens.'
>
> (Arendt 1973: 149)

As will become clear in Chapter 4, through the nineteenth century the developments of democracy in France were far from smooth and long before stable liberal democracy was achieved new ideas had developed in Europe which rejected liberal democracy, as 'bourgeois democracy', and made a theoretical link between democracy and a new kind of revolution – proletarian revolution ending in communism.

The Marxist challenge: revolution and bourgeois democracy

The Communist Manifesto was first published in 1848, the year of European revolutions. By the end of the nineteenth century, some of Marx's followers promoted the idea of social democracy to be achieved through the liberal democratic process. The Marxist interpretation of revolution is that it marks the end of an epoch, the move from one mode of production to the next. The bourgeois revolution brings the move from the feudal to the capitalist epoch, the proletarian revolution from the capitalist epoch to the communist, viewed as the stage that brings an end to history as class conflict. Marx's interpretation of the French Revolution is that it was a bourgeois revolution. Marxist interpretations of the Russian Revolution differ: either it was the predicted proletarian revolution or Russia took the semi-Asiatic route (Melotti 1977). The

Marxist interpretation of the German Revolution is that it was an aborted proletarian revolution, entered through the western route (ibid.). A bourgeois revolution serves the interests of the bourgeoisie, the owners of the capitalist means of production whose interests revolve around private property. A proletarian revolution serves the interests of the proletariat, concerned with the common ownership of property, on which the new system – the communist society – is based. In theory, following a proletarian revolution the majority rather than minority class comes to power, for the first time in history.

In the Marxist analysis, the French Revolution was necessary in order to replace the old feudal mode of production. In serving the interests of landowners, based on peasants paying tithes to the lords and performing duties in their service, the feudal mode of production could not serve the interests of the bourgeoisie. The bourgeoisie wanted to maximize profits, which required the availability of wage-earners free from obligations to the feudal lords, not peasants tied to the land. The bourgeoisie also wanted: property which could be purchased on the open market, with legal protection; a money economy and banking system to accommodate this; and a society based on merit not birth. With such they could have not only economic power but also political power.

With the *ancien régime* representing the interests of feudal landlords the political system had to be overthrown and replaced by one which operated in bourgeois interests, with a government of the bourgeoisie which would free peasants for wage labour, which would uphold private property in law, and which would sustain a monetary and banking system. In supporting bourgeois interests, the government would also be one that would give power and position to those who acquired property and expertise through their merit not their privilege. Few in number at the start of the revolution, because their growth has been constrained by the old mode of production, the bourgeoisie could grow in number and importance under the new political order.

As the new capitalist mode of production with its new system of government to represent the interests of the bourgeoisie becomes established, in turn the class system changes as peasants are replaced by wage-earners both on the land and, more importantly, in the cities. Urbanization grows to accommodate the industry which the capitalist mode of production, with its new-found freedom for invention and investment in technological and scientific ideas, produces. Along with industrialists and proletariat, bankers, lawyers and other professionals also grow in number in order to serve the new capitalist mode of production.

Because the political system serves the interests of the owners of the capitalist means of production (hence 'bourgeois democracy'), the bourgeoisie, rather than genuinely representing the interests of all will have a suffrage restricted to those with private property. The Marxist analysis is concerned, therefore, with the state. The police, the bureaucracy, the army, the judiciary, the legal system as a whole, are viewed as operating to protect, above all, the interests of the owners of capital. And, crucially, bourgeois democracy is not, therefore, viewed as genuinely representative but rather as coercive of the majority. The interests of capitalists are seen as in direct conflict with the interests of those who, lacking property, have to sell their labour.

In Marx's analysis, the values of the new bourgeois society differ greatly from those of the old feudal society. In the bourgeois society individualism, competition, inventiveness, independence of thought, entrepreneurship, respect for property and respect for law are all important. At the same time, the relentless competition to maximize profits, in which the level of wages paid to workers is critical, means that other values are also present in capitalist society. Along with competitiveness and individualism go greed and selfishness. The dominance of self-interest means that the interests of those less able to look after themselves are discounted other than where those interests overlap with those of the bourgeoisie. Wage-labourers are needed for the capitalist system so workers must be alive in sufficient numbers, with health and capabilities sufficient for the work required. Subsistence level wages with minimum training are the basic requirement. These workers develop not simply a conflict of interest with the bourgeoisie but also competing values.

As the bourgeois mode of production develops and the size of factories and units of industrial and commercial production grows, so the size of the proletariat also grows and along with the growing proletariat the towns and cities and size of factories expand. In opposition to the individualism and collectivism of the entrepreneurs, this physical closeness of the proletariat develops values relating not to individualism but to collectivism. In reflection of these collective interests, workers' organizations, trade unions, mutual societies, cooperatives and workers' parties develop (including, so crucial to Marx's analysis, the Communist Party) to serve the interests of workers. In the Marxist analysis, bourgeois democracy itself changes over time, through responding to the organized demands of workers. Eventually, legality is given to trade unions and workers' parties, suffrage is extended, and legislation is introduced which increasingly offers workers protection in the workplace and improvements in standards of health, education and living conditions. Bourgeois interests are served in this because, in order to pursue profit maximization it is necessary not only to have laws which protect property but also a quiescent workforce. Stoppages and riots damage production and profits and, in consequence, some satisfaction of workers' demands is therefore conceded.[9]

In the Marxist analysis, bourgeois democracy can only develop in capitalist societies and it is for this reason that modern democracy must be accompanied by both independent, competing, economic organizations and economic growth. These are inherent aspects of the mode of production itself. What is equally clear, however, is that in the Marxist view of bourgeois democracy the modern aspects of the system – universal suffrage, free trade unions, workers' associations of all kinds, and increases in social welfare – are the product of pressure from the working class. They are not intrinsic to bourgeois democracy. It is liberal democracy, based on freedom of individual competition and suffrage limited to property owners, which constitutes the essential nature of bourgeois democracy.

Russia and Germany: social democracy

The extent to which bourgeois democracy could accommodate workers' demands to the point where it ceased to be a system to represent bourgeois interests without the need for violent proletarian revolution proved a debate which was to affect both the Russian and the German revolutions. The growth of trade unions which developed with the expansion of the working class in capitalist countries and the workers' parties which took form in step with the granting of male suffrage led to a revised interpretation of Marxism. Bernstein, and later Kautsky, both German Social Democrats, argued that it was possible to move to a socialist society without violent revolution. This 'evolutionary socialism', Bernstein argued, could be achieved through the process of workers' movements gaining some social and economic improvements under bourgeois government, and resorting to mass strikes if the way was blocked. The crucial change of government to one that represented the interests of the proletariat, rather than those of the bourgeoisie, could, then, be achieved through the ballot box. Through the very process of election introduced under the bourgeois system, a socialist party could be elected to power to introduce the legislation that would turn the system into a social democracy. (See Mills 1963: 133–5.)

Kautsky specifically argued for the value of elections. Quite in line with the discovery made in Britain, America and France, Kautsky argued,

> Elections are a means to count ourselves and the enemy, and they grant thereby a clear view of the relative strength of the classes and parties, their advance and their retreat. They prevent premature outbreaks and they guard against defeats. They also grant the possibility that the opponents will themselves recognize the untenability of many positions and freely surrender them when their maintenance is no life-and-death question for them.
>
> (Kautsky, *The Social Revolution* (1902) in Mills 1963: 171)

Kautsky's argument makes clear that central to the revisionist view was not only the importance of the growth of the proletariat and the pressure for socialism that this would bring but also the effects of the nature and role of democracy itself. In the revisionist view the workers' movement and workers' party would play an important part in educating workers, an educated and informed electorate seen as an intrinsic part of a socialist democracy. More than that, the socialist democratic society, when it arrived, would be generated through the movement, through the experience of cooperation and collective action, and through the informed understanding and experience of democracy at work. Kautsky also argued as follows:

> But it is not alone the relief of the proletariat from its misery that makes the activity of the proletariat in Parliament and the operation of the proletarian organizations indispensable. They are also of value as a means of practically familiarizing the proletariat with the problems and methods of national and municipal government and of great industries, as well as the attainment of that intellectual maturity which the proletariat needs if it is to supplant the bourgeoisie as ruling class.
>
> (Kautsky, *The Social Revolution* (1902) in Mills 1963: 172)

In social democracy, with universal education and an end to property qualifications there would also be genuine universal suffrage, women as well as men.

Objections to this revisionist view, which amounted to revolution through reform, were principally raised over the capacity of the capitalist political system to divest itself of the primary purpose for which it was set up, namely the function of serving the interests of the bourgeois class. The view that the proletarian revolution could not be achieved by socialist representatives taking over the operation of the bourgeois state was a view shared by Lenin and Luxemburg, but with very important differences in their analyses. In a Russia far more backward than Germany, both politically and economically, where the proletariat was consequently far smaller, where the Russian Social Democratic Party was illegal and where the Tsarist secret police, the *Okhrana*, was highly repressive, Lenin focused on the coercive nature of the bourgeois state.

Central to Lenin's position on the tactics of revolution was that the state had to be smashed. The coercive aspects of the state – the army, police, judiciary and bureaucracy – had to be defeated and they, like the political structures and institutions of bourgeois democracy had to be replaced, entirely. As Lenin expresses it in *The State and Revolution* (1917), it is necessary 'to crush, smash to atoms, wipe off the face of the earth the bourgeois, state machine, the standing army, the police and bureaucracy'

(Mills 1963: 226–7). It also followed not only that the proletarian revolution had to be a violent revolution but that the proletarian party (the Bolshevik Party) had to be tightly organized both in order to act as the vanguard of the revolution and to take over power and construct, organize and consolidate the new revolutionary state.

Rosa Luxemburg's position was in opposition to both revisionism and bolshevism. In Luxemburg's view, as expressed in *Reform or Revolution* (1899), Bernstein's position was 'opportunist' and caught in the stream of early workers' protests, struggling 'against the mode of distribution, instead of basing it on a struggle against the mode of production' (Mills 1963: 195–6). Winning the battle on distribution, she argued, would not be enough, it was necessary to change the mode of production and whereas distribution could be changed by reform, a change in the mode of production (which included the political and legal superstructure) necessitated revolution. Crucially, however, this change had, for Luxemburg, to be achieved through the social democratic movement and it was here that she departed from Lenin.

Luxemburg was opposed to the tight organization of the Bolshevik Party, designed for carrying out 'the dictatorship of the proletariat', the Marxist stage after the revolutionary overthrow. In Luxemburg's (1967: 76-7) view, expressed in *The Russian Revolution* (written in 1918), the dictatorship of the proletariat should constitute 'a dictatorship of the *class*, not of a party or a clique', which she explains is 'on the basis of the most active, unlimited participation of the mass of the people, of unlimited democracy'. This desire for the 'most active unlimited participation of the mass of the people' was at the very centre of her thinking. What Luxemburg criticized in bourgeois democracy was not the political structures and institutions designed to make democracy work in practice but the conditions which these formal structures concealed. She argues as follows:

> We have always distinguished the social kernel from the political form of *bourgeois* democracy; we have always revealed the hard kernel of social inequality and lack of freedom hidden under the sweet shell of formal equality and freedom – not in order to reject the latter but to spur the working class into being satisfied with the shell, but rather, by conquering political power, to create a socialist democracy to replace bourgeois democracy – not to eliminate democracy altogether.
>
> (Luxemburg, *The Russian Revolution*, 1967: 77)

'Socialist democracy', she argues (ibid.: 78), 'must proceed step by step out of the active participation of the masses; it must be under their direct influence, subjected to the control of complete public activity, it must arise out of the growing, political training of the mass of the people'.

Socialist democracy, for Luxemburg then, exists not in the institutions – regular elections, universal suffrage, debating chambers, bureaucracy to implement legislation and so on – though they are necessary, but in the nature of the legislation, which has social equality and freedom at its heart, and in the 'active participation' of people throughout society in both democratic procedures and in the formation of policy. Such active participation is far more than simply voting for representatives at regularly held elections, it is involvement in decision-making, with power flowing, not from the top down, but from the bottom up. The role of a social democratic party within capitalist society, therefore, was restricted to that of opposition:

> Social Democracy is confined by definition to the role of an opposition party; it can only appear as a ruling party on the ruins of that bourgeois society.
>
> (Luxemburg, 1899, quoted in Nettl 1969: 145)[10]

Luxemburg was also clear that socialist parties should not join other political parties in the government of a bourgeois democracy. She was opposed, as a consequence, to the Waldeck-Rousseau cabinet in France, 1899–1902, in which the socialist Millerand became a minister, the first socialist minister in history.

In arguing for organization to grow from mass action and not vice versa, in arguing for social democratic political leadership to spring from spontaneous mass action, and in arguing for the post-revolutionary democracy to be developed 'step by step' and 'subjected to the control of complete public activity', Luxemburg's view of democracy is clearly in sympathy with the ideal of pluralist democracy. At the same time, however, a question mark hangs over her view of the number and kinds of parties to be permitted. Plural parties, but only competing socialist parties maybe. If so, there are concerns about the majority dominating the minority. Nevertheless, in criticizing the Bolshevik form of dictatorship she argued, 'Freedom only for the supporters of the government, only for the members of one party – however numerous they may be – is no freedom at all. Freedom is always and exclusively freedom for the one who thinks differently' (Luxemburg 1967: 69). Logically, this should lead to the inclusion of non-socialist parties. She explicitly defends aspects of 'bourgeois parliaments' arguing: 'The living fluid of popular mood, continuously flows around representative bodies, penetrates them, guides them' (ibid.: 60). She also criticizes the Bolsheviks for disbanding the Constituent Assembly after the elections of November 1917, stressing that '[T]he most important democratic guarantees of a healthy public life and of the political activities of the labouring masses: freedom of the press, the rights of association and assembly . . . have been outlawed for all opponents of the Soviet regime' (ibid.: 66). She adds, 'it is a well-known and indisputable fact that without a free and untrammelled press, without the unlimited right of association and assembly, the rule of the broad mass of the people is entirely unthinkable' (ibid.: 66–7). Interpreting these words, Nettl (1969: 433) comments, 'On the face of it, this could only mean that the existing institutions should have been preserved, full freedom of the press and of assembly guaranteed, and so on.'

While, clearly, Luxemburg's ideal of socialist democracy was opposed to Soviet communism, her ideal remains undeveloped as a practical form of government after proletarian revolution. The practicalities of achieving effective, stable government, with such high participation and likely wide diversity of opinion remain problematic. Whether or not the aim would have been to seek consensus in a way similar to ancient democracy or to develop a form of competition for and alteration of government is not clear. One thing is clear, however – that in moving from the position of social democratic parties being only opposition parties in bourgeois democracies to parties seeking election to government, participating in a system designed for alteration, it is Bernstein who is the proponent of social democratic parties participating in modern pluralist democracy. The difference between parties, whether left or right, which seek election purely as parties opposed to the system, and those that accept alteration in office and stand for election with the aim of becoming the next government or participating in the next government is the difference between a loyal and a disloyal opposition.[11]

Guiding hypotheses

Guiding hypotheses suggested through consideration of the history of revolutions and ideas of democracy, the domain of normative political theory, have proved complementary to those from empirical political theory. They have brought to the fore issues of constitution-making, of the development of competing political parties and of differences between parties in respect of their capacity to participate in loyal opposition. The significance of differences between social democratic parties has been particularly highlighted in this respect. Consideration of normative ideas both indirectly and directly related to democracy has, above all, demonstrated the importance of considering the role played by political actors and movements and the interactions of ideas and actors in making choices on structures and institutions. Clearly, consideration of ideas, both directly and indirectly related to democracy, has shown the importance of revolutions and post-revolutionary state-making. Crucially, consideration of the history of revolutions and the ideas of democracy has demonstrated that ideas should not be viewed in terms of the importance of texts but in terms of how ideas are taken up and put, sometimes incompatibly, together in practice.

Part II

Revolution

Chance for democracy

4 Revolution and the long path to democracy in France

The French Revolution, 1789

To resolve the government's bankruptcy, the decision to recall the Estates-General, for the first time since 1614, produced crucial debates about both the composition and the process of election to the Third Estate, the Estate supposed to represent those who were neither aristocracy (First Estate) nor clergy (Second Estate). The decision to recall the Estates-General also provoked a campaign for a 'National Assembly' in opposition to the resuscitation of the old system. The campaign for a National Assembly, which took place from 1788 to 1789, was carried out by a group, the 'patriots', largely composed of aristocrats who supported the idea of a new assembly something along the lines of the English parliament or the state legislatures in America (Wick 1996). Six of these patriots, most prominent among them Lafayette, had fought in the American War of Independence and 'picked up notions of individual rights, contract theories of government and the rhetoric of popular sovereignty' (Sutherland 1985: 34). The recalling of the Estates-General to preserve privileges provoked, therefore, the opposite of that intended. In place of the reassertion of the traditional absolutist system, aspects of democracy were in the air: ideas of representation for the common people, of a new representative debating chamber, and, not least, of elections.

Elections were held for the Estates-General, which opened on 5 May 1789. On 17 June the Third Estate voted to become the National Assembly. A few days later, in the Tennis Court Oath, in reaction to the soldiers blocking the entrance to its normal meeting hall and in defiance of the threat to the National Assembly's existence, its members vowed to establish a constitution (Sutherland 1985: 46). The National Assembly was saved by the popular revolution, which took hold in July, first in the cities and towns and then spreading, by August, to the countryside. On 11 August, the National Assembly, in the words of the legislation, 'abolished feudalism' (ibid.). On 26 August, the Declaration of the Rights of Man and Citizen was adopted to set down the measure of good government and, as an education to all, to proclaim the revolutionary advances in liberty (ibid.: 80).

The Declaration of the Rights of Man and Citizen was essentially drafted by Lafayette and, with the benefit of his experience in America, it drew both on the Virginia Declaration of Rights and the American Declaration of Independence. Jefferson, American Resident in Paris at the time, helped Lafayette by commenting on the second draft (Sutherland 1985: 81). As explained in Chapter 3, though seemingly similar, in reality the French Declaration differed in important ways from each of the American Declarations. The aim of the French Declaration was to limit the power of the king and to end the powers and privileges of feudalism and, therefore, the church. Because the king was to be retained, to become a constitutional monarch, Article III of the Declaration of the Rights of Man and Citizen stated: 'The nation is essentially the source of all sovereignty.' In the American Declaration of Independence there is no mention of 'nation' and the declared right in the event of the government having ceased to rule with people's consent, rather, is for 'the people to alter or to abolish and to institute new government' (*Declaration of Independence* 1997: 379).

Other contrasts between the Declarations are also found. In the American Declaration, 'life, liberty and the pursuit of happiness' are selected as examples of 'inalienable rights', 'endowed by their Creator'. In the French case, in Article II, drafted in July 1789 around the time of the Storming of the Bastille, and without Lafayette's concern with 'the common good' (Sutherland 1985: 81), 'the natural and imprescriptible rights of man' are given as 'liberty, property, security and resistance of oppression' (ibid.). Furthermore, it is not God and the Creator who are referred to in the French Declaration but the 'Supreme Being', a device to end the Roman Catholic Church's monopoly. In America with its various Protestant dissenters, separation between state and religion was enough (see Paine 1989: 114–15).

The next step was to write a constitution. This was where the split occurred: between the 'monarchiens' or 'Anglophiles', those who, in sympathy with Montesquieu wanted constitutional monarchy and a bicameral legislature, as in the two houses of parliament in Britain; and those, in the assumed mind-set of Rousseau, who wanted a unicameral parliament (Sutherland 1985: 82). As Hampson (1986: 51) comments, 'All of them disregarded Rousseau's warning that the general will could not be represented.' The disagreement was reinforced by their split over the king's veto. Though, in fact, not the practice in Britain, the Anglophiles wanted the king to have the right of veto over laws passed by the legislative assembly. The unicameralists wanted the king to have a 'suspensive veto', that is a veto that could be later overridden by the legislature. This latter thinking was in line with the relationship of the president to the Congress in the American Constitution (Wilson 1997: 386). The Anglophiles lost heavily in the Assembly votes, on both counts; a unicameral legislature with the monarch tied by a suspensive veto was introduced (Sutherland 1985: 82). As such, the outcome followed neither the English nor the American example. The king refused to promulgate any of these decisions – single legislature, suspensive veto, bill of rights, end of feudalism – until forced to do so in October 1789 (ibid.: 85). The new unicameral legislature became known as the 'Constituent Assembly' and the question of how it was to be elected became pressing.

In the committee set up, in July 1789, to produce a constitution, Abbé Sieyès had argued for distinguishing between 'active citizens' and 'passive citizens', only the former to be given the vote. Sieyès excluded from active citizenship: 'Women, at least in the current circumstances, children, foreigners and those who make no fiscal contribution to the state.' In justification, Sieyès argued 'only those who pay taxes are real stakeholders in the great social enterprise. They alone are true active citizens, full members of the association.' (For Sieyès's quotations see Crook 1996: 30.)

Debates quickly developed over the nature of suffrage with the decision taken, in 1790, for a limited franchise given only to 'active citizens' defined as men, of 25 or older, born in France (or naturalized), having lived in the locality (canton) for a minimum of one year who paid annual direct taxation to the equivalent value of three days' local wages. This taxation qualification ensured that neither the unemployed nor those without property got the vote (Crook 1996: 31). Further debates ensued. Robespierre was the major objector to the taxation qualification arguing that not to give all men the vote contradicted the Declaration of the Rights of Man and Citizen, 26 August 1789, under which all men were equal. His view was rejected. Arguments for inclusion of men with religious and racial differences were made more successfully. By September 1791 the vote was agreed for all religions and 'free men of colour'. Condorcet stood alone in advocating not only votes for all religions and races but also for women (ibid.: 34–5).

Direct elections on this suffrage of 'active citizens' were, however, restricted to the local level. In the first year of the revolution, France had been divided into eighty-three departments. Following the precedent of the Estates-General indirect elections, through electoral colleges, were chosen for both the departmental assemblies and the Constituent Assembly. For these purposes, the 'active citizens' were divided into those who could only vote (those paying the three-day labour tax), those eligible (and so known as 'eligibles') for municipal office and for the electoral colleges in the departments (those paying a tax equivalent to ten days of wages) and those who could serve as national deputies (those paying an annual tax of 50 livres) (Crook 1996: 36).[1] In all, around

15 per cent of the population were classified as active citizens and received the vote, which amounted to approximately 60 per cent of all adult males (ibid.: 36–7). This was proportionately wide in comparison with Britain at the time and with most of the American states (Sutherland 1985: 92). The Constitution of 1791 increased the property qualifications and set the implementation of these changes for 1793 (ibid.: 48).

Votes cast were for individual names, not parties, and there was no secret ballot. The voters were expected to engage in informed discussion with votes being cast publicly, at times out loud. The burdensome nature of voting, which required first the certificate of taxation, then registration for jury service and then for the National Guard and then the need to spend a whole day waiting to present credentials before voting, kept turnout lower than the term 'active citizens' might suggest. Turnout was further lowered by the sheer number of elections. Between 1790 and 1792 at least eight elections were held everywhere in France; Toulon had fourteen (Sutherland 1985: 71).

The First Republic

In August 1792, in the face of threatening civil and foreign war the king took flight, and so the constitutional monarchy ended and the First Republic began. The Constitution of 1791 was thrown out and with it went tax restrictions on votes. A National Convention replaced the Constituent Assembly and elections were held for it on an expanded suffrage of all men of 21 years and over, other than servants and the unemployed. The indirect elections, through electoral colleges, remained, with the lower age limit at 25 for eligibles (Crook 1996: 48). The debate over whether the king should be executed led to the fall of the liberal Girondins and the rise of the radical Jacobins, in March 1793. In that month the Committee of General Security was set up followed, in April, by the Committee of Public Safety, headed by Robespierre from July. The two committees together presided over what became known as the Reign of Terror. Robespierre was impressed by the ideas of Rousseau, with his *Social Contract* at least, to which he referred often (Cobban 1971: 153). Theory, however, did not correspond to practice.

A new constitution, drafted by Hérault de Séchelles, was adopted by the Convention in June 1793. The Constitution of 1793 replaced the Convention with a new Legislative Assembly and introduced universal male suffrage from the age of 21, without tax qualifications or other qualifications of any sort other than six months' residence in the canton. Electoral colleges and indirect elections were ended. Voters were to elect representatives directly to the Legislative Assembly (Crook 1996: 103). The constitution was put to a referendum with the electorate, appropriately, constituted under the existing rules (ibid.: 106). Voting took place in July and August and the constitution won overwhelming support. Elections, however, were never held under the new constitution. Faced with escalating civil war, intensifying foreign war and aggravated economic pressures the reign of terror took hold, ending less than a year later with Robespierre's execution in July 1794.[2]

The reign of terror ended, the Convention, now restored to its old name, set to writing a new constitution. Though the Constitution of Year III (1795) retained the 1793 age qualification of 21 it reintroduced tax qualifications, making the tax requirements more stringent than in 1791, and also restored the electoral colleges and the two-tier system of the 1791 Constitution (Sutherland 1985: 272; Crook 1996: 117–18). Though the terms 'active' and 'passive' to differentiate citizens were dropped, the property qualification for those eligible to serve as electors was increased and the number of members in the electoral colleges was reduced.

The overriding aim of those framing the Constitution of 1795 was to prevent a dictatorship and to do so through the separation of powers. A bicameral legislature was therefore introduced, divided into a 'Council of Five Hundred', for which members had to be over 30 years old and a 'Council of Ancients', made up of 250 citizens over 40 years old. The Council of Five Hundred, one-third of which retired each year, initiated legislation; the Council of Ancients approved the legislation. The executive was to be a 'Directory' and to consist of five members, one to retire each year, by lot (Sutherland 1985: 273). The Directory was allowed neither to introduce nor to veto laws but only to suggest that issues be discussed by the legislature. Crucially, however, the Directory was given the power to make appointments, to control the military and to execute the laws. A referendum was again used for this Constitution of Year III (1795).

The introduction of the Constitution of 1795 began what Sutherland (1985: 325) terms a period of 'failed consolidation'. Turnout in the first election, in 1796, was 20 per cent; in subsequent years annual elections fell further, down to 9 per cent in the elections of 1799 (Crook 1996: 124). The decline in turnout at elections was partly attributable to the fact that if the results were not what the Directory wanted they changed them (Sutherland 1985: 32). Faced with the continuing pressures of foreign war and disorder both in society and in the National Assembly the Directory determined 'to outlaw schisms' (Crook 1996: 189).[3] The Directory's aim was to strengthen the middle ground in the Assembly in order to combat what they viewed as the damaging polarization between royalists and Jacobins. They rigged elections essentially to conceal Jacobin gains. The Directory failed to achieve its objective. It was to end this political turmoil, the idea being to install a strong executive over the legislature, which the 1795 Constitution had glaringly failed to do, that the decision was taken to invite General Napoleon Bonaparte to stage a coup in 1799 (Sutherland 1985: 333).

Assessing the first ten years

Though elections were a crucial feature of the decade following the revolution, the governments they produced were not cases of modern democracy, not even examples of early forms of modern democracy. This is so not simply because elections were indirect and because election results were so frequently rigged and turnout, in part consequence, so low. Under the right conditions such might indicate the start of suffrage expansion and the first tentative moves in the direction of free and fair elections. What prevented these elections from being early indicators of modern democracy was essentially that the system was devised for 'the pursuit of unanimity' (Crook 1996: 195), the goal so clearly distinguished by Sartori as that of ancient, not modern, democracy. As Crook concludes, the chosen electoral systems were designed 'to fabricate a false unity and to exclude any real form of opposition'. This was the motive for choosing indirect elections and this was why the elections were postponed indefinitely in 1793 (the one election that would have been direct) and why, after 1795, there were 'a constant succession of annulments' (ibid.).

Electoral competition in the modern sense of representation was not the purpose of the electoral systems chosen, neither under the constitutional monarchy, nor the First Republic, whether under Robespierre or the Directorate. As Hayward (1991: 114) explains, 'Parties were equated with uncompromisingly divisive factions . . . Opposition was regarded – as it was in practice – to be by definition disloyal.' This call for uniformity followed from the revolution. As Tombs (1996) explains:

> The Revolution, with its ideologies of the general will and the sovereignty of the nation, and its own struggles against internal and external enemies, had stressed 'the One and Indivisible Republic'. Awareness of that unity in reality and the universal fear of renewed conflict, meant that all regimes and parties after the revolution embraced in varying degrees the unitary aspiration. Individual freedom was only legitimate within a framework of common purpose.
>
> (Tombs 1996: 62)

Under the Directorate, the minority view, a very small minority, was argued strongly by the liberal, Benjamin Constant, who stood against the pervading view that 'diversity is life, uniformity is death'.[4] Constant's modern view, based on the English model, was for the right to opposition with a system designed on checks and balances, competitive parties, freedom of speech and freedom of the press with the judiciary (not Montesquieu's aristocracy) as a countervailing check, plus a bicameral legislature (Hayward 1991: 121–2). The meaning of liberalism in France, Benjamin Constant and this small minority of like-minded thinkers apart, was not the same as in Britain where individualism was admired and went hand-in-hand with free trade and utilitarianism. In line with the Declaration of the Rights of Man and Citizen, individualism in France concentrated, rather, on the rights and duties of the citizen to the state and nation.

Constant made the distinction between 'the liberty of the ancients' and the 'liberty of the moderns'. The former, characteristic of France at the time and of ancient Athens, is the public liberty of participation in the political life and marketplace of the community; the latter is the private liberty of being able to conduct one's affairs away from the public gaze. As Tombs (1996: 64) comments, France 'never accepted the Scottish Enlightenment, the "birth certificate of modernity", with its principles of economic liberty, utilitarianism and liberalism'. Significantly, Constant had studied in Edinburgh (ibid.). This call for uniformity also served the interests of a new political group, the 'notables', those who were eligible for public office. These notables brought together property and political power. As Crook (1996: 196) concludes: 'The "invisible aristocracy" of the departmental assemblies points to the hidden agenda which elections were designed to serve: the legitimisation of a new political class.'

This dominant view of the rights and duties of the citizen to the state and nation in combination with the desire to serve the interests of the new political class puts into perspective the decision to invite Napoleon Bonaparte to take power to end schism and so to bring the revolution to its conclusion. The American solution for post-revolutionary political consolidation, with a president as a strong executive in a country where differences between states were built into the federal system and elections for both lower and upper Houses were direct, was not an option for the 'one and indivisible republic'. Least of all was it possible for the move to organized political parties, which began in America in 1800, the year after Napoleon's coup.

Republic to empire: the political system under Napoleon I

The day after Bonaparte's coup on 18–19 brumaire, year VIII, work began on a new constitution. Abbé Sieyès was the main drafter, his aim to achieve, as he stressed, 'confidence from below, authority from above'. The Constitution of Year VIII introduced elaborate devices to ensure separation of powers, concentrated executive authority in the 'First Consul' (Napoleon) and sharply reduced the role of elections. The Tribunate, consisting of 100 members, was given the role of discussing bills but not of voting on them; the Legislative Body, consisting of 300 members, was given the role of voting on bills, but not of discussing them. Any bill voted on and supported was then to go to the Senate, which had sixty members, where it was to be checked thoroughly to ensure that the bill was constitutional. Not one of these bodies was elected other than in the most indirect and contrived way. (See Sutherland 1985: 338.)

Elections based on universal male suffrage were to be held in each 'communal arrondissement', where one-tenth of their number were to be elected to a communal list. These 'communal notables' were then to elect one-tenth of their number to a departmental list. In turn, these 'departmental notables' then elected another tenth of their number to a national list. The members of both the Tribunate and the Legislative Body were chosen by the Senate from a list of 6,000 'notabilities'. (See Sutherland 1985: 338.)

Executive power was held by the Consuls. Bonaparte was appointed First Consul for ten years. Beneath the First Consul were two other Consuls to act as executives, one with control over foreign affairs, the other over internal affairs. These two Consuls, Camacérès and Lebrun, had only advisory powers with Article 42 of the constitution stating, categorically, that 'the decision of the First Consul shall suffice'. As Sutherland (1985: 339) remarks, 'At a stroke, Bonaparte acquired staggering powers of appointment in the local, national, military and civil spheres of government', adding, 'In no sense were the Consuls or the ministers responsible to the legislature.' To aid the First Consul there was to be a Council of State, the role of which was to prepare bills and its members in turn to put the case for the bills before the Tribunate and Legislative Body; it was also to act as a court for judging purely administrative matters (ibid.: 338–9).

Following Sieyès's dictum of 'confidence from below, authority from above' and to avoid meddling by the Councils of the old legislature, which were to be replaced, it was decided to put the constitution to a plebiscite. Rather than achieving a ringing endorsement, however, the result demonstrated the growing apathy of the electorate. Only around 1.5 million participated in the election, though with the vast majority in favour and only 1,500 against. To conceal this low participation, the election results were fiddled to double the totals. Officials added between 8,000 and 14,000 yes votes to every department's returns. In addition soldiers' votes were entirely fabricated, as none were actually given the opportunity to vote, and sailors voted in highly questionable circumstances.[5] In any case, the Constitution of Year VIII was implemented before all the results were known, in fact when only those from Paris were ready (Sutherland 1985: 361).

With the constitution in place, appointments were made. Appointments made to the Senate, Tribunate and Legislative Body were mostly political, rewards given for their support of Bonaparte's coup while, in contrast, those made to the Council of State demonstrated the importance given to expertise. As Sutherland (1985: 347) comments, 'they were chosen less for their political background than for their expertise in legal, financial, educational or administrative areas which they had acquired in the royal or revolutionary bureaucracies'. By centring on the Council of State and the Consuls, the constitution concentrated power in the hands of experts. The roles of the Senate, Tribunate and Legislative Body were essentially to play their designated part (checking with the constitution, discussing bills and voting on them, respectively) in ratifying legislation. Debate was built into the system for the purpose of unification not division ('authority from above'). The elaborate system of election in the *arrondissement* for the list of notables was designed to develop 'confidence from below'. What the constitution was not intended to do was to direct debate towards division or, worse, towards coalitions of divided opinion and interests – parties. In protest against opponents to a bill in 1801, Bonaparte stated the government's aim as being 'to destroy the spirit of faction'; 'I am a national', he declared (ibid.: 357).

In 1802, a plebiscite was again employed, at the instigation of the Council of State, to make Bonaparte 'Consul for Life'. The votes less than free and less than accurate, on extrapolation from the conduct of the first plebiscite, this second plebiscite was won overwhelmingly. The irrelevance of a true vote may have been indicated by the fact that the new constitution was drafted in anticipation of the required plebiscitary support, drafted before the votes were counted. The plebiscite, in any case, was of dubious worth for it was only concerned with an amendment to the existing constitution, not its replacement with an entirely new one, which was what transpired. (See Sutherland 1985: 358–61.)

The Constitution of Year X was promulgated in August 1802. Bonaparte to be Consul for Life, he also gained greater power of appointment over the Senate, quite sufficient to control the majority. The contrived system of electoral lists was replaced by the election of electoral colleges, the choice of members from a list of the 600 men in the department paying the heaviest taxes (Sutherland 1985: 359). Election was for life. With a system of elections ended and a constitutional guarantee for Bonaparte to weight assemblies in his favour, the Constitution of Year X is seen as the start of Bonaparte's dictatorship. After the purge of the government bodies which followed in Year X, a bill was never again rejected in the Legislative Body and the Tribunate achieved only inconsequential opposition to any bill (ibid.: 359-60). The Senate simply acquiesced (ibid.: 361). The institution of the Legion of Honour in May 1802, the system of rewards and titles, proved too enticing to risk the consequences of making a stand (ibid.: 366-7).

On 18 May 1804, Napoleon Bonaparte became Emperor, no longer simply consul for life but a hereditary position, the position of emperor after his death to be passed on to his chosen heirs. Agreement was readily given by all the government bodies and a further plebiscite, again, gave support (Sutherland 1985: 365). He was crowned in December of that year. From 1805, expression of free opinion in the press began to decline (ibid.: 390).

Under Napoleon Bonaparte the revolutionary aspiration of citizens' government was finally abandoned altogether. It is Bonaparte, nevertheless, who is credited with laying the foundations of modern government.

The Bonapartist system of administration

The establishment of state centralization is a crucial feature of a modern state (Skocpol 1979). Though centralized administration could also be a feature of traditional societies and can, as Bonaparte clearly showed, serve dictatorship as well as democracy, the essential aspect of the modern state which differentiates it from previous states is that it is legal-rational, based on and run according to proper laid down rules (Weber 1964: 329–41). For the uniform administration of law, a modern bureaucracy is essential, one that approximates Weber's ideal type – an organized hierarchical structure and a proper career system with laid down salaries, duties and required educational qualifications. By design, Bonaparte's administrative system was quintessentially hierarchical. Authority was centralized in the ministries in Paris, from whence instructions descended to the prefects, in their newly created posts. A prefect held individual control over one of the eighty-three departments into which France had been divided since the first year of the revolution. Officials within each of these departments were themselves positioned within a strict hierarchy and the whole bureaucratic system was internally regulated by the Council of State. (See Tombs 1996: 98.)

Prefects, though combining administrative with political roles in the departments, were appointed officials earning excellent salaries of between 8,000 and 24,000 francs plus allowances (Sutherland 1985: 345). Under the law of 28 pluviôse, year VIII (7 February 1800), each prefect was to be appointed by the First Consul (Napoleon) and was directly responsible to the Minister of the Interior.[6] The prefect system replaced the collapsing local government system, begun in 1790, which had had elected posts. Now outside of the control of local citizens the prefect, accountable only to the Minister of the Interior, supervised all local affairs, including the police, conscription, tax payments, hospitals and roads (ibid.). The prefects also made by-laws, decided on the use of common lands, awarded contracts, made appointments of even those such as road-menders and postmen, decided on water distribution, provided scholarships and poor relief, and set food prices in lean times (Tombs 1996: 98–9). Tax collection, the army and the law courts, however, were outside the prefects' control (ibid.: 100).

Below the prefects came the sub-prefects, in charge of the *arrondissements*, the newly devised sub-areas of the departments. The sub-prefects had no independent authority, their role being to execute the prefect's instructions. In place of the municipal cantons put in place by the Directory, the communes, which had been first introduced in 1790, were reinstated. Each one of the communes, 36,000 in all, was administered by a mayor who, similarly, was now an appointee of the prefect in communes of under 5,000 people and an appointee of the central government if in a larger commune.[7] The prefects, as for appointments to the Council of State, were mostly drawn from those with legal qualifications or with previous administrative experience, whether in civil or military affairs (Sutherland 1985: 345). Experts were specially sought in the area of tax collection.[8] As Sutherland comments, 'Although this had a crusty Old Regime air about it, the system worked extremely well. For the first time in a decade, the bulk of the taxes of the Year IX [1801] were collected in the year they were assigned' (ibid.: 346).

Napoleon's aim of centralization with top–down organization and, in theory, problems solved rationally from above, could not be fully realized in practice. The central bureaucracy, in Paris, had only between 2,000 and 3,000 civil servants spread around ten or so ministries to serve the whole country (Tombs 1996: 99). It was impossible to know precisely what was happening in the localities except through the information provided by the local officials, and such information was not objective. Prefects particularly and also the sub-prefects and the mayors in the communes became the focal point of local wealthy society and subjected to considerable pressure to protect local interests (ibid.). Initially, Napoleon's bureaucracy also lacked a career structure based on examinations. In 1806, however, Napoleon introduced a restricted higher education system – the *Université* – under state not church control, which was primarily designed for training in state service (ibid.: 132). In addition to constructing the centralized legal-rational administrative system, Bonaparte also rationalized the monetary system.

Economic foundations

The Bank of France was established on 24 pluviôse, year VIII (13 February 1800). It issued notes above 500 francs and was run by an elected board of rich shareholders and, among its roles, made loans to the treasury and managed some of the government's financial assets (Sutherland 1985: 346). Of more relevance for day-to-day exchange, in 1803, the law of 7 germinal, year XI, established the *franc de germinal*, which introduced the decimal system, fixing the metal content, denomination and circulation of coins (ibid.).

After 1799, as after 1789, the expressed aim was to remove all vestiges of the traditional economy, that is of feudalism, and to establish the conditions needed for a modern rational economic system of production and exchange. As Tombs (1996) explains,

> This meant uniformity in law, markets, money, taxation and measurement: freedom to work and trade; and the recognition of property, on the Roman Law model, as an 'inviolable and sacred right', unencumbered by ancient regulations and customs.

> (Tombs 1996: 147)

These aspirations had been first given form through the d'Allarde and Le Chapelier laws of 1791, and were established, under Napoleon, through the Civil Code (or *Code Napoléon*) of 1804 and the Commercial Code of 1807 (Tombs 1996: 147). Important restraints, however, were imposed which particularly affected the labour market. The formation of and participation in a workers' organization was a criminal offence. Under the d'Allarde and Le Chapelier laws also, all 'corporations, monopolies, restrictive practices and combinations of citizens' had been prohibited and such 'combinations' included both those of employers and of workers (ibid.: 160). The effect was to limit the size of enterprises to that of family firms. Employers' interests were served through the workings of the chambers of commerce and consultative councils. Under the law of 22 germinal, year XI (1803) both employers and employees were forbidden to take actions to restrain trade by conspiring to lower salaries, on the part of employers, or to raise salaries, by workers striking. The harsher penalties fell on the workers rather than on the employers. (See Sutherland 1985: 375.)

Wage-earners (the term 'proletariat' dates from the 1830s) were controlled through a system of documentation – *livrets*. All workers were required to carry these identity documents which carried their record of work and employment (Tombs 1996: 160). These *livrets* remained officially in operation until 1890. A system operated to resolve industrial disputes, heavily weighted towards the interests of the employers. Only the employers could elect the arbitration council and courts involved in wage disputes were only obliged to accept the testimony of the employer (ibid.). This remained the case until 1864 when workers' organizations were also allowed, though they were not to be made fully legal until 1884.

The Civil Code of 1804 was especially important in setting a rational system of law, one that applied to everyone and everywhere in France. Its concerns were primarily those of property ownership and inheritance (Sutherland 1985: 374–5). The uniformity of law was also achieved through the Code of Criminal Procedure and the Penal Law of 1810 (Harvey 1968: 59). As Harvey (ibid.) observes, the codification of law was an 'enduring contribution by Napoleon'.

Freedom of worship and toleration

The Concordat of 1801 together with the Organic Articles of 1802 made the Catholic Church subordinate to the state and permitted freedom of worship (Tombs 1996: 132). As Eisenberg Vichniac, focusing on Jews, argues,

> The logic of the 'Declaration of the Rights of Man' made it impossible to maintain discrete categories of individuals who were excluded from French society, just as the logic of the emerging capitalist economy made it unthinkable to limit Jews to specific professions.
>
> (Eisenberg Vichniac 1998: 179)

As explained, by September 1791, 'free men of colour' and men of any religion became citizens like other Frenchmen. Although in some departments some restrictions on Jews returned under Napoleon, they lapsed in 1818 (ibid.).

Toleration for Jews had been achieved in France before the revolution of 1789, in the south-west at least if not fully in Alsace, but, crucially, under Napoleon the institutional means, the consistory system of governance, was created through which Judaism could be protected as a religion while at the same time achieving integration of Jews. This system of governance, under the Ministry of Cults, acted to negotiate between the state and the Jewish community. Through this system the state protected Jews against the prejudice which continued within society, particularly in Alsace.[9] (See Eisenberg Vichniac 1998: 179–80.)

After the empire of Napoleon I: constitutional monarchy to 1848

Napoleon was deposed in 1814, a fall brought not by internal collapse but by defeat in war which led to the Senate being asked by the allied forces occupying Paris to form a provisional government. Constitutional monarchy replaced the emperor. Napoleon returned briefly, for the Hundred Days, in 1815, ended by his final defeat at Waterloo. The restoration of the monarchy was based on a constitutional Charter, 'granted' by the king rather than 'the nation', in which a Chamber of Deputies and a Chamber of Peers replaced the previous assemblies. Bonaparte's strong system of centralized bureaucracy remained. In the upper house, the Chamber of Peers, members (unlike in Britain) were to be appointed by the king. (The Chamber returned to the name of Senate in 1851.) (See Sutherland 1985: 428.) The lower house, the Chamber of Deputies, was elected but the franchise was the most restricted of all the constitutions. The law of 1817 gave the vote to men paying 300 francs or more in taxes, a total of just over 110,000 men (Tombs 1996: 102). To be eligible to stand for election to be a deputy the minimum tax payment was 1,000 francs. The Council of State remained, but 40 per cent of its members were purged and 28 of the 87 prefects were similarly dismissed (Sutherland 1985: 430).

The consequence of the political revolution of 1830, following riots in Paris and calls for Napoleon's son as 'Napoleon II', was that constitutional monarchy stayed but the Bourbon king was replaced by the Orleanist monarchy. The constitutional Charter was revised. The highly restricted suffrage was little affected, the tax qualification was reduced to 200 francs, thereby increasing the electorate to 166,000 (Tombs 1996: 103). This approximated to the right to vote being held by just 33 out of every 1,000 of the population (ibid.). The refusal of both the new king, Louis-Philippe, and his chief minister, Guizot, to extend suffrage gave fuel to the revolution of 1848 (ibid.).

François Guizot, the head of government from 1840 to 1848, was a Protestant and the leading liberal politician in the 1820s and 1830s. Guizot, however, held to the elitist view of liberalism in which the vote was viewed not as the right of the individual private citizen but as a public duty to the state (Tombs 1996: 69). Guizot supported a narrow suffrage restricted to the educated property owners and he justified his view in terms of this 'middle class' being ideally placed between the prejudices of the privileged nobility and the undemocratic urges of the masses. The view was that those with property gained through their own hard work were uniquely capable of reasoning in a public-spirited way. This was in line with Sieyès's position, as expressed at the time of drafting the first constitution of the revolution, in 1789, on taxpayers as 'stakeholders' who 'alone are true active citizens' (Crook 1996: 30). Guizot's liberalism was Constant's 'liberty of the ancients'.

By 1848, the pressure for widespread male suffrage could no longer be resisted. The age of the democracy of the ancients was passing. The binding idea of the French Revolution of 1789, the one and indivisible republic which sought government based on unanimity, the general will, was destined to be replaced. The pressure for these political changes came from the economic and social changes that followed the revolution of 1789.

Economy and social structure to 1848

The end of the feudal system brought by the French Revolution in 1789, and the sale of land confiscated in the revolution led to a hugely increased number of people (including large numbers of peasants) becoming landowners, land rather than industry seeming the safest investment. Indeed, France was to remain a largely agricultural nation until after the Second World War. In Britain the number of workers employed in manufacturing exceeded those working in agriculture in 1840, more than a century earlier than was to be the case in France. France did not achieve the dramatic growth in economic production witnessed in Britain during the nineteenth century, though when France's relatively slow growth in population is taken into account economic performance approximated the European average. (See Tombs 1996: 148–50.)

The consequence of the retention of agriculture as the major feature of the economy after the revolution of 1789 was that a strong and powerful bourgeoisie and a large proletariat did not develop, as they had in England. In contrast to Britain, at the time, where rapid industrialization led to a sharp increase in urbanization with the consequent upheaval of population, in France the growth of cities was less marked than the expansion of small towns. In France, small-scale enterprises were the norm in both country and town, and labour-intensive methods were retained, bringing lesser disruption to patterns of life than the large factories of Britain. In agriculture, the fallow system of feudalism was replaced by the modern method of crop rotation but on the small farms self-employment was far more common than employment of workers for wages. Wage earning for many in the rural areas was in the form of supplementary income in rural industry.[10]

In France, it was not the bourgeoisie, as big capitalists, but the petit-bourgeoisie which grew most strikingly following the revolution: people buying farms, including peasants buying the land on which they worked; workers who were self-employed; entrepreneurs of small-scale enterprises. In Weber's (1964: 424) terminology, rather than Marx's, in France it was the 'acquisition classes' that grew after the revolution, those between the owners of large properties – landowners, entrepreneurs, rentiers – and those without properties – the proletariat.

1848: the turning point

In February 1848, faced with rioting in the streets of Paris, King Louis-Philippe abdicated, Guizot was ousted and monarchy was finally ended by another revolution which, in March, brought the introduction of universal male suffrage with 20 the minimum age and a huge increase in the electorate to 9,900,000. In December 1848, the newly enfranchised voters elected Louis-Napoleon Bonaparte, the nephew of Napoleon Bonaparte, as president. Workers played a major part in the 1848 revolution and, along with calls for political change, they demanded guarantee of work, a demand met by the provisional government in setting up national workshops (Gould 1995: 39–40). Following the elections in April, and the new government's decision to end these workshops, an insurrection broke out in June in defence of their 'democratic and social republic' (ibid.: 49). After four days the insurrection was put down. A new constitution was approved in November in which not only the legislature but also the president of the republic was to be elected by universal manhood suffrage (Bury 1970: 22). Further elections were held in December.

Marx's assessment of the December 1848 election of Louis-Napoleon Bonaparte, in *The Eighteenth Brumaire of Louis Bonaparte* is that it served the interests of the peasants: 'Bonaparte represents a class, and the most numerous class of French society at that, the small-holding (Parzellen) peasants' (Marx 1964: 123). Marx emphasizes that, 'The Bonaparte dynasty represents not the revolutionary, but the conservative peasant: not the peasant that strikes out beyond the condition of his social existence, the small holding, but rather the peasant who wants to consolidate his holding' (ibid.: 125). For Marx, Louis-Napoleon Bonaparte represented the interests of 'bourgeois order', but, he explained, in 1848, 'the strength of this bourgeois order lies in the middle class' (ibid.). The Bonapartes, he argued no longer represented the minority interests of 'the big landowners' as the Bourbons had or 'the dynasty of big money' as the Orleanists had, but 'the dynasty of the peasants, that is, the mass of the French people' (ibid.:123).[11] This mass, this middle class, consisted of those owning some property and was epitomized by the small-holding peasants.

Both the elections of April and December 1848 confirmed the importance of the acquisition classes. As Tombs (1996) comments,

> Owning a plot of land, however modest, was an incentive and a means for small farmers, artisans, industrial workers and traders to resist economic change. Their numbers meant that governments worrying about elections (especially after the introduction of manhood suffrage in 1848), public order and even revolutions, dared not ignore demands for protection of *les intérêts acquis* (vested interests).

(Tombs 1996: 162)

After 1848: politics and economy

Manhood suffrage was soon reduced again by the Assembly, down by 3 million in May 1850. The president unable to seek re-election after the end of his four years of office under the terms of the constitution, and the Assembly unwilling to make constitutional changes, Louis-Napoleon Bonaparte staged a *coup d'état* on 2 December 1851 (see Bury 1970: 30–3). After the coup, the male franchise was fully restored and the elected chamber (re-named *Corps Legislatif*) was greatly reduced in importance 'to a subordinate and silent role' (Tombs 1996: 104). In 1852, Louis-Napoleon declared himself Emperor Napoleon III.

It is Tombs's argument (1996: 104) that, through 'unwittingly converting his opponents, Napoleon III became something he had never intended: the godfather of a parliamentary democracy'. Between 1851 and 1860 this 'unwitting conversion' occurred through negative reactions. In the 1850s desires for the 'liberty of the ancients', based on the goals of unanimity (the one and indivisible republic), were frustrated as the realization dawned that, once again, an emperor viewed himself, not parliament, as representative of the general will. Between 1860 and 1870, foundations for 'the liberty of the moderns' were laid by positive reactions to increasing opportunities developed for opposition that was not perceived as a threat to the system. During the 1860s, the parliament began to be restored to its pre-1851 role, with crucial legislation in 1860, 1867 and 1870. For example, the Chamber of Deputies was given the right to question ministers and to demand that details of debates be published. Similarly, the Senate was given powers of legislation equal to those of the Chamber of Deputies and gained the right to public debate, and the Chamber of Deputies was given the rights to initiate bills, to consider and vote on the budget and to appoint its officers. Though harsh in his approach to strikes, in 1864 Napoleon III also repealed the statute of 1791. This had the effect of conceding the right to strike and allowing trade unions. (See Harvey 1968: 99.)

In respect of the economy, Louis-Napoleon encouraged free trade, a development marked by the Anglo-French commercial treaty of 1860 (Tombs 1996: 153). Public works, most notably the re-building of Paris, ensured full employment and boosted the economy (Harvey 1968: 100). Nevertheless, with the freeing of trade, French economic growth slowed or stagnated to the end of the century, protectionism finding greater support as a consequence. Wages in France grew slowly in comparison with Britain and Germany, weakening the consumption power of the home market.[12] Failure to invest in modern production methods made imports more competitive. By 1913, French exports accounted for 12.6 per cent of all exports from the Continent; in 1860, France's share had been 60 per cent (Tombs 1996: 154).

France's economy was also severely damaged by the war with Germany in 1870–71. The high costs of fighting the war together with the crippling indemnities paid to Germany after the defeat led to a damaging national debt and the loss of Alsace-Lorraine, a very important industrial region (Tombs 1996: 159). The indemnities paid to Germany, amounting to 5 billion francs, were equivalent to two and a half times France's annual state budget (ibid.: 160).

The Third Republic

Following serious defeat in the Franco-Prussian War, in September 1870, which resulted in the capture of Napoleon III, a new Government of National Defence restored the empire to a republic. In early 1871, the government accepted an armistice and elections were held in February. The war was officially ended in March and the Treaty of Frankfurt signed in May. The government's insensitive handling of Paris, where citizens did not want peace and where they reacted strongly against the downgrading of the importance of Paris, led to the setting up of the Paris Commune. The Paris Commune demanded not a centralized republic but a federal republic. After two months, in May 1871, the commune was defeated.[13]

The crushing of the commune, in 1871, led to the disbanding of organizations and associations and the discrediting of socialistic ideas for the remainder of the decade (Harvey 1968: 153). So began a provisional government, dominated by monarchists deeply split over who the new monarch should be. The end to this absurd situation came in 1875. By the narrowest of votes, the decision was made for a presidency.

In 1875, organic laws were introduced, together known as the Constitution of 1875, which framed parliamentary democracy. These laws confirmed the provisional arrangements of 1871–75. Having learnt the consequences of kings and emperors, the president was to be elected for seven years, but not by popular vote; the American presidential procedure was not adopted. In France, the president was to be elected by an absolute majority of votes of the Senate and Chamber of Deputies (Harvey 1968: 122). The president had considerable powers, including that of dissolving the Chamber of Deputies before the end of its term of four years, though only with the Senate's agreement (ibid.). The Senate consisted of 300 members of which 225 were to be indirectly elected by electoral colleges of notables in each department. The senators served nine-year terms and Senate's support was required for amendments to the constitution (ibid.: 123). The Chamber of Deputies also had weight, being able to initiate financial bills and ask pertinent questions at critical times (*interpellation*). By such means the Chamber could bring down governments (Harvey 1968: 122; Tombs 1996: 105). This republic, the Third Republic, lasted until 1940 when French history was again to be affected by German invasion.

Instituting democracy piecemeal

Between 1875 and 1940 important adaptations were made both to the political system and to civil society. The power of the Chamber of Deputies was put to the test and significantly hardened following the *Seize Mai* of 1877. On 16 May, President MacMahon, having dismissed the Chief Minister, Simon, and then, having sought and gained the consent of the Senate, dissolved the Chamber of Deputies and ordered new elections; instead he was obliged to resign (Harvey 1968: 124–5). The Chamber reasserted itself, making MacMahon first accept the Chamber's choice of chief minister and then face such strong opposition in the Chamber that resignation became the only option. From that time the presidency was weakened, and fulfilled more of a symbolic function. The balance between the Senate and Chamber of Deputies was also changed, the elected Chamber becoming the more powerful. Monarchism was defeated. As Harvey (1968: 126) comments, by 1880, France was fully a republic with 'republicans in charge of republican institutions'.

In the 1880s, a new openness developed. In 1882, free, secular education for all children between the ages of 6 and 13 was introduced, which reduced the power of the Catholic Church, and a wider secularization of society took place (Harvey 1968: 129–30). During the Third Republic, after Jews had already been permitted into the army during the Second Republic, the way was opened for Jews to reach even top posts in the state bureaucracy. Geographical mobility also occurred with large numbers of Jews, as Frenchmen first, beginning to move out of their communities to the cities (Eisenberg Vichniac 1998: 180–2).

In 1884, freedom of association was restored. As a consequence, all sorts of pressure groups developed to lobby for economic interests, whether workers' organizations or groups representing financiers, industrialists, wine-makers, farmers, and so on. Crucially, these groups outside parliament developed links with groups within the parliament (Tombs 1996: 117). Importantly, though workers' organizations had first been allowed in 1864, trade unions became legal in 1884. A public works programme introduced by the government in 1879, the Freycinet plan, which aimed to stimulate the economy mainly through road and railway building, failed; the result was increased taxes and further bankruptcies.

In 1889, following the real possibility, not in the end attempted, that General Boulanger, elected to the Chamber of Deputies in 1888, might, with substantial right-wing support, dissolve the Chamber and revise the constitution to re-establish a strong executive (perhaps even king or emperor), changes were introduced in the electoral laws (Harvey 1968: 130-2). In the 1889 elections, candidates were no longer allowed to stand in more than one district and the *scrutin de liste* was replaced by the *scrutin de arrondissement* under which voters could choose only one candidate (ibid.: 133).

The threat to the republic again reared its head in 1894 with the Dreyfus Affair. The arrest, in 1894, and conviction, in early 1895, of a Jewish army officer, Captain Alfred Dreyfus, for spying led to a wave of anti-Semitism, which peaked in violent street-battles between Dreyfusards and anti-Dreyfusards in 1898–99. The sentence was eventually acknowledged as a miscarriage of justice and Dreyfus was pardoned in 1906. Though the events provide certain evidence of intolerant beliefs and actions among some of the population, the anti-Semitic movement of 1898–1900 fell apart through lack of widespread popular support. There is also no evidence that Dreyfus was arrested and convicted because he was Jewish (Lindemann 1997: 231). The Affair, crucially, was resolved through parliament and anti-Semitism never formed the basis of a political party separate from conservatives, as it was to do in Germany in the National Socialist German Workers' Party, NSDAP. In the elections of both 1898 and 1906, the Dreyfusards gained the majority. (See Lindemann 1997: 234–5.) The Dreyfus Affair also played a part in the development of voluntary associations that cut across social cleavages. In particular, the League of the Rights of Man (pro-Dreyfus) and the League of Patriots (anti-Dreyfus) cross-cut social classes (Harvey 1968: 139–40). By the end of the nineteenth century the rule of the notables, Crook's new 'political class', had given way to the pressure of pluralist groups (Lindemann 1997: 237).

Organized political parties

By the end of the nineteenth century, the Third Republic had instituted power in the Chamber of Deputies, the elected chamber, modernized the electoral laws and overseen the development of pressure group politics. Crucially, the government and parliamentary representatives as a whole had become answerable to the electorate, if still imperfectly. Elections were not fully free and fair until 1914 when the ballot became 'truly secret' (Tombs 1996: 106). Before 1914, under the Third Republic, in addition to the continued use of bribery, sometimes intimidation and the shifting of polling stations and constituency boundaries, voting returns had sometimes been falsified. Furthermore, electoral expenses were not limited and barrels of wine at polling stations and rounds of drink for weeks before were quite common. As late as 1902, in one election, voters were said to have averaged 500 glasses of free wine (ibid.: 109).

Not only were elections not 'free and fair' in the nineteenth century, French political parties did not have permanent national organizations until the twentieth century. From the days of the revolution and through the century which followed, organized parties continued to be looked upon with suspicion and until 1901 all associations of over twenty people remained under legal restrictions. These restrictions were removed by the Law of Associations of 1901 from which point permanent nationally organized parties were set up. Before this time, organization existed only at election times, formed around ad hoc local committees set up to choose a candidate, raise money for election leaflets, drinks, and so forth. From the turn of the century, groups within parliament began to correspond to party organization outside parliament, but before then deputies formed clubs, coalescing around individual politicians or broad differences and usually deputies belonged to more than one group and the groups within the Senate differed again. (See Tombs 1996: 114–16).

The lack of organized parties within parliament before 1901 led to the instability of short-lived governments. Continuing in the pattern since 1814, majorities were too unstable to guarantee the passing of legislation and the average life of a government from 1814 to 1914 was only around eight months (Tombs 1996: 119). Guizot's government (1840–48), in lasting for eight years, was the notable exception. Before this, only the governments of Villèle (1822–27) and Perrier (1831–32) had lasted for more than a year. After 1848, only the governments of Thiérs (1871–73), Ferrys (1880–85) and Meline (1896–98) lasted longer than a year, though from the turn of the century three years became more common.[14]

Neither a majority party nor a firm coalition of parties could be guaranteed to support a body of legislation and ministers could control parties no more than parties could control ministers.[15] It was in this that the attraction had lain, for some, of a strong executive, whether king, emperor or president. Such a person, these advocates argued, would be capable of disciplining proceedings. The alternative was to develop party government in which, for others, lay the attraction of the Westminster model, though the sheer number of rival parties made France inherently different from the two-party system of Britain and America. As Tombs (1996) comments in respect of all the regimes between 1814 and 1914:

> But what no assembly under any regime did was to provide a means for *alternance*, the peaceful alternation of parties in power, for which generations of French parliamentarians regarded Westminster as a model.
>
> (Tombs 1996: 105)

Encouraged by the popular participation in politics stimulated by the Dreyfus Affair together with the passing of the Law of Associations, modern, nationally organized, permanent political parties began in 1901: the *Parti Républicain Radical et Radical-Socialiste* (the Radical Party, radical -socialists), the *Fédération Républicaine* (conservative republican), the *Action Libérale Populaire* (Catholic). The *Section Française de l'International Ouvrière* (SFIO), the French Socialist Party, formed in 1905 as an amalgamation of the earlier socialist groups such as, the *Fédération de Travailleurs Socialistes* (1879), the Marxist *Parti Ouvrier Français* (1883) and the *Blanquist Parti Ouvrier Socialiste Révolutionnaire* (1890). (See Tombs 1996: 115–16.)

The formation of the French Socialist Party accompanied the development of the *Confédération Générale du Travail* (CGT), which formed in 1895 and merged, in 1902, with the craft unions, the *Bourses du Travail* (Harvey 1968: 153). By 1912, the membership of all trade unions totalled around 1 million. The figures of 4.5 million members in Britain and the 3 million members in Germany are in line with France's continuing relatively slow rate of industrialization (ibid.). Reactions to the Russian Revolution led to a split in the SFIO in 1920. The majority, favouring the revolutionary route to socialism, formed the new French Communist Party. The minority, which favoured the evolutionary route, remained the SFIO, headed by Léon Blum. A similar split took place in the CGT in 1921, though in this case it was the minority that founded the communist-dominated union, in 1924 (ibid.: 224).

After the First World War, in July 1919, a new electoral law was passed with a 'winner-takes-all' provision (Harvey 1968: 220). The party that won a majority within the department was to be awarded all of the seats. This new law provided an incentive for parties to enter elections with pre-formed coalitions. The 1924 election was fought between the *Bloc National* (nationalists and conservatives) and the *Cartel des Gauches* (the SFIO plus the radical-socialists but not the communists, who were excluded) (ibid.: 225). The election was won by the Cartel des Gauches and alteration in power between pre-formed coalitions continued. At the time of the World Market Crash in 1929, a strong centre coalition was in power (ibid.: 231). Following the collapse of the Weimar Republic in Germany, the French communists decided the 'Republic was to be defended against the right' (ibid.: 239). The Communist Party joined a centre-left coalition to form the Popular Front, which won the election in 1936. Following Germany's invasion of Poland, the French allied with Britain and the United States and declared war against Germany in September 1939. Following France's defeat, in June 1940, the Third Republic ended.

Looking back

As has become clear, there was no easy association between the French Revolution of 1789 and the development of modern representative democracy. Organized political parties were not in place until 1901 and elections were not fully free and fair until 1914 when the ballot became truly secret and the 'buying' of votes with free drinks had been ended. Furthermore, it was not until the Third Republic that, from 1879, the elected house (the Chamber of Deputies) became truly answerable to the electorate as their representatives. Only then did the Chamber become a forum in which politicians practised the art of oratory within the constraints of the possible, Weber's requirement for *Sachlichkeit* (Beetham 1985: 23). The cases of both MacMahon and Boulanger demonstrated this. MacMahon learnt the hard way; he thought that he could do what he liked and found that he could not. The lessons from Boulanger are very different. General Boulanger, the genuinely charismatic figure who commanded following by his natural charm, chose not to exploit his electoral victory.

Though, from the 1880s, deputies were able to topple a government through *interpellation* they were aware of their own vulnerability in the next government (Tombs 1996: 105). They lacked the assurance of support, which would have been provided by party obedience. Without modern organized political parties, the French system remained associated with disorderly assemblies. Against the recent history of revolutions, restorations, empires and disorderly assemblies, elections became accepted as the means of avoiding further revolutionary upheaval and dictatorship and became viewed as the means through which crises could be weathered, even solved. Elections could settle immediate crises and offer a fresh start. Even if the elections were not fully free and fair, the free drinks all round were a welcome alternative to revolution and dictatorship and gratifying compensation for the disruptions to ordinary life, which such frequent elections brought. Practical experience of elections also proved the means through which people, both inside and outside parliament, learnt the value of parliamentary democracy.

Practical experience of elections, for a substantial portion of men at least, had been the legacy of the revolution of 1789. Demands for the universal manhood suffrage expected by many from 1789, promised in 1793 and thwarted so many times from that point on finally burst out into the political revolution of 1848 in protest against the highly restricted suffrage with its severe property qualifications. The 1848 revolution represented a crucial break with the past in far more than levels of suffrage. Before the removal of Guizot in 1848, liberalism was not the same as in Britain and America. French liberalism was not Constant's 'liberty of the moderns' concerned with private enterprise and one's life private, 'one's own business'. In France, individualism was viewed as selfish and liberalism was the 'liberty of the ancients' with citizenship a public duty. In France it was not until 1864, under Napoleon III, that free trade became policy and it was not until the 1860s that the beginnings of the democracy that France was to become, though as yet an empire, are to be discerned.

In France, furthermore, the revolution of 1789 did not lead to an economy like the capitalist system in Britain with its large factories, large cities and consequent large proletariat and bourgeoisie, in the strict sense of owners of industrial capital. In France it was Weber's acquisition classes that grew most: owners of small enterprises, owners of small plots of land and self-employed workers. The absence of free trade aside, this description of small enterprises, ownership of small plots of land and the importance of self-employment does, however, come close to the United States at the time, outside the Southern states that is. As de Tocqueville makes so clear, however, France lacked the society of pluralistic groups which were so crucial to American democracy. Not until 1901 were groups of more than twenty allowed to be organized and pressure groups did not develop until the 1880s.

As de Tocqueville (1862, First Part: 210) also argues, whereas in America groups were formed for the purpose of persuasion in the recognition that they represented only a minority, in France groups formed for conflict in the claim of representing the majority. De Tocqueville also stresses the importance of universal suffrage (of manhood suffrage at least) as the means to 'mitigate the excesses of political association' (ibid.: 211) through demonstrating that they represent only a minority. Serving the interests of the new political class before 1848 through indirect elections, falsified results and highly restricted suffrage, held back the development of modern democracy in France, for which the revolution of 1848 became essential.

Though Napoleon Bonaparte replaced the semblance of democracy with dictatorship, it was, nevertheless, his codification of laws together with the introduction of a modern monetary and banking system which provided the foundations of a modern, rational economy and a modern rational bureaucracy on which the future modern democracy was to rely. The revolution of 1789 also laid the foundations of religious toleration in setting down the Rights of Man and Citizen and granting the vote so early to Jews as well as to men of other religions and to 'free men of colour'. It is in the light of the granting of the vote to these groups so soon after the revolution of 1789 that the absence of female emancipation weighs so heavily against a designation of France under the Third Republic as a fully modern democracy.

5 Revolution and the failure of democracy in Russia and Germany

The Russian Revolution, 1917

Though over one and a quarter centuries had passed between the French and the Russian revolutions, in many ways Russia in 1917 was remarkably similar to France in 1789. Like France, in Russia the economy was predominantly agricultural, the social structure largely made up of peasants. Russia was similarly ruled over by an autocratic monarch with divine right, and, also like France, the state was highly bureaucratic and the government heavily repressive. Reforms had been introduced in Russia, under Alexander II (1855–81): serfdom had been ended; the courts had been reformed; and local government institutions, the *zemstvos*, had been introduced. Following Alexander II's assassination, however, the state returned to its earlier levels of repression and, in consequence, pressures for liberalism grew, particularly in the zemstvos. These pressures for liberalism, however, were not for liberalism of the modern kind; as in France before 1848, liberalism in Russia was against individualism (Sakwa 1998: 9).

The revolution of 1905, though defeated, led to the setting up of a parliament, the State Duma, which allowed trade unions (Sakwa 1998: 13). For the first time soviets, local workers' councils, were set up, spontaneously. Though illegal and suppressed within the year, they were to arise again in 1917. A constitution (Organic Laws) was set in place in 1906 for a constitutional monarchy, though under the new constitution few restrictions were put on the powers of the monarch and suffrage was narrow, favouring the large landowners (Beetham 1985: 195). Political parties competed in elections for the first time.[1] Though the Tsar had anticipated an Octobrist majority, that is a majority on the right, the Kadets (Constitutional Democrats), a liberal party formed in 1905, proved the largest party after the elections, with 196 of 478 seats (Sakwa 1998: 13). Zemstvo participants were important in both parties. The Socialist Revolutionaries (SRs), formed in 1900, boycotted the elections, as, too, did the Social Democrats.

The Duma first met in 1906. In Weber's assessment, the Duma was set up by the Tsar not for the purpose of satisfying demands for liberal democratic government at home but for creating the required image of constitutional government for securing loans abroad (Beetham 1985: 193). The Duma was a very weak parliament, with neither the right to petition nor the right to approve the budget. All that it could do was to veto legislation (ibid.: 194).[2] The first Duma was disssolved in less than three months for being too radical (Sakwa 1998: 13). In 1907, the Second Duma lasted just over three months. In the Second Duma the socialists participated and won 113 seats while Kadet seats fell to 92. As in France under the Directorate, the 'solution' was to manipulate the electoral system to achieve the parliament desired; landowners dominated the Third Duma, which lasted from 1907 to 1912 (ibid.). In the Fourth Duma, 1912–17, liberal opposition to the monarchical system of rule grew, forming the 'Progressive Bloc' in 1915, pressing for a government that was accountable to parliament, a demand made more pressing by the country being at war. In the end, even the Octobrists joined the Progressive Bloc in frustration with the Tsar's incapacity to work with parliament (Ulam 1969: 14). During these years, state repression continued to increase.

In spite of the reforms, from ending serfdom to the introduction of the Duma, in respect of Tsar Nicholas II's powers and hold over the country, Russia remained similar to France under Louis XVI. There were, however, important differences between the cases and, not least, in respect of war. In February 1917, Russia was embroiled in the First World War and had been so since 1914. France was not engaged in foreign war in 1789 and was not to be so until 1792, when the king declared war on neighbouring European countries with the aim of securing his position at home. In this, there is, perhaps, similarity with the Tsar's decision to enter the war in 1914. Both revolutions moved to their radical stages under war, though in contrast to France where war continued through to 1815 the Bolsheviks sought an end to war. After their take-over in October 1917 (7 November on the new calendar), the Bolsheviks negotiated a peace in March 1918.

Russia and France also differed in other crucial respects. Though around 75 per cent of Russia's population were peasants and over 80 per cent of the total population lived in rural areas (Kotz with Weir 1997: 17), the levels of industrialization in Russia contrasted sharply with France in 1789. Late in development and state-sponsored, the factories in Russia were the largest in the world and the proletariat, therefore, were very different from workers in France who, more than a hundred years before, had been predominantly artisans. In consequence, whereas in France urbanization had grown slowly, in Russia the cities had expanded rapidly, Moscow and Petrograd most strikingly.

Not only had the spread of capitalism in Europe during the years between the French and Russian revolutions created significant social and economic differences between the two cases, political events and workers' organizations had impacted on political ideas. As the Dumas showed, ideas of liberal democracy aspired to no more than the adoption of the structures of contemporary modern democratic states, notably that of Britain but also those of France and America. As explained, Russian liberalism, however, remained similar to that found in France in the first half of the nineteenth century, epitomized by Guizot's ideas, quite opposed to the individualism and private enterprise of the 'Scottish School' admired by Constant and characteristic of America and Britain, and France in the latter half of the nineteenth century.

In respect of radical ideas, however, the differences between France and Russia were striking. The ideas of the radicals of the Russian Revolution were no longer those of Rousseau mixed up with those of Montesquieu, but those of Marx whose ideas of proletarian revolution and of communism had been formed and developed, in important part, through reflection on the French Revolution of 1789 and the consequent revolutionary events of 1830, 1848 and 1870–71. In the year 1848, in addition to France, where the king was overthrown, revolutionary events of lesser success also swept through virtually all of Europe. Those in Italy, Germany, Hungary, Austria and Bohemia were the most notable; only Russia and Spain were unaffected. The year 1848 was the year in which Marx and Engels first published their *Manifesto of the Communist Party*. The Communist Manifesto was published in Russian in 1882 and in 1898 the Russian Social Democratic Party was formed.

The Russian Social Democratic Party was illegal before the overthrow of the Tsar in February 1917 (Ulam 1969: 423). In 1903, the party had split over party organization: generally, in reaction to Lenin's *What is to be Done?* (1902); specifically, in reaction to the halving of the number of editors of *Iskra*, their socialist newspaper (ibid.: 249–50). The split Russian Social Democratic Party became the Bolshevik and Menshevik parties. Neither Bolsheviks nor Mensheviks were members of the Provisional Government, set up in February 1917. With the overthrow of the Tsar, Russia ceased to be a monarchy but no new constitution was introduced. The plan was that the Constituent Assembly would do this, but its first meeting was not to be until January 1918.

At the same time as the Provisional Government was installed by the Duma, a second government was set up by the Petrograd Soviet of the Workers' Deputies (soon to be Workers and Soldiers' Deputies) (Ulam 1969: 410–11). The leaders of the Soviet were members of the socialist parties – Socialist Revolutionaries, Mensheviks and Bolsheviks – and the ratio of members of the Executive Committee reflected the importance and support given to these parties. The Socialist Revolutionaries were the largest in number, the Bolsheviks fewer than the Mensheviks. On 1 March 1917, the Soviet issued Order Number One which commanded all military and naval units to form local councils, soviets. Through these soldiers' and sailors' councils every military and naval unit and their weapons were under the control of the Petrograd Soviet (ibid.: 419).

The Provisional Government was headed by the liberal nobleman Prince Lvov, who had been head of the local government association, the Union of Zemstvos (Ulam 1969: 421). Lvov's government was made up of members of the Kadet Party and of moderate conservatives. There was one exception: Kerensky, Socialist Revolutionary and vice-president of the Soviet, became the Minister of Justice in the Provisional Government. In May, Kerensky became Minister of War and five other socialists (Socialist Revolutionaries and Mensheviks) joined the Provisional Government (ibid.: 441–3). In July, Kerensky became the head of government in place of Prince Lvov.

The see-saw events of June to September 1917, beginning with a failed Bolshevik-led uprising in Petrograd and ending with the failure of the coup led by the Minister of War, General Kornilov, led to the gaining of pro-Bolshevik majorities in both the Petrograd and Moscow soviets. In Moscow the Bolshevik majority was absolute and in the local elections in other industrial cities majorities made up of Bolsheviks and Left Socialist Revolutionaries were reproduced (Ulam 1969: 469–70). In contrast to the Menshevik and Socialist Revolutionary dominated First Soviet Congress, the Second Soviet Congress had 390 of the 650 members either members of the Bolshevik Party or Bolshevik sympathizers, such as Left SRs (ibid.: 487–8). Between February and October 1917, membership of the Bolshevik Party had grown from around 25,000 to around 300,000 (Sakwa 1998: 21). This Second Soviet Congress which met in Petrograd in October received the news of the fall of the Provisional Government.

After the Bolshevik coup led by the Military Revolutionary Committee of the Petrograd Soviet on 24–5 October 1917, a temporary central government, the Council of People's Commissars, *Sovnarkom*, was set up by the Soviet Congress (Ulam 1969: 495). Sovnarkom was dominated by Bolsheviks but also included members of the Left Socialist Revolutionaries. The Chairman of Sovnarkom was Lenin. Alongside Sovnarkom the soviets retained a form of dual power through the All-Russian Central Executive Committee (VTsIK) of the Congress of Soviets, which had first met in June (Carr 1966, Vol. 1: 156). Within days of the overthrow of the Provisional Government, Sovnarkom decreed itself interim powers of legislation (until the Constituent Assembly could be formed) with VTsIK, given the right to 'defer, modify or annul that legislation' (ibid.). Unlike the dual power situation under the Provisional Government, Bolsheviks sat on both Sovnarkom and VTsIK but there was friction between the two organizations and Sovnarkom soon took on the right to issue urgent decrees without consulting VTsIK. This condition became written into the constitution for the Russian Socialist Federal Soviet Republic (RSFSR), which was approved in July 1918 (ibid.: 157).

The elections to the Constituent Assembly, promised by the Provisional Government, went ahead, as planned, on 12–14 November. Suffrage was universal, both men and women voted in the election. Forty million votes were cast but less than a quarter of them for the Bolsheviks; the majority of votes went to the Socialist Revolutionary Party (Ulam 1969: 516). The Constituent Assembly met on 18 January 1918 (31 January on the western calendar). It was dissolved the next day. The Bolsheviks had decisively rejected the liberal democratic route.

Following the signing of the Brest-Litovsk Treaty on 3 March 1918, which ended the war with Germany, the Left SR members, being opposed to the treaty, withdrew from Sovnarkom. Thus Sovnarkom became a single party government. On 8 March, on Lenin's insistence, the Bolshevik Party was re-named the Communist Party (Ulam 1969: 532–3). Left SRs, however, remained in both the soviets and VTsIK and continued to do so after June 1918, when Right SRs and Mensheviks were banned.[3] From the signing of the Brest-Litovsk Treaty through the summer of 1918 violent opposition to the government grew; in September it turned into outright civil war.

During the civil war the Communist Party expanded and enhanced its importance. The Politburo, the Political Bureau of the Communist Party Central Committee had become a kind of 'court of appeal' against Sovnarkom decisions (Rigby 1979: 183). Three of the Politburo's five members were Lenin, Trotsky and Stalin. In spite of the relatively small membership of the party and the problems of communications, local party committees had become important organizations in the provinces (Mawdsley 1987: 274). When the civil war ended, the move from emergency government by Sovnarkom to a new permanent government of Communist Party rule began (see O'Kane 1991: 111–14). At the Tenth Party Congress, in March 1921, all opposition parties and trade unions were banned, Left SRs having last been admitted to VTsIK in December 1920. Discipline within the Communist Party was also made compulsory; opposition within the party, permitted by a statute in 1919, was banned (Carr 1966, Vol. 1: 208). The concerns that Luxemburg had had about Lenin's tactics of revolution had proven well founded, mass democracy in which people have the freedom to act in concert had never been given a chance and, in October 1921, 24 per cent of party members were expelled from the party (ibid.: 211–13).

From mid-1921 the Politburo and Central Committee of the Communist Party began to displace the importance of Sovnarkom.[4] In

April 1922 Stalin, already a member of the Politburo, was appointed General Secretary of the Central Committee. In December 1922, the RSFSR adopted the new title of the Union of Soviet Socialist Republics (USSR). In January 1924 Lenin died and from that point on the general secretary's power grew (Deutscher 1968: 236). By 1928, Stalin, having outmanoeuvred possible alternative successors to Lenin, had emerged in full control of both the party and the state.

Chances for democracy

Though we know from history that a communist system happened in Russia the question remains as to whether, had the Bolsheviks not taken over in October, a multi-party democracy could have taken hold and become permanently established. An answer to this question is usually sought in the class structure. In the Marxist analysis of the day, the question was whether a bourgeois revolution was a necessary stage before the proletarian revolution and whether the bourgeoisie was strong enough to sustain a bourgeois revolution. The evidence of the Provisional Government's failure swung the argument in Lenin's support, playing a crucial part in swaying Trotsky from Menshevik to Bolshevik Party. In the Bolsheviks' analysis the bourgeois revolution of February could not be sustained and Russia could jump straight to proletarian revolution. The issue was not only the weakness of the bourgeoisie but also that of the large peasantry (Sakwa 1998: 18–19). In Moore's (1969) analysis the peasantry support communism or reaction (fascism) but not democracy. In the Marxist analysis, as discussion of France in 1848 in Chapter 4 has shown, peasants, as owners of small plots of land, have petit bourgeois interests and will support bourgeois democracy, as they had in the election of Louis-Napoleon in December 1848. In the Russian edition of the Communist Manifesto, published in 1882, the argument is made that where peasants have experience not of private ownership but of communal ownership, as in the Russian *obschina*, then they will support communism. These arguments were taken up and developed by Lenin (see Mills 1963: 226–40).

These various arguments about a weak bourgeoisie and a large peasantry both relate to Russia's late, rapid and state-led capitalist development. During the 1890s, industrial growth averaged 8 per cent per year. Between 1906 and 1913, it continued to average a 6 per cent growth rate (Skocpol 1979: 91). Such considerations were also central to Weber's analysis of Russia in 1905 and the development of his argument in 1917. For Weber, what the bourgeoisie lacked in Russia was the individualist, entrepreneurial spirit that had accompanied the earlier development of modern capitalism, as in America. In contrast, late capitalism was large-scale, needing, therefore, more organization, more bureaucracy, and was more likely to be involved with the state (in cartels), rather than being independent of the state as in early capitalism (Beetham 1985: 203–4). As discussed in Chapter 2, for Weber, in the tendency of state bureaucracy to grow lay the path away from freedom through the thwarting of the individualist, entrepreneurial spirit through which people took personal responsibility for their actions whether in the economic or the political sphere.

Weber also drew attention to the absence of experience of democratic institutions in Russia. In the earlier cases of industrialization, he argues for the advantages of the bourgeoisie becoming familiar with parliament and gaining confidence in its workings before the proletariat developed as an independent political force with separate interests. In Russia, he contends, the bourgeoisie were afraid of parliament (Beetham 1985: 205). There was, in any case, he argues, a culture of authoritarianism: the Russian Orthodox religion was inherently authoritarian and encouraged submission to authority and, therefore, to the state (ibid.). In short, in Russia, the desire for order was greater than that for constitutional rights (ibid.: 209). Though evidently somewhat more sympathetic to the bourgeoisie, of the modern hard-working kind, than was Marx, it is clear that it was not Weber's argument that the bourgeoisie had any natural affinity with liberalism or liberal democracy. Rather, it is his contention that their enthusiasm for (as opposed to fear of) parliament and for civil liberties was itself the product of the specific historical circumstances in which the bourgeoisie arose. Democracy and freedom, Weber argued, occurred where people were determined 'not to be ruled like a herd of sheep' (ibid.: 210).

What is so central to our concerns here is that in his comparative analysis of contemporary Russia and Germany in 1905 and 1917 Weber found only similarities.

Germany 1918: failed revolution and democracy through reform

Germany, like Russia, had been late to industrialize and had similarly modernized rapidly. Following the foundation of the German Reich in 1871, rapid industrialization took place in the 1870s and 1880s. For example, steel production in 1870 had grown by a factor of 13 by 1890 and was thirty-nine times greater than the 1870 level by 1900. In comparative terms, with production of steel in Germany in 1870 at less than 60 per cent of that being produced in Britain, by 1910 German steel production was more than double that being produced in Britain and almost four times that produced in France.[5] In Weber's view, as a consequence of this late and rapid industrialization, Germany, like Russia, had missed out the early stage of capitalism taken by Britain,

Weber

America and France, and, consequently, lacked the conditions for bourgeois democracy. Germany, like Russia, therefore, he viewed as bureaucratic, hierarchical and state-dominated, with a bourgeoisie lacking confidence in parliament.[6]

Germany before 1918, is described by Weber as an '*Obrigkeitsstaat*', an authoritarian regime, with, as Beetham (1985: 152) summarizes, 'its political direction in theory in the hands of the monarchy but in practice determined by the bureaucracy, with a façade of parliamentary institutions, or "token parliamentarianism"'. In summary, the *Obrigkeitsstaat* sounds not only like Russia after the introduction of the Duma, 1905 to 1917, but also like France at the time of the calling of the Estates-General. Yet, given Weber's position, the German political system appears surprisingly different from those of pre-revolutionary Russia and France and the more strikingly so as 1918 approaches.

The Frankfurt Assembly

Germany's first flirtation with modern parliamentary democracy occurred in 1848. Following revolutionary uprisings, set off by economic recession and given impetus by the events in France, a National Assembly was set up in Frankfurt in April 1848. It was the first central government of a federation. Before 1848 the German states formed a confederation. In May, the Assembly, consisting of 380 elected representatives of the German states, set about drafting a democratic constitution. Their priority was to establish basic rights and in this they were heavily influenced by the American Constitution but also made some very progressive additions (Hahn 2001: 143).

The basic rights, approved in March and incorporated in the Frankfurt Constitution when drafting began in October, included freedom of speech, freedom of the press and freedom of religion (para. 145). Rights to trial by jury, to independent courts and to equality before the law were also included. The end of feudal dues and other aristocratic privileges was to be guaranteed (para. 137). Local self-government and open government in each of the German states were to be rights (para. 187). Capital punishment was also to be abolished (para. 135). Education also featured: schooling was to be supervised by the state (para. 153) and basic education was to be free (para. 157). In addition, the tax system was to be equitable (para. 173). (See Hahn 2001: 144; Stearns 1974: 186.) Under paragraph 189, the constitution also gave state protection to every German citizen abroad. The problem was that Germany did not have clearly defined borders, notably in respect of Austria and the areas next to Denmark and Poland. Austria stayed outside. (See Hahn 2001: 144.)

The American Constitution also provided a model for the relationship between federal and state law as well as areas of international law and war and peace. The Frankfurt Constitution set up a federal system with a bicameral parliament, the upper house representing the states, the lower house to be elected by universal male suffrage (Stearns 1974: 188). Rather than a president, as in America, the king of Prussia, Frederick William IV was to be offered, as the constitution put it, 'the hereditary headship of a united Germany' (ibid.).

The drafting of the constitution was also informed through debates, drawing lessons from other parliamentary systems. Contemporary events in Britain, such as the Chartists' charter with its demands for universal suffrage and regular elections and Cobden's reforms were also influential, as too were contemporary writings, in particular the works of the philosopher and conservative member of the British parliament, Burke, and those of the liberal historian, Macaulay. France also provided a source of inspiration: the *Code Napoléon* was used for the concept of citizenship and the idea of civil marriage. Montesquieu and Robespierre were also quoted, and those supporting constitutional monarchy quoted Mirabeau. In addition to these models and ideas from abroad, ideas were drawn from German writings and philosophers. (See Hahn 2001: 143.)

In April 1849, however, Frederick William, King of Prussia, refused the imperial crown, refused to rescind his divine right and to become a constitutional monarch. The Frankfurt Assembly was dissolved for being too radical and the direct elections were replaced with indirect elections for a new assembly. The results of these elections, too, were viewed as too radical and a new electoral system was devised to ensure the greater conservatism of the parliament. Similar to what had existed in France, before 1848, a three-class system of voters was introduced, the classes divided according to taxes paid. The first class, consisting of the wealthiest 5 per cent of voters, elected one-third of the deputies. The second class, approximately 20 per cent of the voters, elected another one-third of deputies. The third class, approximating 75 per cent of votes, elected the final third of delegates. (See Stearns 1974: 190.) Like the British House of Lords, the new upper house was unelected. It was composed of aristocrats, top officials of church and state and members for life, appointed by the king. The powers of the lower house were also greatly limited. In 1851, the basic rights set down by the Frankfurt Constitution were abolished (ibid.: 194).

Rather than federal democracy, the outcome of the failed revolutions of 1848/9 was a return to confederation and to the increased powers of the state bureaucracy and the army. The state bureaucracy was used to destroy progressive ideas and to re-establish authoritarian rule (Hahn 2001: 188). Obedience and discipline, not free thought, became the order of the day in state education. Bureaucracy was employed to increase police control and to support a secret police force (ibid.: 189). Civil society was under suspicion and censorship became oppressive (ibid.: 190). Though the *Junker* landlords lost feudal rights they gained police rights over their estates (Stearns 1974: 239).

The end of the 1848–49 revolution in Germany was the start of Weber's *Obrigkeitsstaat* and in it Prussia became the dominant political force. From 1862, Bismarck manoeuvred, from within the Prussian parliament, for a policy of German unification under Prussian leadership. From 1866, the Prussian army fought to achieve this, first in the south then in the north. With the defeat of France in 1870, German unification was achieved.

The Second Reich: Imperial Germany

Following unification, under the Constitution of 1871, the German Chancellor, Bismarck, introduced near universal male suffrage, for all men over the age of 25 with a few exceptions including those dependent on charity.[7] Thus, in 1871, Germany came close to the level of suffrage present in France from 1852. For elections to the state assemblies, however, things were far closer to the way they were in France in 1792. In most of the states, *Länder*, the electorate was divided into three levels of tax payment (the three-class voting system) – a system that was retained in Prussia right through to 1918. As in France, too, in most states votes were oral, a public declaration, a public duty. It was a situation, therefore, open to the abuse of the dominant over the subordinate. In contrast, the national vote was by secret ballot, but again in ways similar to post-revolutionary France, state elections were indirect and the system two-stage with those elected from each tax class then selecting the deputies. Anderson (2000: 7) contrasts these state and national systems in terms similar to Constant's ancient and modern liberalism: 'Although constitutional scholars insisted that voting was not the "right" of an individual, but a "public office entrusted in him as a whole", direct elections with secret balloting implied that a man's political decision was indeed a private one.'

The unification of Germany in 1871, like the uniting of the thirteen states in America after the War of Independence, was resolved by a federal system first envisaged in the aborted Frankfurt Constitution. There were, however, crucial differences between the German and the American federal systems. Under the new Imperial Constitution, Germany was neither to be a republic, like America, nor even a constitutional monarchy. The king of Prussia, the Kaiser, was to be the Emperor of all Germany and was given rights to appoint and to dismiss the chancellor and to veto legislation. Through his Prussian support in the upper house, the Federal Council (Bundesrat), he also had executive power. (See Bartolini 2000: 345–6.) In addition, the German Emperor also appointed and dismissed the chancellor, without recourse to the lower house, the Reichstag (Ginsberg 1996: 89). Bartolini (2000: 346) comments, 'Thus Imperial Germany not only did not have the principle of parliamentary responsibility, but even the legislative role of the lower house was restricted, and not only on military and fiscal matters.'[8] As Beetham (1985: 51) emphasizes, 'Under the German Constitution the government was neither chosen from the Reichstag nor responsible to it.' In strong contrast to America, with its frontier mentality, dissenter spirit and republican attitudes, Germany was ridden by status, dominated by the Prussian Junker class, and hierarchical and authoritarian in consequence. As discussed in Chapter 2, such contrasts had earlier been observed between America and France by de Tocqueville.

There were yet further striking differences between Germany and America in respect of the nature of their federal systems. Whereas in America, the Federalists, Madison and Hamilton, had won the argument in drawing up the American Constitution for a strong central government, in Germany, federalism was based on a weak central government and strong states. The upper house, Bundesrat, consisted of delegates from the states and the upper house had the power of veto over Reichstag legislation. As such, the states had the dominant position over the federal government (Bartolini 2000: 345). In addition, one state – Prussia – was dominant over all others. Prussia constituted more than half of the area of Germany and included over half of the population. In addition, not only was the king of Prussia to be the emperor of all Germany, it was also customary for the prime minister of Prussia to be the imperial chancellor, the chancellor of all Germany (ibid.). Furthermore, the Prussian Army formed the vast bulk of the German forces (ibid.). How different too was the balance and separation of powers in the American Constitution as compared with the German Constitution of 1871. As explained in Chapter 3, in America not only was the president elected by the people and had powers separate from the Senate and House of Representatives, in America the Senate had two representatives for each state, irrespective of their size of population. In Germany, the members of the Bundesrat were in proportion to the size of each state. By far the largest was Prussia with 17 members.[9]

In the tradition of ancient democracy, unitary not pluralist, Bismarck was opposed to political parties and in the Constitution of 1871 there was no mention of parties, references were made only to voters and deputies. In Article 29 each deputy was a representative of 'the whole people' (Anderson 2000: 287). Nevertheless, Germany had political parties, though not just two as in America and Britain. In Germany, the establishment constituted the conservatives and along with the conservatives three competing organized political parties came to predominate over the years from 1871 to 1918: the National Liberal

Party, the (Catholic) Centre Party (Zentrum)[10] and the Social Democratic Party, SPD.

Social democracy

The German Social Democratic Party was first set up as the Social Democratic Labour Party (Socialist Workers' Party, SAP) in 1875, bringing together earlier workers' associations (Bartolini 2000: 254). Between 1878 and 1890, under the 'Socialist Law', renewed every two years, the party was outlawed and along with it the connected associations including trade unions. Only moderate unions, liberal not socialist, remained legal (Arends and Kümmel 2000: 190). The sugar to sweeten the anti-socialist blow was the introduction of welfare policies (ibid.). In spite of the anti-socialist legislation and the repression suffered by SAP supporters and sympathizers, socialists continued to be represented in parliament. Ironically they were able to exploit Article 29 of the Imperial Constitution of 1871 under which each deputy represented 'the whole people'. Once elected, they also benefited from parliamentary immunity (Anderson 2000: 287). Furthermore, given free range on the floor of the Reichstag and debates officially recorded, the words of socialist deputies, taken from the printed recordings, could then be quoted, legitimately, in newspapers (ibid.).

There was also a very useful loophole in the Electoral Law in an amendment that had been passed in 1869. This amendment gave the right to anyone standing for election to form 'election committees' and 'election clubs', the freedom, that is, to campaign and form associations (Anderson 2000: 289). All that needed to be done to overcome the Socialist Law during election time was to drop 'socialist' and to change 'Socialist Worker Committee' to 'Worker Election Committee' and so on. Even socialist leaflets and the like could not be legally confiscated during the designated 'election time' (ibid.: 290). Election time lasted around a month and there were also run-offs, adding around two weeks, and also many by-elections (ibid.: 291).

In spite of the Socialist Law, and through taking advantage of the protections available to be exploited in the constitution, between the elections of 1887 and 1890 the votes for the Social Democratic Party doubled. In 1891, at the Party Congress in Erfurt, the SAP changed its name to the German Social Democratic Party, SPD, and also adopted a new programme, the Erfurt Programme (Anderson 2000: 294). It was at the Erfurt Party Congress that Bernstein launched his revisionist strategy of seeking to attract middle-class votes and to be part of bourgeois government rather than having the goal only of replacing it, wholesale, with a socialist government (Bartolini 2000: 73). The Erfurt Programme also adopted the policy of an electoral system based on proportional

representation (PR). The view was that a PR system was more truly
representative of voters' wishes and therefore more democratic
(Anderson 2000: 342).

With the Socialist Law at an end, the Erfurt Programme with its new
strategy brought dividends. Votes for the SPD continued to rise and in
the election of 1912 the SPD gained a third of the votes, giving them the
largest number of seats in the Reichstag (Weitz 1997: 28; Nettl 1969:
144). The success of the SPD reflected the growth of industrial workers.
In 1910, 40.1 per cent of the workforce were employed in industry
(Bartolini 2000: 133).[11]

Contrasting Germany

Kautsky compared Germany of the day with France in 1789:

> The struggle is no longer, as in 1789, a battle of unorganized mobs
> with no political form . . . It is a battle of organized intelligent masses,
> full of stability and prudence, which do not follow every impulse, or
> explode over every insult, or collapse under every misfortune.
>
> (Kautsky, *The Social Revolution*, 1902 in Mills 1963: 171)

German workers (in industrialized Germany rather than agricultural
France of 1789, with its vast peasant population) had the benefit, in
Kautsky's and Bernstein's view, of both education and elections. In 1870,
Germany had one of the highest literacy rates in Europe with only 8–13
per cent illiterate as compared with 31 per cent in France, 25–30 per cent
in England and Wales, and 69 per cent in Italy (Bartolini 2000: 195). As
explained in Chapter 3, the advantages of elections in the revisionist,
German Social Democrats' eyes lay in their value for resolving conflicts of
view. As also explained in Chapter 3, the revisionist social democrats
were not simply concerned with the advantages of liberal democracy.
Their view, shared with Social Democrats opposed to revisionism, such as
Luxemburg, was that elections also have the benefits of providing the
means for educating the proletariat in the workings of the democratic
political system and, of course, in creating governments with a
programme for the improvement of workers' social and economic
conditions.

Failed revolution, 1918

As is clear, the nature and role played by the German Social Democratic
Party before Kaiser Wilhelm II's forced abdication in 1918 were very
different from those of the Bolshevik Party in the Russian Revolution. In
Russia, the Bolshevik Party had been illegal at the time of the February

Revolution, in Germany the SPD was not only a legal party but had the largest number of seats in the Reichstag. Furthermore, in complete contrast both to the spontaneous, violent uprising of February 1917, in which the Bolsheviks (and Mensheviks) played only a small part, and to the Bolshevik *coup d'état* in October 1917, in Germany the SPD was handed power. With defeat in the First World War a foregone conclusion, sailors in Kiel refused to go to sea and mutinied on 28 October 1918. Revolts began to spread to other ports and cities from 3 November, reaching Berlin on 9 November. On the same day the abdication of the king was announced and the Imperial Chancellor handed power to Friedrich Ebert, the leader of the largest party in the Reichstag, the SPD (Moore 1978: 291–2).

In certain respects, the immediate outcome of November 1918 was similar to that of Russia in February 1917. A provisional government was formed, the Council of People's Representatives, RdV, in which the SPD shared power with the Independent Social Democratic Party, USPD. The USPD had been formed in April 1917 by members of the SPD who retained their internationalist stance and opposed the SPD's patriotic support of the war. Members of the USPD included Kautsky and also the radical Marxist group Spartacus, which was led by Karl Liebknecht and Rosa Luxemburg (Bartolini 2000: 105–6). At the point of the formation of the provisional government in November 1918 the Spartacus group split from the USPD, becoming the Spartacus League, and on 30 December 1918 formed the German Communist Party, KPD (Weitz 1997: 92–3).

As in Russia, initially a form of dual power emerged. Workers' and soldiers' councils had begun to form in various cities and, in this spirit, on 10 November, councils were elected in the Berlin factories and barracks. Delegates were sent by these councils to the Circus Busch meeting, the same day. The purpose of this meeting was to ratify the provisional government, the Council of People's Representatives, and to set up their own Executive Council, much in the same way as the Petrograd Soviet (Moore 1978: 293; Weitz 1997: 85). Unlike the Russian case, however, not only was there no separation between parties participating in the two halves of power, socialists being in both, but also the Executive Council never had the equivalent of Order Number One. In fact, rather than having, in effect, control over the army and navy through the local councils, Ebert actually made a deal with General Groener, the head of the armed forces, for the government to continue to rely on the support of the officer corps. This deal was made immediately after the Circus Busch meeting. Furthermore, Ebert kept this agreement secret from the members of the SPD because the other half of the deal was to fight Bolshevism. (See Moore 1978: 294.)

In Russia, in November 1917, the Bolsheviks, with their own armed wing, the Military Revolutionary Committee of the Petrograd Soviet, took power at a time when the Russian army was not simply weak but otherwise engaged in fighting in the First World War. In Germany, in November 1918, the German Army having been defeated in the First World War, was about to return home, its high command intact and with a deal having been made to rely on the existing army for state coercion.

Chances for communist revolution

Whether or not there was a real possibility for communist revolution in Germany, as had happened in Russia, is debatable. Before the Kiel mutiny on 28 October 1918, there had been strikes, the first in June 1916 (see Moore 1978: 289). There was in the Spartacus League/KPD if not a tightly organized Leninist party at least a potential revolutionary organization which had an armed brigade. The Red Soldiers League was set up on 15 November 1918 and, in addition, in the Revolutionary Shop Stewards, there was strong workers' support. On 5 January 1919, a vast mass demonstration took place in protest against the dismissal of Emil Eichhorn, who was both the Berlin Chief of Police and member of the USPD. On the following day the demonstrations turned into an uprising (Moore 1978: 306–7). Over the following days the uprising was savagely suppressed by *Freikorps* troops, right-wing paramilitary forces, under Noske, the new Berlin Chief of Police.[12] On 15 January 1919, Luxemburg and Liebknecht were captured and murdered.

The potential for the violent revolutionary takeover of government to be found in revolutionary organizations and support has to be weighed against the repressive capacity of the state. The Freikorps went on during 1919 to violently suppress workers' movements, most notably in the industrial Ruhr. In defence, the Red Ruhr Army was formed by workers, in March 1920, and it quickly established control of some large cities (Moore 1978: 313). The Red Ruhr Army formed in consequence of the Kapp Putsch, 13–17 March 1920, the attempt to overthrow the government with the support of the Freikorps and regular army units. The putsch was defeated by a general strike in which even members of the state bureaucracy in Berlin participated. In its turn, however, the Red Ruhr Army was then defeated on 30 March.

The strikes and demonstrations before the Kaiser's abdication had each been provoked by one or more of three things: the repressiveness of the regime (such as the protest in June 1916 over Liebknecht's trial for treason); food shortages (such as the cuts in the bread ration which led to rioting in April 1917); and the demand for peace (as in the demonstrations of January 1918) (Moore 1978: 289). The demands for bread and peace were similar to those made in Russia, but the demands for land, so central to protests in Russia, were missing.[13] Crucially, unlike Russia with its overwhelmingly peasant population, in Germany agricultural workers constituted less than a third of the working population, at 32.9 per cent in 1910 (Bartolini 2000: 13). The contrast between the Russian and German social structures is notable in other ways too. Not only, as mentioned on page 101, did industrial workers constitute 40.1 per cent of the workforce in 1910, white collar workers constituted 26.4 per cent of the workforce.

The protests against the repressive nature of the government and opposition to the war were met by the Kaiser's abdication in November 1918. In Russia, even after the Bolsheviks had taken power in October 1917, it was nearly five months before the peace treaty was signed. With the war ended the German provisional government was able to move swiftly to the introduction of political changes demanded. These included the demand for an eight-hour working day and for free trade unions. The right to strike had been made illegal at the start of the war. In addition to the demand for an end to the three-class voting system, which still continued in Prussia, there were also demands for proportional representation to be introduced. In contrast to Russia, in Germany elections were organized swiftly, the outcome respected and a democratic constitution was set in place. In Germany, with its long experience of elections and parliamentary representation, so unlike Russia, the path chosen was democracy. As Anderson (2000) concludes:

> The most widely shared demand of the citizenry, including the majority of the representatives of the workers' and soldiers' councils, was for national elections, the sooner the better. After fifty years of going to the polls, Germany assumed that democracy was both desirable and inevitable.
>
> (Anderson 2000: 399)

The Weimar Republic

On 19 January 1919, elections took place for the Constitutional Assembly to frame a new constitution. Initially, Weimar parties were either those of the Reich or splits from them, similarly grouped into Catholic, socialist, liberal and conservative. On the left were the SPD, USPD and KPD. From the liberal group (the Liberal Party having split into left and right under the Reich), in November 1918 the German People's Party, DVP, was formed, to represent the interests of big industrialists. At the same time the German Democratic Party, DDP, was formed, succeeding the Progressive People's Party. The DVP was opposed to the revolutionary changes, the DDP was a strong supporter of the Weimar Republic and played a main part in drafting the constitution. (The DDP was replaced by the German Party of the State, DStP, in 1930.) The conservatives became a variety of parties of which the main one was the German National People's Party, DNVP, founded in 1919. This was a monarchist party, representing the large landowners, strongly opposed to democracy and anti-Semitic. (See Arends and Kümmel 2000: 193–7.)

The January 1919 elections were held on the basis of genuine universal suffrage: no tax qualifications, everyone over the age of 20, women as well as men. The SPD received the largest share of the poll with 37.9 per cent of the votes and formed a coalition with the Centre Party and the German Democratic Party, DDP. Together the three coalition parties gained over three-quarters of the votes. The USPD gained 7.6 per cent of the votes. (See Arends and Kümmel 2000: 200–5.) The KPD did not participate (Bartolini 2000: 106).

The Weimar Constitution established a democratic federal republic, retaining the two houses of parliament, the Reichstag and the Reichsrat with a president instead of a monarch. As before, the upper house, Reichsrat, was to be made up of deputies appointed by the states' parliaments, *Landtäge*. The three-class system of suffrage was ended and elections, as for the Reichstag, were to be conducted on the basis of universal suffrage for all men and women over 20 years of age. The balance of power was shifted from the upper house to the Reichstag, which was given the powers to make laws, set budgets and to consent to the appointment or force the resignations of ministers and the chancellor. The chancellor was the head of the cabinet, the prime minister (Ginsberg 1996: 90).

The Weimar political system is classified, by Sartori (1997: 121), as 'semi-presidentialism', a popularly elected president in dual power with a prime minister reliant on parliamentary support. Both presidential and parliamentary elections were to be based on universal suffrage and parliamentary elections were to be through a 'pure' system of proportional representation, one, that is, with a single national constituency (ibid.: 128). For its time, the Weimar Constitution was very progressive. Both women's suffrage and proportional representation were the hot contemporary debates in Europe. The president was to be popularly elected rather than elected within parliament, as a device for the parliamentary system to be counterbalanced by a strong presidency (ibid.: 127). The president was to be elected every seven years, the Reichstag every four years (Ginsberg 1996: 90).

The power of the president was strengthened through four devices: the capacity to rule through decree in times of emergency (Article 48); the right to appoint and dismiss the prime minister (chancellor) and also individual cabinet ministers, and to form governments; the power to dissolve parliament; and authority to refer any law passed in the parliament to popular referendum (Sartori 1997: 128).[14] At the same time, to achieve a balance, the parliament had the power to bring down governments by a vote of no confidence and to force individual ministers to resign. The bulk of legislation was also to be carried out through parliament (through the elected house that is, the Reichstag). Under Article 159 of the constitution the right to form free associations was provided and an eight-hour workday was introduced. Under Article 165, workers' councils were allowed. (See Arends and Kümmel 2000: 191.)

In the first Reichstag elections held under the new Weimar Constitution, in June 1920, the SPD-Zentrum-DDP coalition lost its absolute majority and the new coalition government was Zentrum-DDP-DVP. The Bavarian People's Party, BVP, had split from the (Catholic) Centre Party, Zentrum, in 1920 and, also in 1920, the left of the USPD joined with the Communist Party, KPD, the ultra-left communists having broken from the KPD. The SPD later (in October 1921) replaced the DVP in the coalition. (See Arends and Kümmel 2000: 205.) In the June 1920 election, the SPD vote fell to 21.6 per cent, large numbers of socialist supporters switching to the USPD which gained 17.9 per cent. The Communist Party, KPD, also stood in the election and gained 2.1 per cent of the votes (Bartolini 2000: 106). The left vote had remained above 40 per cent of the total votes but was split, nearly in half.

As mentioned, proportional representation had been a policy of the Social Democrats since the Erfurt Programme of 1891. PR was also supported by the liberals. The view, at the time, was that PR produced representation closer to the ratios of votes cast and was, therefore, more democratic (Anderson 2000: 342). PR had been introduced for communal elections in Bavaria in 1903, Württemberg in 1906 and Oldenberg in 1908 and in the state elections in Württemberg and Hamburg in 1906. In the wider context of the Weimar Republic, however, in practice the operation of the 'pure' system of PR led to the spawning of large numbers of parties and polarized extremes (Sartori 1997: 128–9). For example, further splits from the German National People's Party, DNVP, occurred in 1922 (when the radical anti-Semitic group left) and again in 1928. Other parties also developed outside these main Catholic, socialist, liberal and conservative groupings, including, in 1922, the National Socialist German Workers' Party (NSDAP), the Nazi Party. (See Arends and Kümmel 2000: 193–8.)

As a consequence of the large number of parties and the strength of cleavages between them clear coalitions of opposition failed to emerge, which weakened the party system (Lepsius 1978: 42–3). The proliferation of parties was such that following the 1928 election, eighty-eight seats were held by parties that polled less than 5 per cent of total votes cast (ibid.: 45). In the 1930 election, fourteen such parties gained seats and nine of them gained between 3 and 30 seats, each playing their role in forming and bringing down governments (Ginsberg 1996: 92).

Highly unstable governments were therefore produced, with frequent government alterations and the need for expenditure of enormous efforts to manage tensions.

From the first parliamentary government of the Weimar Republic, 13 February 1919, to its end, 30 January 1933, there were twenty cabinets (see Arends and Kümmel 2000: 205). Not only were governments short-lived but also only during about half of this time did the governments have a parliamentary majority (Lepsius 1978: 43–4). Firm coalitions did not exist for any designated length of time, but rather had to be coalesced for each issue as it arose. Over time this had the effect of separating government from parliament, with government constituted around a few leading personalities dependent on the president, Hindenburg (ibid.). In the reality of a fractionalized and weak Reichstag the constitutional design of the presidency was too strong. Ironically, the Weimar Constitution, in theory designed to achieve a high level of democracy, in practice sapped the vitality of parliamentary democracy and Article 48, intended to balance powers, tragically proved instrumental in securing Hitler and the NSDAP in power in 1933.

Questioning democracy

Following defeat in the First World War, Germany was under external pressure to be a democracy, pressure exerted particularly by US President Wilson (Balfour 1992: 41), but irrespective of external constraints democracy was a chosen path. As explained above, after fifty years of voting, 'Germans assumed that democracy was both desirable and inevitable' (Anderson 2000: 399). Importantly, too, the SPD was not a revolutionary party. As the Erfurt Programme made clear it was a party of representation. Contemporaneous events in Russia, not least the dissolution of the Constituent Assembly and the anarchy and terror of civil war, made the attractions of democracy, the peaceful path, the greater. The Weimar Constitution sought to correct what was at fault with the old system – the monarchy, the weak Reichstag, the three-class voting system still remaining in Prussia – and to do so through previously debated solutions – proportional representation, independent parties, free trade unions and other voluntary associations, and the 'Australian' option of truly universal suffrage. From the example of the French Third Republic, with its president elected by the parliament and its disorderly assemblies, the lesson was also drawn that parliamentary government needed a strong president (Sartori 1997: 128). Such was the context of Article 48, which gave the president the capacity to rule through decree in times of emergency.

In any new political system there are bound to be unforseen consequences that require adaptation of procedures. In Lepsius's

(1978: 45) view, had the Weimar system of proportional representation been adapted in a modest way to deny parties polling less than 5 per cent of the votes then the parliamentary system would have been significantly strengthened. As will be explained in Chapter 9, this rule would apply in the German Federal Republic from 1949. As an alternative solution, Sartori (1997: 129) observes that the defects of PR were remedied in the Fifth French Republic with the double ballot majority system. Sartori (ibid.) also argues that the Weimar system would have been strengthened had the president not been elected by plurality, for it stopped the development of a race between just two presidential candidates, which could have aided what he terms 'bi-polar moulding' to help solidify opposing coalitions. Bi-polar moulding which would, in other words, have approximated the American presidential running system.

While suggesting improvements to the Weimar system, based on comparative observations, Sartori (1997: 127) argues, similarly from comparative observations, against the view that the constitution was to blame for the downfall of the Weimar Republic. Semi-presidental systems have survived elsewhere: in Finland from 1919, in France from 1958, Portugal from 1974 and Sri Lanka from 1978. In respect of Article 48 and also the referendum procedures and the means for dissolving parliament, which have also been blamed for Weimar's collapse, he argues similar inclusions are found in other constitutions and have not produced collapse (ibid.: 129). 'All in all', Sartori concludes, ' I definitely would not say that the Weimar Constitution carries the blame for the unhappy and short life of the first German republic, and especially for its downfall at Hitler's hands in 1933' (ibid.) Indeed, he adds that had Germany adopted a constitution of a parliamentary rather than a semi-presidential type of system, Weimar would probably have collapsed in 1923 following the dramatic escalation of inflation.

If it was not the political system itself, not the nature of the Weimar Constitution that is, that led to the end of democracy in Germany then two possible explanations or some mixture of the two remain. Either there must have been something in the nature of Germany society that worked to prevent the constitution from achieving its designed democratic outcome or something happened after the constitution was in place, which would have disastrous consequences for virtually any democracy.

As explained, Weber's view is that, as a consequence of late and rapid industrialization, Germany before 1918 was an *Obrigkeitsstaat*, an authoritarian regime, lacking a sufficiently strong and independent entrepreneurial class with confidence in parliament. As a consequence of the first stage of capitalism being missed, not only was this class too dependent on the state, it was also, he argues, unpractised in parliament before strong workers' organizations developed and therefore unsure of the merits of democracy. It is not without irony that Weber was both involved in the drafting of the Weimar Constitution and failed to be adopted as a candidate for the Liberal Party. If the pessimism of his writings were in accord with the collapse of the Weimar Republic his concerns over workers' organizations and the SPD in particular were not borne out. If the bourgeoisie were too weak to sustain democracy, the working class provided its strongest and most reliable supporters.

Weber did not live to see the Social Democratic Party working tirelessly with the Centre and Liberal parties, each 'bourgeois' parties, to sustain democratic government throughout the duration of the republic. The SPD formed part of the coalition governments from February 1919 to June 1920; May 1921 to November 1922; August 1923 to November 1923; and June 1928 to March 1930. It is noteworthy too that the Communist Party, KPD, never gained more than 16.9 per cent of the votes, scored in June 1932, and that the gains made by the NSDAP were largely at the expense of the bourgeois-Protestant parties (Arends and Kümmel 2000: 202, Figure 8.2). Over the years, the declines in support for the DDP, the German Democratic Party, and the DVP, the German People's Party, are the most pronounced. The DDP, at 18.6 per cent of the votes in January 1919 and 8.3 per cent in June 1920 was at just 1 per cent by June 1932. The more right wing DVP, which vied with the DDP, was similarly down to just 1.9 per cent in June 1932 from a high point of 13.9 per cent in June 1920 (ibid.: 203, Table 8.4).

Arguments, similar to Weber's, for the inherent unconduciveness of German society to the proper workings of democratic institutions, are also found in Dahrendorf's (1968) view of post-First World War Germany as having undergone a 'suspended revolution'. In Dahrendorf's analysis, Imperial Germany was an 'industrial feudal society' (1968: 61) which had failed to produce an independent bourgeoisie as a class for itself (ibid.: 54) and which had retained the authoritarian patriarchal system of the traditional landowning class, the Prussian Junkers. Their dominance in the military and the state bureaucracy, status groups, had combined with the bourgeoisie, he argues, to form a 'power elite' (ibid.: 223). This 'power elite' sought monopoly in the economy (the cartels) and, in politics, nationalism: 'a desire for unity' (ibid.: 209).

Dahrendorf (1968: 246) argues that though defeat in the First World War and the setting up of the Weimar Republic brought important political changes, crucially the state carried on 'insisting on serving a master who no longer existed'. Stressing, in particular, lawyers and the bureaucracy, he argues that state personnel continued to behave as if they were still under Junker dominated authoritarianism. As a consequence, he stresses 'the dissolution of established uniformity' brought by the events of 1918–19 did not lead to what he terms 'liberal diversity' (ibid.: 231). Dahrendorf's position is not simply that the old authoritarian, militaristic and nationalistic ways of behaving carried on but that society was inherently unsupportive of democracy: 'Society and democracy not only remained incompatible in the Weimar Republic, social reality provided a basis for the militant protest against the political form of democracy' (ibid.: 399).

Support for Dahrendorf's position is found in Berger (2000). In respect of the army, Berger (2000: 107) observes that, 'The Reichswehr in Weimar continued to espouse the Prussian virtues of blind loyalty and obedience; and army leaders continued to believe in strict social hierarchies and celebrated great traditions of the Prusso-German army.' In respect of the industrial elites, he comments how quickly after the agreement between the industrialists and the socialist trade unions, the Stinnes-Legion Agreement of 1918, they moved 'to reinstate the authoritarian "master-in-one's-own-house" attitude that dominated industrial relations before 1914' (ibid.: 108). Not only did the employers' federation reject workers' participation in industry, they also undermined the workers' principal economic achievement of an eight-hour day. Their contempt was evident in their coining the phrase for the Weimar Republic of 'trade union state' (ibid.). As Berger (ibid.) argues, 'the old elites commanded insufficient popular support to replace Weimar democracy with an authoritarian government of their own, but they were still powerful enough to undermine the basis for successful democratization'.

Nevertheless, the question remains open as to whether or not anti-democratic sentiment might have been reduced over time and been bolstered by democratic ones if favourable conditions had enabled Weimar to last longer. As in France, given sufficient time and favourable experiences opposition to democracy might have been won over by its proven advantages. Germany also had an extensive array of voluntary organizations and, indeed, had had so for over a century. In short, Germany had a strong civil society and a society, therefore, that should have played a crucial role in 'making democracy work' (Putnam 1993). Berman (1997), however, as mentioned in Chapter 2, has drawn attention to the failure of memberships of these voluntary organizations to cross-cut and to the effect that the weakening of the institutionalization of the Weimar Republic had on the civil society. She argues,

> Because weak national political institutions reinforced social cleavages instead of helping to narrow them, moreover, associational activity generally occurred within rather than across group lines. Under these circumstances, associational life served not to integrate citizens into the political system, as neo-Tocquevilleans would predict,

but rather to divide them further or mobilize them outside – and often against – the existing political regime.

(Berman 1997: 411)

Rather than protecting democracy, making it work, the reinforced structure of the civil society contributed to the rise of the Nazi Party; the party members infiltrated associations as part of their strategy to win support (see Berman 1997: 422–3). Berman concludes, therefore, that the effects of civil society are dependent on the political context rather than vice versa, associationalism contributing to the working of democracy only when democracy is working.

It is Sartori's (1997: 129) view that 'what fatally injured Weimar was the "great depression" of 1929, which hit Germany more devastatingly than any other Western country'. There is no dispute that the Great Crash hit Germany in a devastating way. Most strikingly, unemployment rose to 5 million by the winter of 1930/31 and 6 million by the winter of 1931/32 (Balfour 1992: 49). That is, from 8.4 per cent in 1928, unemployment had soared to a rate of 30.1 per cent in 1932 (Arends and Kümmel 2000: 201, Table 8.3). The new unemployment insurance, introduced in 1927 could not cope without adjustment. It was the question of how to reform the unemployment insurance that led directly to the fall, in March 1930, of the last democratically legitimated government (Berger 2000: 109). From that point on, presidential cabinets were formed. Furthermore, exports fell dramatically, from 12.3 billion Reichsmark in 1928 to 5.7 billion in 1932. This export crisis, which was bound to follow for a while, accompanied overproduction and coincided with a severe crisis in agriculture. Gross Domestic Product fell from 88,100 million RM in 1928 to 56,700 in 1932. Industrial production, at 15 per cent higher in 1928 than it had been in 1925, was, in 1932, only 71 per cent of what it had been in 1925. (See Arends and Kümmel 2000: 208 and 200.)

Germany's severe suffering after the Great Crash cannot, however, be separated from both the underlying economic problems within Germany and the country's post-war political and economic history which affected both government actions and people's perceptions more widely. The hyperinflation of 1922–23, when the cost of living, based on 100 in 1921, rose to 1,123 in 1922 and to 1,187,076 in 1923 (Arends and Kümmel 2000: 201, Table 8.3), remained in recent memory. Though the economy stayed in good shape from 1924 as a consequence of foreign loans (the Dawes Plan) (ibid.: 200), the fear of hyperinflation had much to do with Chancellor Brüning's choice of deflationary measures to tackle the effect of the 1929 Great Crash. In practice, the deflationary policies, while avoiding inflation, created problems at least as bad as inflationary policies, as the unemployment figures, discussed above, clearly demonstrate. Brüning's economic policy was also designed to strengthen his hand in negotiating an end to reparation payments still being made to the Allies. In this he was successful. In June 1932, the Allies accepted an end to the payments, but by this time Brüning had resigned.

Not only did the inflation of 1923 stay in the public consciousness, so too did the defeat in the First World War. The harsh settlement of the Versailles treaty associated the new republic with humiliating defeat and the harsh reparation payments burdened the economy. The Allies failed to nurture and support the new democracy and pursued, rather, hostile and isolationist policies against Germany. (See Ginsberg 1996: 92–3.) What also stayed in minds were the post-war political events: the revolutionary uprisings and strikes in the early years; the experience of the succession of Weimar governments collapsing. The record of democracy, both politically and economically and, with the unemployment, socially, was one of instability.

What happened in Germany, however, was not simply the collapse of democracy and a return to the authoritarianism that had existed in Germany before the First World War. What arose in Germany was a totalitarian regime. That it was not, purely and simply, the workings of the Weimar Constitution that led to the Nazi regime is supported by the glaring lesson to be drawn from comparison with the Soviet Union. Though having taken not the path to democracy but to communism, both the Soviet Union and Germany developed totalitarian regimes.

Part III

Totalitarianism

Antithesis of democracy

6 The rise of totalitarian regimes

Contrasting France

In spite of choosing very different paths, the one to democracy the other to communism, both Germany and the Soviet Union developed totalitarian regimes. Neither case simply reverted to being authoritarian governments, neither case constituted simply the rejection of liberal democracy; the totalitarian regimes set out to destroy not only political pluralism but social pluralism too. Added to this destruction they substituted government, even as dictatorship, with rule through terror. Consideration of what was common between Germany and the Soviet Union before their totalitarian regimes but absent in France where such a regime did not occur holds the potential to provide two important lessons about democracy. The first is to gain understanding of how and why countries manage to stay on a path to democracy. The other is to gain perspective on democracy being set up after the experience of the very antithesis of pluralist democracy.

In *The Origins of Totalitarianism*, Arendt contrasts the similarities between the histories of Germany and of the Soviet Union with differences in the history of France. Arendt (1958) traces the 'origins of totalitarianism' to developments in Europe in the nineteenth century, highlighting the emergence of the nation-state and the growth of imperialism. Nineteenth-century imperialism, she argues, used two devices to rule over people: 'bureaucracy as a principle of foreign domination' and 'race as a principal of the body politic' (Arendt 1958: 185). 'Race-thinking' (ibid.: 158) is not equivalent to anti-Semitism.

Central to Arendt's argument is that in imperialist thinking the differences between race and nation undermined the ideas of citizenship within the nation-state. In the form that it took in Europe in the nineteenth century, imperialism both developed the ideas to justify the denial of rights to people within a country and identified the peoples to whom such rights could be denied. Lacking colonies abroad (in contrast to the cases of Britain and France) Russia and Germany looked for 'colonies on the continent' (Arendt 1958: 222). She explains that, 'Nazism and Bolshevism owe more to Pan-Germanism and Pan-Slavism (respectively) than any other ideology or political movement' (ibid.). What Arendt terms 'tribal nationalism' developed in Europe and with the pan-movements including some people, though outside the state's borders, and excluding others, though inside the state's boundaries, 'race-thinking' became a powerful political force (ibid.: 223).

The number of these 'stateless' people, Arendt (1958: 267–9) argues, crucially escalated as a consequence of the First World War. As a result of the post-war treaties, which artificially drew boundaries such that all sorts of people found themselves in new states, the newcomers were resented (ibid.: 261). Stateless people, lacking rights, became a characteristic of Europe after the First World War with refugees, beggars, Jews, Trotskyists and so on, all denied citizenship and viewed as 'undesirables' (ibid.: 269). The presence of stateless people, the 'undesirables', she argues, was exploited both by Hitler and by Stalin. As she explains, 'an ideology which has to persuade and mobilize people cannot choose its victims arbitrarily' (ibid.: 7).

The opportunity that allowed Hitler and Stalin into power was provided by the respective political systems in Germany and the Soviet Union. Drawing on her two themes of imperialism and citizenship, Arendt (1958: 243) argues that a political system historically structured around a strong bureaucratic state, 'government by decree', will be the one best suited to a totalitarian leader; in such systems, nationalism is encouraged.[1] The system that cannot be undermined by a totalitarian leader is the 'Anglo-Saxon' two-party system based not on a strong state but on a strong parliament and strong government with an opposition organized as the future party of government (ibid.: 252).

In a system designed for alternating parties in government, the state bureaucracy, Arendt argues, is organized for the purpose of 'alteration' and does not, therefore, stand above government and citizens (Arendt 1958: 252). In contrast, in what she terms the 'continental party system' with proportional representation and coalition government, the state is above parties, for 'each party defines itself consciously as a part of the whole, which in turn is represented by state above parties' (ibid.: 253). A consequence is that in the continental party system nationalism is encouraged. In arguments similar to Weber's, she also criticizes the coalition system for undermining the taking of responsibility, whether by any one politician or any particular party (ibid.: 254–5).

Arendt stresses that France differs from Germany and Russia. France had colonies abroad and did not, therefore, seek them on the continent. As the oldest nation-state in Europe, France had no pan-movement similar to those in Germany and Russia. There was anti-Semitism in France, certainly; indeed she points out that in 1898, there were nineteen members of parliament 'elected through antisemitic campaigns' (Arendt 1958: 46). But, she stresses, though France had anti-Semitic parties, and though violent, they had 'no supranational aspirations' (ibid.: 45). In respect of the Dreyfus Affair, Arendt argues that anti-Semitism in France in the nineteenth century stayed 'a domestic issue', it was not part of 'imperialist trends' (ibid.: 90). Indeed, she points out that 'parliament became a champion of Dreyfus' (ibid.: 119). As explained in Chapter 4, in France, Jews had the protection of the state.

Arendt's claim that Pan-Slavism was more important to developments in the USSR than was communism is challenged by Friedrich and Brzezinski (1965: 364); certainly, 'race-thinking' in the Soviet Union was not equivalent to its importance in Germany. Furthermore, though the general argument about the strength of the state bureaucracy and the political systems not being organized for alteration may apply to both Russia (as a single party system) and Germany (as a PR, coalition system with a decree clause in the constitution), the specific arguments about PR do not apply to the Soviet Union. Furthermore, as discussed in Chapter 5, the arguments about the dangers of PR and specific weaknesses of the Weimar Constitution can be questioned. As noted, Lepsius (1978: 45) argues that had the Weimar system of PR been adapted in a modest way, to deny seats in parliament to parties polling less than 5 per cent of the votes, then the parliamentary system would have been significantly strengthened. Sartori (1997), challenging the significance of the Weimar Constitution for the Nazis coming to power in 1933, argues that there are plenty of similar cases where democracy has survived and in respect not only of similar PR systems but also of similar decree clauses. As explained, he also finds examples of similar semi-presidential systems, which are successful. It is this rejection of a political explanation for the collapse of Weimar democracy that leads Sartori to argue, rather, for the primary importance of the effects of the 1929 Great Crash.

Arendt underplays the importance of economic conditions. In O'Kane (1996), I argue that economic conditions played a significant part in respect of both the nature and the origins of totalitarianism and figured prominently in both Hitler's and Stalin's motivations. Each held in their thinking the same immovable conviction of the value for the economy of the intensive use of labour under state control and, more particularly, of the use of forced labour at minimum financial expenditure. The totalitarian regimes moved from rational planning, Weber's 'substantive rationality', to wild schemes, what I term 'substantive irrationality'. This economic thinking is central to understanding the centrality of concentration and labour camps to the terror of their totalitarian regimes. Economic crisis also provided conditions able to be exploited both by Stalin and by Hitler in their securing of power. In Germany, certainly the Wall Street Crash in 1929 propelled the country into economic crisis. In the Soviet Union in late 1928 and 1929 the country was hit by serious and unexpected economic shortfalls. Crucially, however, I argue that what was so significant about these economic crises was that they each followed an earlier crisis. Their real significance lay in that they were renewed economic crises and that these crises reoccurred in societies that had been dislocated.

A 'dislocated society' is a society full of movement. The dislocations, demographic, social and geographic, resulted from combinations of the effects of foreign war, civil war, revolution, famine and rapid economic modernization. This emphasis on the importance of movement in society is in contrast to Marx and Weber's class analyses and sympathetic rather to Arendt's stress on the creation of outsiders. Dislocated societies provide ripe conditions for the victimization of innocents.

Dislocated societies and economic crisis in Russia and Germany

As explained in Chapter 5, both Germany and Russia experienced late and rapid industrialization. Important dislocations also followed. In Russia, rapid movement occurred from rural to urban areas. From 800,000 industrial workers in 1860 (one-third of them still serfs), by 1900 the figure had reached 3 million and the concentration of workers in large factories by the turn of the century was the highest in the world. By 1912, 43 per cent of Russian factories employed more than 1,000 workers (Wolf 1973: 74–5). As in Russia, in Germany the consequence of rapid modernization too was social and geographical mobility, but in Germany there was a difference. The growth in factories did not simply lead to rural workers migrating to urban areas: as the rural workers moved out, so landowners replaced the migrating workers with seasonal foreign labour, particularly in Eastern Germany. By 1914 half a million foreign agricultural workers were seasonally employed in Germany (Homze 1967: 3). Late and rapid modernization, however, was not the only factor that brought dramatic changes to the German and Russian societies.

From 1914 to 1918, both Russia and Germany were embroiled in foreign war. The loss of German soldiers in the First World War is estimated at 1,808,545, the greatest number of any of the countries involved and approximately 1,700,000 Russian soldiers were killed (Bullock 1993: Appendix 2). As explained, Russia then had a revolution, in 1917, followed by a civil war, lasting from 1918 to 1921. Germany, as has become clear, similarly experienced growing disorder from 1916, culminating in revolutionary action from November 1918 to 1920 and further outbursts occurred in 1921 and 1923. The civil war in Russia was then followed, in 1921, by famine. In the period of revolution and civil war, 1917–18, an estimated 10 million people lost their lives in Russia (Rummel 1990: 50–4, Table 2A). Furthermore, the number of people living in the cities dropped from 19 per cent of the population in 1917 to 15 per cent in 1920. The population of Petrograd fell by two-thirds and that of Moscow by half (Lewin 1985: 211). The severe drought in 1921 brought famine to the Volga basin, the Southern Urals and areas of the Ukraine and 27 million people faced starvation, resulting in 5 million deaths (Levytsky 1972: 43).

Russia had negotiated itself from the First World War in March 1918 and Germany had been defeated in November 1918; the economies of both countries suffered badly as a consequence. In the Brest-Litovsk Treaty, March 1918, Russia lost to Germany: the Ukraine, which was the main wheat growing area; the rich industrial areas of the Baltic; Finland and the Polish territories. In all, 27 per cent of the arable land, 33 per cent of the manufacturing industries and 26 per cent of the population passed to Germany (Bradley 1975: 46). In the Treaty of Versailles, June 1919, it was Germany that lost, forfeiting all of its colonies and 27,000 square miles and 6 million people in order to separate East Prussia from the rest of Germany and provide Poland with access to the coast (Balfour 1992: 42). Other treaties also created new states, including the Baltic States, and imposed new borders. For example, in the Treaty of Riga, in 1920, part of the Ukraine and part of White Russia were given to Poland. Reparation payments were also demanded from Germany of 33,000 million dollars (Harvey 1968: 205).

What is significant is not simply the similarity of experiences in Germany and Russia but also the similarity of the repercussions for their economics and societies. Economic crisis ensued, which further aggravated social dislocation and its consequences. In Russia, during the civil war the war communist economy, which aimed at central control over distribution and production, 'collapsed' (Sakwa 1988: 240). The purchasing price of money in circulation at 1 July 1921 was worth little over 1 per cent of what it had been worth at the time of the Bolshevik Revolution, November 1917 (Carr 1966, Vol. 2: 259). In Germany, the immediate economic effect of defeat in the First World War was runaway inflation, the consequence of loans raised by the Imperial Government. The problem was added to by the reparation payments demanded by the Allies. By June 1922, the value of the Mark had similarly dropped to just 1 per cent of its value in 1914. (See Balfour 1992: 44.)

In turn, the experiences of living in a dislocated society together with those produced by the economic crisis faced by each of the two countries set in tow similar socially tense conditions. In Russia during the civil war, under war communism, grain requisitioning set worker against peasant, town against country (Carr 1966, Vol. 2: 152–65). In Germany, at the end of the war, unemployment for German workers returned and all the foreign workers ceased to be employed (Homze 1967: 4). The presence of dispossessed foreigners in times of economic hardship gave fuel to racist scapegoating. Jews were a group traditionally blamed for economic problems and waves of anti-Semitism had hit Germany from the 1870s (Moore 1978: 414; Pulzer 1992: 345). With the events of revolution in both Germany and Russia, Jews and Bolshevism/communism became intertwined in anti-Semitic minds. Those blamed for the economic crisis after the First World War became the scapegoats for the economic crisis that returned in the late 1920s.

France: the contrasts

In France, capitalism had been neither late nor rapid nor bound-up with the state as in Germany and Russia. As explained in Chapter 4, industrialization and commercialization began earlier in France and took place at a slower rate. In France between 1870 and 1914, the rates of change lagged behind those in Germany and, as a consequence, though social changes occurred, society was not radically altered. By 1914, around half the population of France was still working in agriculture and neither urban areas nor factory sizes had expanded in the same way as in Germany and Russia. Family-sized firms remained the norm and in 1914 around a quarter of the population lived in towns of between 2,000 and 20,000 people.[2]

France also differed from Russia and Germany in respect of the consequences of war. While Russia had negotiated itself from the First World War in March 1918 and Germany had been defeated in November 1918, France emerged victorious. In stark contrast to Russia and Germany, rather than losing territory and suffering consequent economic loss, France gained. The penalties for war aggression imposed on Germany had been similar in design to those imposed by the Germans on the French in the Treaty of Frankfurt of 10 May 1871, which followed France's defeat in the Franco-Prussian War. Under that treaty France lost the whole of Alsace and part of Lorraine and was obliged to pay the equivalent of 1,000 million dollars (Harvey 1968: 117). With French victory and German defeat in 1918, Alsace-Lorraine was returned to France.

France, like both Germany and Russia, suffered enormous losses of life in the 1914–18 war. In total, 1,327,000 French soldiers died (Bullock 1993: Appendix 2). As a victor of the war, however, the country had no reparations to pay and benefited from the regaining of the territory lost in 1871. In contrast to both Germany and Russia, France neither faced revolutionary upheaval, in 1917 or 1918, nor suffered under consequent civil war. Though France came close to a general strike in 1920, it was quickly suppressed (Harvey 1968: 222–3).

Loser or victor, war brings a level of economic devastation. Comparing France in 1919, the year after the war ended, with 1913, the year before war broke out, industrial production was down 40 per cent and exports were down by 75 per cent. By 1926, however, the economy had recovered fully from the war (Harvey 1968: 229). Again, compared with 1913, in 1926 industrial production was up by 25 per cent and exports had improved by 66 per cent (ibid.). Not only were new factories built to replace those destroyed but new industries were also developed: the automobile industry, chemical and hydroelectric industries and the tourist industry, which was booming. In 1926, France benefited from full employment to such an extent that 2 million foreign workers were also employed (ibid.: 230). Though a financial crisis faced the government in 1926, it was successfully concluded in 1927 (ibid.: 227–8).

In both Russia and Germany, too, the post-war economic crisis at first gave way to economic improvement. In Germany, in 1924, the currency was stabilized and negotiations achieved a reduction in the reparation payments and a package of American loans, the Dawes Plan (Conradt 1989: 7). This phase, known as the 'golden years', lasted until 1929 (Arends and Kümmel 2000: 199). Between 1924 and 1929, GNP per capita increased an average 4 per cent a year, though not everything reflected well, unemployment rates continued to average around 10 per cent and falling world market prices adversely affected the agricultural sector (ibid.: 200). In the Soviet Union, Lenin introduced the New Economic Policy (NEP), in 1921, under which the currency was stabilized. (For full details see Carr 1966, Vol. 2: 282–322.) Economic reconstruction, needed after the devastation brought by the civil war on top of that brought by the war and revolution, was completed by 1927 (Siegelbaum 1992: 203–11). Crucially, however, when the Great Crash came, in 1929, hitting everywhere in Europe, it fell on France with a softer blow.

In France, though foreign markets contracted, the franc stayed relatively buoyant and gold reserves were substantial. Industrial growth, rather than going into immediate decline as elsewhere, continued well into 1931. Strikingly, too, in the middle of 1931, in contrast to the 8 million registered unemployed in the United States, the 4.5 million in Germany and the 2.5 million in the United Kingdom, there were only 55,000 in France. (See Dobry 2000: 174.) In addition, the effects of unemployment were cushioned by the social welfare legislation, which had been introduced in 1927 and was in force by 1930, in which, hitherto, France had lagged behind. Furthermore, in contrast to the situation in Germany where social welfare was closely associated with the SPD, in France the social welfare legislation had been introduced after the financial crisis had been successfully concluded, in 1927, with deputies of the right and centre joining those of the left to develop the legislation (Harvey 1968: 227–8). Though the government of 1928–32 engaged in some measures aimed at balancing the budget, the economic system was left largely to market forces (ibid.). The government of the left that took over in 1932 was similarly cautious (Dobry 2000: 174). By 1934, official unemployment figures had risen to half a million, still a relatively low total and kept down by the departure of the 2 million foreign workers (Harvey 1968: 231).

In respect of economic crisis and dislocated society France contrasts sharply with both Germany and the Soviet Union. There are also other clear contrasts to be made between France, Germany and the Soviet Union in respect of anti-Semitism and the workings of the political system, both viewed as significant by Arendt (1958).

Anti-Semitism

As in the rest of Europe, anti-Semitism was present in France and growing during the 1880s, aggravated by the decline in the economic growth rate from the 1.6 per cent in the 1870s to 0.6 per cent a decade later. In France, facing particularly strong competition from Germany and America, a view of bankers became epitomized by the Rothschild family who were not only Jewish but also of German origin. (See Lindemann 1991: 65–6.) During the 1880s, anti-Semitism was also heightened by the debates over the separation between church and state and, in particular, by the move to secular education. As explained in Chapter 4, in politics, anti-Semitism coalesced around General Boulanger, the Minister of War dismissed in 1887. The Boulangist movement, however, collapsed in 1889 when only forty Boulangists were elected to the Assembly. The recognition of the weakness of this support was to affect the right's calculations from then on (Dobry 2000: 182–3). Furthermore, it is noteworthy that, in contrast to the rightward tide in Germany and Russia, in the elections of 1893 France moved to the left.

As also mentioned in Chapter 4, in 1894 the arrest and wrongful court martial and conviction to life imprisonment of Dreyfus, a Jewish captain in the French army, produced the catharsis of anti-Semitism. The Dreyfus Affair led, by 1898, to violent attacks on Jews and on supporters of Dreyfus and on their properties. Street brawls between the Dreyfusards and anti-Dreyfusard Leaguers and their student supporters became a common feature in France through 1899 (Harvey 1968: 137). Dreyfus was finally exonerated in 1906, by which time the same mob who had supported the anti-Dreyfusards had reversed their position and had begun to use violence against them (ibid.: 123). In the same year, the left also won a decisive victory in the election. As Lindemann (1991: 123) comments, 'France seemed to many observers, in spite of all the excitement in 1898–9, a tolerant country, one where Jews could rely both on the state and on the people, in contrast to the situation in Germany, Austria, or Russia'.

There is, however, debate over whether anti-Semitism receded at this point or, rather, went underground (Lindemann 1997: 234). If underground it was ready to reappear once the state lost its hold, as it did after France's defeat in 1940. One thing is clear, however, in contrast to Germany it was the left not the right that gained from the Dreyfus Affair. In line with Arendt's position, anti-Semitism, in France, settled within conservatism rather than in separation from it as in Germany and the NSDAP (Lindemann 1991: 126). In Lindemann's (ibid.: 128) view, too, the Dreyfus Affair also crystallized political changes, towards a modern pluralist democracy, based on free associations. In particular, the League of the Rights of Man and the League of Patriots were developed and trade unions and business and professional organizations became strengthened (Lindemann 1997: 237). As Dobry (2000: 167) comments, there is 'a paradox, given the anti-parliamentary origin of the *Ligues*' that they led to the development of mass participation within parliamentary democracy. Indeed, he credits the 'reactivation of the *Ligues*' together with the 'birth of new organizations' with a crucial role in shaping politics between the wars and especially in reconfiguring politics of the right.

In Germany, anti-Semitism was well served within conservative parties and organizations and, as mentioned in Chapter 5, especially so by the German National People's Party, DNVP, founded in 1919. Support for the DNVP, however, which was at its highest in 1924, at 20.5 per cent of the votes and 103 seats, declined from then on. Support went down to 14.2 per cent in May 1928 and was at its lowest point in July 1932 with 5.9 per cent, rising a little to 8.3 per cent in November 1932 and 8 per cent in March 1933. (See Arends and Kümmel 2000: 203, Table 8.4.) As in France, anti-Semitism within conservatism, within an ordinary nationalistic-monarchist party, like the DNVP, was not a means for totalitarianism in Germany. The National Socialist German Workers' Party (NSDAP), the Nazi Party, made illegal between 1923 and 1925, following Hitler's attempted coup in Munich (ibid.: 197), achieved electoral breakthrough in September 1930 when it received 18.3 per cent of the votes and 107 seats in parliament. In the May 1928 election the NSDAP had won only 2.6 per cent of the votes and only twelve seats, and at that point had only 80,000 members. (See Arends and Kümmel 2000: 203, Table 8.4.)

The Nazi Party was not a conventional political party. From 1921, when Hitler became chairman of the party, the NSDAP had a paramilitary force, the Storm Division, SA. Between 1931 and 1932, the SA grew from 77,000 to 470,000 (Arends and Kümmel 2000: 197). Commenting on the political and economic disorder in Germany in the early 1930s, which took protest onto the streets and into violent confrontations, Arends and Kümmel (ibid.: 209) nicely understate that 'Here the SA turned out to be a very useful instrument for the NSDAP'.

As a relatively new party which offered all things to all people (ibid.: 197), exploiting existing ideas and prejudices with actual policies vague enough to conceal incompatible promises and to avoid detailed questioning, the Nazi Party stood as the party that challenged all parties. In sum, the party promised to return Germany to its earlier greatness, to the greatness that, as the superior people, was the destiny not simply of Germany but of all, true, German people. As such, the Nazi Party positioned itself to benefit best from the political and economic crisis which arose and it was especially sure to present its nationalist credentials to the DNVP. The NSDAP never gained a majority of votes in a free election. Once the majority party within a coalition, one with the DNVP, the Nazis destroyed democracy.

Political safeguards

In contrast to France with its early nation-state and long history of republicanism, in both Germany and the Soviet Union the end of monarchy was recent. In the Soviet Union, where communist revolution and civil war had not simply ended the monarchy but totally destroyed support both for the monarchy and for conservative authoritarianism, in Germany, as explained in Chapter 5, supporters of both monarchy and conservative authoritarianism remained in opposition to democracy. They were 'semi-loyal oppositions' at best (Lepsius 1978: 45).

In practice, though both Germany and France were liberal democracies with presidents and coalition governments at that, the Weimar Republic contrasted with politics under the Third French Republic. Over time, whereas the rules of the Weimar Republic served to undermine parties, to diminish the importance of parliament and to enhance the power of the president, in France quite the opposite was the case. As explained in Chapter 4, following the crisis of 'Seize Mai' in 1877, by 1879, the presidency became 'a decorative post, with its powers severely curtailed' (Harvey 1968: 126) and parliament, especially the Chamber of Deputies, gained a predominant position in the Republic with ministers paying more heed to parliament than to the president (ibid). As also discussed in Chapter 4, a significant change to the political system also took place.

In July 1919, an electoral law was passed in France, which included a provision that had similar effects to the first-past-the-post rule of the British system. Within each department, all the seats were awarded to the party or coalition group that secured a majority of votes (Harvey 1968: 220). As discussed in Chapter 5, such a rule could have helped to overcome the weaknesses posed by proportional representation in the Weimar system. Crucially, in France, the new law provided incentives for coalitions to be made before elections, and they held. As a consequence, not only were governments more secure than in Weimar Germany but opposition was also strengthened in France.

Like Weimar Germany, governments in France changed frequently. Between the wars there were forty cabinets, some lasting only a few weeks (Dobry 2000: 168). Dobry (ibid.) argues, however, that it is a mistake to interpret this instability as constituting a weakness of the system for a number of reasons. Mostly, the same politicians were to be found in succeeding cabinets, sometimes even the leaders were the same. Crucially, in practice, rather than creating instability the frequent changes served to manage political crises, those stemming from financial crisis in particular. It is also significant that both houses of parliament had the power to overturn governments, thus adding to the number of changes (ibid.). Dobry (ibid.: 168–70) also highlights the role of the Radical Party, important since 1902, in these changes for so frequently swapping sides, while at the same time support for it was declining.

The effect of the electoral law of 1919 was also to produce another difference. The government of France from 1919 to 1924 – the Bloc National – was, in contrast to Weimar at the time, not a coalition of the left but a coalition of the right. In 1924, however, a left coalition, the Cartel des Gauches, which did not include the Communist Party, won the election (Harvey 1968: 225). Financial problems for the government of the Cartel des Gauches came to a head in 1926 and the coalition broke down, but rather than producing a polarization between left and right, as was to happen in Germany, a broad coalition government of centre and right was created. As explained, the financial crisis was resolved by 1927 (ibid.: 227). In 1928 the electoral system was, again, modified with a return to plurality ballot (Dobry 2000: 173).

Socialist parties

France contrasted not only in respect of the workings of proportional representation. Socialism in France began before the publication of the Communist Manifesto in 1848, and was, therefore, separate from Marxist social democracy. French socialist ideas can be traced back to the French Revolution, but it was in protest against the Bourgeois monarchy of Louis Philippe, 1830–48, that French socialist leaders and groups developed. By 1848, there were several kinds of socialism. For example, there were Fourier's 'utopian' socialism, Lamennais's Christian Socialism, Saint-Simon's technocratic socialism, and Louis Blanc's social workshops (*organisations du travail*) which were so important in the 1848 revolution. As explained in Chapter 4, with the French system lacking permanent nationally organized parties before 1901, the Socialist Party, SFIO, which, as also explained, brought together various socialist groups, was established in 1905. The Communist Party was founded in 1920 following a split in the SFIO through disagreements over the Russian Revolution. The minority remained the SFIO under Leon Blum's leadership and pursued socialism through evolution not revolution (Harvey 1968: 223).

Drawing lessons

In sum, France, unlike Germany and Russia, had neither late, nor rapid, nor state-led modernization and did not experience a dislocated society in the 1920s. Between the wars France had a stronger economy than either Germany or the Soviet Union, and was relatively unscathed by the Great Crash. Also in contrast, France's political system had a longer history and, in the 1920s, in contrast to Germany, was not polarized and had a strong centre. In addition, the political appeal of anti-Semitism had been tested by the Dreyfus Affair and been found lacking in significant support and the Affair had also confirmed the lesson which France, with its long path to democracy interspersed with revolutions and dictatorships, had learnt the hard way. The lesson was that the best way for resolution of difference was through elections and parliament. Furthermore, the history of socialism in France was long and pluralist.

In contrast to Germany's move to the right in the election of 1930, in France, in 1932, the left-centre coalition, the Cartel des Gauches won (Harvey 1968: 231). The Cartel des Gauches lasted until 1934, but by the time right-wing riots and demonstrations led to the resignation of the centre-left government in France, on 4 February 1934, the benefits of lessons from Nazi ascendancy to power in the Weimar Republic were also available to be drawn, by the communists especially. In this sense, French history was affected by German history, just as German history had been coloured by contemporary events in Russia. Rather than splitting the opposition to fascism, as happened in Germany, in France, the communists joined the socialist organized general strike on 12 February and forged the basis of a future coalition of the centre-left, which included the communists (Harvey 1968: 238–40). This Popular Front won the election in May 1936 with 55 per cent of the popular vote and 65 per cent of the seats (ibid.: 241).

Anti-Semitism reappeared in 1936 with 'streetfighters and hoodlums' (Harvey 1968: 244) – the *Cagoulards*. The government dissolved the Fascist Leagues.[3] Following the Senate's refusal to endorse the Chamber of Deputies' decision to grant Blum extraordinary decree powers to bring in a radical programme, Blum resigned in June 1937 (ibid.). Decree powers were then granted to his successor who, as one of the Allies, declared war on Germany in September 1939. In the same month the Communist Party was made illegal (ibid.: 259). In June 1940, unable to repel invasion, France surrendered to Germany.

Following the defeat, an armistice was concluded under which three-fifths of France was under German occupation with the remainder under a French government, the Vichy Republic under General Pétain. The new government ruled under emergency powers until a new constitution was in place. The aim of producing a new constitution was abandoned in 1942 but under the Twelve Constitutional Acts introduced between 1940 and 1942 both the presidency and the parliaments were ended and corporate institutions replaced the pluralism of free trade unions and of social and economic organizations more widely. In the new political thinking, 'family, work and fatherland' replaced 'liberty, equality and fraternity'. Along with these ideas, associated with fascism, there was also 'virulent anti-Semitism' (Harvey 1968: 274), anti-Semitism that was especially harsh on non-French Jews. At the end of the war officials were to make excuses on the grounds of Nazi insistence, though later investigations have challenged the claim and demonstrated the virulence of French anti-Semitism. (See Harvey 1968: 262–74.)

The intensity of French anti-Semitism in the Vichy Republic indicates the importance of state protection for religious and ethnic minorities provided by democratic political systems. It also suggests that the contribution of ideas of toleration, so important to liberalism, is not wholly independent of the political system and cannot, therefore, alone at least, be used as explanation for democracy. Lack of toleration is, of course, characteristic of authoritarian regimes but, as argued, both Germany and Russia went beyond authoritarianism, beyond the mere denial of liberal democracy and set up, rather, systems of terror under which not simply pluralism was destroyed but millions of innocent people died. This contrasts with Italy.

Totalitarian dictatorship versus totalitarian regime

Italy became a totalitarian dictatorship. 'Totalitarian dictatorship', is viewed by Friedrich and Brzezinski (1965) as a new phenomenon of the twentieth century and is conceptualized as a syndrome, which involves political dictatorship, over society and economy, based on a new total ideology, through a 'system of terror', using modern technology and single mass party organization (ibid.: 22 and passim). Friedrich and Brzezinski view Nazi Germany, the Soviet Union along with other communist regimes, and Fascist Italy as totalitarian dictatorships. Arendt (1958), however, includes only Nazi Germany and Stalin's Soviet Union as totalitarian regimes. Italy under Mussolini she allows as a totalitarian dictatorship and then just from 1938. For Arendt, totalitarianism proper is a 'regime' run from behind the state, not through it.[4] Italy, she argues, never moved to the final stage, explaining 'Mussolini who was so fond of the term "totalitarian state" did not attempt to establish a fully-fledged totalitarian regime and contented himself with dictatorship and one-party rule' (Arendt 1958: 308).

Italy was like Germany, but unlike France, in experiencing deep economic recession after the First World War (Clark 1984: 206). As in Germany, proportional representation was introduced in 1919 and, similarly, the result was a series of weak short-lived coalitions. Again as in Germany, polarization between the left and the right occurred and, like Hitler, Mussolini came to power through a combination of politics and violence, with the Fascist squads attacking socialists and communists. In France, in contrast, the government retained a strong centre. Like France but unlike both Germany and the Soviet Union, however, Italy did not experience rapid modernization before the war and, helped also by being a victor in the war, neither did Italy experience a dislocated society after the war. Though starting from a lower base, Italy was also like France, but unlike Germany and the Soviet Union, in achieving growth rates of crucial economic indicators above those of other capitalist countries through 1922-1938 (Gregor 1982: 153-5). Avoiding both a dislocated society and renewed economic crisis helps further to explain why Italy never made Arendt's 'last stage' to the totalitarian regime.s

In Arendt's totalitarian regime 'real power' (as opposed to the 'ostensible power' of state institutions) belongs to the secret police, with concentration camps at the core of their operation. In her conception, the system of terror operates independently, in secrecy, the whole system characterized by lawlessness.[5] Arendt holds that the 'last stage' of totalitarianism, which is the totalitarian regime, began only in the Soviet Union in 1930 and Nazi Germany in 1938 (Arendt 1958: 419). In a totalitarian regime, she argues, the state is a façade, a shapeless creation of 'multiplication of offices' and 'duplications of function' (ibid.: 399) that even has 'fake departments' (ibid.: 371). It is a far cry from the centrally organized party-bureaucracy of Friedrich and Brzezinski's (1965) syndrome of totalitarian dictatorship.

Again in contrast to Friedrich and Brzezinski's view of the importance of a new total ideology, it is crucial to Arendt's (1958: 188) argument that rather than developing an entirely new totalitarian ideology the leader exploits existing ideas, prejudices and beliefs. Such ideas included those, mentioned above, of anti-Semitism, Pan-Germanism, Pan-Slavism and Marxism-Leninism, but stripped of ideological principles (ibid.: 222). Not being a dictatorship based on ideological principles, the leader's orders are 'deliberately vague' (ibid.: 404), the system is based on 'systematic lying' (ibid.: 423) and the leader's hold is operated through 'prophetic infallibility' (ibid.: 348–50).[6] In the changing and arbitrary society the leader, never admitting an error, appears as the one firm presence to whom people can attach themselves.

With the regime operated from behind the state by the secret police with concentration camps at the centre of their operation, the kind of terror which Arendt (1958) posits as characteristic of the totalitarian regime contrasts significantly with Friedrich and Brzezinski's view. For Friedrich and Brzezinski (1965) the system of terror, which can be 'physical or psychic', is operated through the state, through the bureaucracy of party and secret police, and is directed at dissenters with the aim of intimidation. They define terror as 'a process in which activities of deliberate violence are undertaken by the power wielders to strike general and undefined fear into anyone who dissents' as 'a deliberate policy to intimidate' (ibid.: 170). This contrasts with Arendt's (1958: 6) position for whom: 'Terror as we know it today strikes without any preliminary provocation.' She continues, 'its victims are innocent even from the point of view of the persecutor' and adds, 'This was the case in Nazi Germany when full terror was directed against Jews, i.e. against people with certain common characteristics which were independent of their specific behaviour.'

For Arendt (1958: 437–59), the primary purpose of terror in a totalitarian regime is not that it is aimed at dissidents in order to create fear, as Friedrich and Brzezinski argue, but that it is directed deliberately at innocents, its aim to destroy spontaneity and to achieve perfect obedience for the purpose of 'total domination'. The years 1930, for the Soviet Union, and 1938, for Germany, are chosen by Arendt as the crucial points of separation between totalitarian dictatorship and totalitarian regime as government because these years mark the dates when the concentration camps were overwhelmed with 'completely "innocent" inmates' (ibid.: 450).

Though Friedrich and Brzezinski allow that 'unpredictability' (1965: 163) plays a part in terror and therefore innocents may be affected, their definition of terror as violence essentially aimed against 'anyone who dissents' in order 'to strike a general and undefined fear' into them (ibid.: 170), does not fit the Nazi case, certainly after 1938. Jews did not 'dissent' by being Jewish. It was not an attribute that they could alter through a change in their behaviour. They were not, for example, given the choice of being Aryans instead or to claim their conversion to Christianity and so escape the Holocaust. As will become clear, in Chapter 7, the absence of choice in behaviour is equally characteristic of the other groups victimized by the Nazis such as the mentally ill and gypsies. Similarly, as will also become clear in Chapter 8, in the case of de-kulakization in the Soviet Union, which began in 1930, the classification as a *kulak* could not be affected by any present change of behaviour (Viola 1993: 73).

In contrast, in Fascist Italy, though violence was part of the Fascist philosophy, the difference between guilt and innocence turned on actual voluntary conduct. It was possible to avoid punishment by not performing proscribed acts. People could be intimidated through violence because they knew what they had to do in order to avoid it. In Italy, the function of the Special Tribunal for the Defence of the State, instituted on 25 November 1926 was to intimidate, to stop people carrying out behaviour proscribed by the regime. Its purpose was not to kill innocents, this is clearly shown by the evidence (Gregor 1982: 152–68). From 1926 until 1943, when the Fascist regime collapsed, only forty-seven death sentences were passed by the Italian Special Tribunal and of the 5,619 people prosecuted, 998 were found innocent.[7] Gregor contrasts this with the Special Boards in the Soviet Union which gave defendants no right to defence and where cases were brought in absentia and against groups of people at a time without specific charges. Crucially, too, in Stalin's Soviet Union at times thousands of executions a week took place and 'corrective labour' mostly meant death in a labour camp.

Gregor (1982: 161) also points out that while 7,495 Jews were deported, of whom 6,885 were killed by the Germans, 'none were executed by the Fascists'. The contrast is stark not only with Stalin's Soviet Union but also with Hitler's Germany. Mussolini did introduce anti-Semitic legislation in 1938, but under it 'mitigations' were allowed and many Jews were 'Aryanised' (ibid.: 163). After the Italian government surrendered to the Allies in 1943, implementation of the Nazi Final Solution took place under the Italian Social Republic in the north of Italy, the execution of Jews only beginning with the arrival of German SS units for the purpose (Steinberg 1991: 158–63). The Italian Social Republic was set up in September 1943 and controlled by the Germans and headed by Mussolini, now freed (Clark 1984: 308–10).

Ironically, proof that Fascist Italy, was not a totalitarian regime but became only a totalitarian dictatorship, run through the state, is found in the refusal of state personnel to carry out the German Foreign Minister Ribbentrop's request, in 1942, to deport Jews to German concentration camps. It was to this that Mussolini had no objection – the famous 'nulla osta ... M' which he was later forced to revoke after the refusals to obey those orders. The 'resistance' involved the very highest generals and members of the state, beginning with Count Luca Pietromarchi, the senior diplomat responsible for Italian-occupied territories, and Colonel Cigliani, the colonel in charge of the office of civilian affairs at the headquarters of the VIth Army Corps. On 27 November General Roatta visited the largest of the Jewish concentration camps, at Kraljevice, and formally told them that they were under Italian protection (Steinberg 1991: 84). As the facts of the Holocaust became clearer the Italians also defended Jews in Greece and France, between November 1942 and July 1943, by which time the fortunes of war had turned (ibid.: 85–134).

7 Totalitarian regime

Nazi Germany

The collapse of the Weimar Republic

The immediate condition that led to the collapse of the Weimar Republic and the rise of Hitler was the Great Crash of October 1929. The consequent rise in unemployment, which reached 5 million by the winter of 1930–31, put intolerable pressures on the new system of unemployment pay and strains on the Great Coalition Government (Balfour 1992: 49). On 27 March 1930, Chancellor Müller, Social Democrat and head of the five-party coalition government, resigned over reform of the unemployment insurance.[1] Brüning (Centre Party) was given the task of forming a new government. In an effort to solve the economic problems he embarked on a policy of deflating the economy through cutting expenditure and wages in an effort to balance the budget, with the longer term aim of reviving foreign investment in the German economy. Following the high inflation of 1918–24, a reflationary policy looked dangerous but in practice the deflationary policy reintroduced the harsh conditions of those years. Political crisis ensued and in July 1930 President Hindenburg invoked Article 48 of the constitution, the provision for emergencies under which rule became by presidential decree.

In the Reichstag elections of September 1930, the NSDAP polled 6,409,600 (18.3 per cent) of the votes moving from 12 to 107 seats (Broszat 1966: 138; Frei 1993: 32). Brüning resigned in April 1932 and two elections followed: in the July election the Nazis took 37.4 per cent of the votes cast and in the November election they took 33.1 per cent.[2] On 30 January 1933, Hitler became Chancellor with a nationalist coalition cabinet in which Nazis were a minority. The coalition was designed to ensure control over the Nazis but what the nationalists failed to take account of was that, as Balfour (1992: 53) observes, 'the Nazis effectively controlled the police and troops'.

Control over the police and army was exactly what Ebert had lacked in 1918 and, critical to their hold on power, the Nazis quickly expanded their own coercive forces in the form of the Storm-Troopers (the Nazi paramilitary organization), SA, and its subsection, the SS (the 'Protection Squads' of the NSDAP), headed by Himmler. By 1931, the SA had a strength equivalent to the 100,000 strong Reichswehr, the state army (Frei 1993: 9). In January 1933, the SS had 52,000 men and was subordinate to the SA leader Röhm (Burleigh and Wippermann 1991: 60). In February 1933, 40,000 SA and SS members were made auxiliary policemen (Broszat 1966: 141).

Nazi dictatorship, 1933–38

Destroying political pluralism

Hitler's position as chancellor enabled the NSDAP to increase its vote from the 33.1 per cent in November 1932 to the 43.7 per cent of March 1933. In protest at the National Socialists' rise to power the communists called a general strike for 31 January. It failed and the Nazis exploited the event to the highest degree. When a fire broke out in the Reichstag, it was interpreted (in spite of the lack of any evidence) as the start of a communist revolution. The fire opened the way for the German Communist Party, KPD, to be destroyed and a systematic persecution of communists began immediately (Frei 1993: 36).

In the run-up to the new election called for 5 March, and from his new position of power within the system Hitler ensured that the air waves carried Nazi broadcasts. He also employed violence and intimidation to the full. The SA and SS, together with the 40,000 Nazi police auxiliaries, launched their violent campaign on the streets. Against their expectations the NSDAP failed to gain an overall majority, winning only 43.7 per cent of the votes cast in a turnout of 88.7 per cent of the electorate. Furthermore, the Communist Party lost only nineteen seats (representing a loss of 1.1 million votes) and 13 million of the total 32 million votes cast went to the democratic parties. In particular, votes for the Social Democrat Party, SPD, held firm. Support from the German Nationalist Party gave the Nazi Party the necessary majority, with 51.9 per cent of the vote (Frei 1993: 38).

The Nazis immediately set about constructing a dictatorship. On 13 March all the Länder parliaments were dissolved and reconstituted to reproduce a Nazi majority everywhere. On 7 April, Nazi Federal Commissions (Reich Governors) were appointed to run the Länder governments. (See Broszat 1966: 142–3.) On 23 March, the Enabling Act was passed by the Reichstag with only the Social Democrats voting against it. By then the Communists were proscribed. The Enabling Act enabled the government to rule by decree until April 1937 (when it was renewed); it turned Hitler into a dictator. The Act authorized him to issue laws without reference to the president or regard to the constitution.

Also in March, special courts were set up for the prosecution of 'political enemies'. Prisons soon proved inadequate to contain all the political prisoners and concentration camps were set up, using buildings such as disused warehouses and factories (Noakes 1986: 79). These concentration camps, Balfour (1992: 55) comments, 'though not yet slaughterhouses, soon earned an ugly reputation'. On 26 April 1933, a secret police, the Gestapo, was created to deal with political crimes (Broszat 1968: 146). The state police forces were made subordinate to the SS (Balfour 1992: 55).

On 14 July, the National Socialist German Workers' Party was declared the single legal party, all other parties were banned. Under Goebbels, the Minister of Popular Enlightenment and Propaganda since 13 March, the Reich Chamber of Culture was established, on 22 September, to control the press and all other forms of media. On 12 November the Reichstag elections, the last to be held by the Nazis, returned 95.2 per cent of votes to the NSDAP giving them 661 deputies. (See Broszat 1966: 142–4; Frei 1993: 32–49.) On 30 January 1934, all the remaining independent powers of the Länder were abolished, so completing the centralization of power.

By the spring of 1934, the SA numbered nearly 3 million men, without counting the reserves (Frei 1993: 9). On 30 June 1934, 'the night of the long knives', the leaders of the SA were shot on Hitler's orders and in the changes which resulted the SS ceased to be commanded as a section of the SA and was made an independent agency of the NSDAP on 20 July 1934. At this point the SS 'Reichsführer', Himmler, came under Hitler's 'personal and direct' command (ibid.: 26). By this act against the SA Hitler not only began the process of the SS developing as a state behind the state, he also subordinated the law to his will. Speaking to the Reichstag, on 13 July 1934, on the shooting of the SA leaders, Hitler made the following declaration: 'I gave the order to shoot the main culprits in this treason . . . and every man should know, and for all time, that if he raises his hand to strike at the state, his fate will be certain death' (quoted in Frei 1993: 24).

On 1 August 1934, the aged President Hindenburg on the verge of death, Hitler passed a law to merge the offices of president and chancellor. Under this law the title 'Führer' (leader) became official. On the following day, when Hindenburg died, the title of Reich President was abolished, and command of the army, hitherto under the President of the Reich, came under Hitler's command. On 19 August, Hitler's new position of supremacy as Head of State, Government, Party, and of the Army was confirmed in a referendum with 89.9 per cent of the votes in favour, with a 95.7 per cent turnout. From that point on ministers no longer swore allegiance to the 'constitution and to the law' but to the 'Führer of the German Nation and People'. (See Frei 1993: 27; Broszat 1981: 282–3.)

Destroying social pluralism: racial thinking

In April, only nine days after the Enabling Act, a boycott of Jewish professional and business people started. Legislation against the employment of Jews soon followed and began with the 'Restoration of the Civil Service', which was not only anti-Semitic but also anti-communist in design. Similar measures and legislation then followed to cover other professions and students. In 1935 the Military Service Law made 'Aryan' ancestry compulsory for the armed services. In September 1935, the Nuremburg Laws were introduced forbidding inter-marriage or sexual relations under any circumstances between 'Aryans' and Jews. Jews were deprived of citizenship by the Reich Citizenship Law of September 1935. Not only did it take away their citizenship, it also deprived Jewish families of welfare measures. Welfare was similarly denied to families with 'hereditary mental or physical illness'. (See Burleigh and Wippermann 1991: 44–8.)

Other legislation and decrees directed at 'alien' races and 'racially less valuable' members of the population added alcoholics and dangerous habitual criminals (Burleigh and Wippermann 1991: 46). The last of such legislation was the Law on the Punishment of Juvenile Offenders of 22 January 1937, under which a 'racial-biological' examination determined the length and nature of the sentence. A similar law was planned for the 'asocial' but it never materialized. As Burleigh and Wippermann (1991) remark:

> However, like its analogue – a law on 'Gypsies' – no comprehensive law on the 'asocial' was ever promulgated. This was due not to the collapse of the Third Reich, but rather, as was the case with the Jews, to the fact that the regime preferred to solve the 'question' without resorting to formal legislation or decrees.
>
> (Burleigh and Wippermann 1991: 49)

This was consistent with lawlessness as a defining characteristic of a totalitarian regime.

Destroying economic pluralism: labour control and price-fixing

Policies concerned with control over labour were also of fundamental importance to the Nazi system, and they began with control over trade unions. Trade unions were abolished on 2 May 1933 and their leaders were arrested, their funds, properties and newspapers taken over by the Nazi-controlled German Labour Front, DAF. Workers were organized into specialized unions: those working on farms into the Reich Food Estate, schoolmasters into the Teachers' League, women into the *Frauenschaft*, youth into the Hitler *Jugend* and so on (Balfour 1992: 55). On 19 May the Law on Trustees of Labour ended negotiated wage rates and instituted compulsion (ibid.). The thirteen Reich Trustees of Labour were, in practice, rather more in tune with employer than employee needs and the Law on the Regulation of National Labour of 20 January 1934 formally confirmed this. It gave the employer the role of 'leader' (Führer) and employees only that of 'retinue' (*Gefolgschaft*). DAF was explicitly denied the role of acting on any individual's behalf. (See Frei 1993: 54–5.)

The destruction of the trade unions, in containing both actual and potential opposition, was clearly a politically motivated policy but control over labour also enabled the Nazis to tackle unemployment, the one economic issue that had featured in Nazi electoral propaganda (Frei 1993: 50). Employers were encouraged to employ as many workers as possible and in getting the employers to agree to this the destruction of the trade unions and wage control were crucial (Homze 1967: 6–8). There were large wage cuts, for example in the Upper Palatinate wages in the porcelain and glass industry were halved in a year (Frei 1993: 4). A large drop in unemployment in 1933 was also achieved through the huge numbers of people in the prisons and the newly set up concentration camps, mostly around Berlin.[3] New posts were vacated too as Jews were removed from their positions and Jews did not figure in the official unemployment statistics. A further significant cut in unemployed was achieved by the introduction of conscription into the armed forces (Frei 1993: 73).

In 1934, free movement of labour was stopped and the system of Reich labour offices became the sole authority for allocation of labour (Homze 1967: 8). In February 1935, the Work Book Law was introduced. Under this law every wage-earner had to register with the local Labour Office and obtain a work book, a copy of which was to be held at the Labour Office, the original to be given to the employer. Under later regulations the employer could keep the work book for the length of a contract and under this situation any worker breaking a contract would be unable to obtain another job. The work book contained personal information about the employee (age, name and so on) together with a record of training, previous jobs, wage and 'rating' and it also contained any history of 'disciplinary measures' taken against the worker (Homze 1967: 10 and fn. 5).

The work book scheme gave the government the potential for total control over labour mobility and the information contained within these work books could be used in planning. Regulations were also passed which ensured that skilled workers could not leave the Reich (ibid.: 11 and fn. 17). In June 1938, the Compulsory Labour Decree was passed. Under this decree anyone living in the Reich had to accept any job anywhere within the Reich or do the vocational training ordered by the Labour Office. Under the Emergency Service Decree of October 1938, the police authorities (under Himmler) could conscript people to deal with emergencies (Homze 1967: 11–12).

Concerned not only with controlling labour and wages but also with controlling the prices of commodities generally, the Reich Food Estate, RNS, a marketing organization which fixed prices for each agricultural good and standardized sales, was set up to increase farmers' profits and to end the 'tyranny of free prices' (James 1987: 357). The Reich Entailed Farm Law was introduced to keep workers on the land and to stop them from migrating to the towns (Frei 1993: 5).[4]

State plans and economic crisis

The low wage economy and price controls together produced steadily worsening quality in consumer goods (James 1987: 417). Furthermore, even as early as 1934, shortages of supplies were a problem. Shortages and erratic supplies in dairy products and cooking oils were of the greatest concern to consumers; rubber and fuel oils, which fell far short of production needs, presented the most serious problems for industrial producers. The Nazis chose to cut consumer demand and to do so through import controls (Frei 1993: 6). In place of the Four Year Plan announced in May 1933, a 'New Plan' was introduced, in September 1934; it sought to control foreign trade through the allocation of foreign exchange (James 1987: 395). The New Plan failed and foreign exchange problems continued to get worse and increasing world market prices contributed to food shortages (Frei 1993: 75). Military expenditure also took an increasing proportion of state expenditure: 18 per cent of the total public budget in 1934, it reached 58 per cent by 1938, amounting to over 20 per cent of national income (ibid.: 74).

Labour shortages continued to worsen and in November 1936 the second Four Year Plan was introduced, with Goering its Commissioner. Under the plan 'business groups' were set up for each of the four problematic areas of shortage – raw materials, foreign exchange, labour, agricultural production – and for price controls (Frei 1993: 76). The plan also gave Goering, through the labour offices, full control not simply over the allocation of workers in industry but even to individual factories (Homze 1967: 13).[5] A General Council of the Four Year Plan was set up at the same time with an increasing number of important posts given to industrial managers and to officers of the armed forces. As Frei (1993:

76) remarks, 'any remaining illusions about a proper demarcation between the state administration and private business were finally dispelled when, in 1938, Carl Krauch was appointed General Plenipotentiary for Chemicals'. Krauch was the foremost scientific expert on synthetic fuels and rubber, but was also a director, soon to become chairman, of I.G. Farben. I.G. Farben was the German chemical cartel, which had a monopoly on the production of synthetic fuels and rubber, and which later produced Zyklon B for use in the gas chambers.

Setting up the terror organization

During the years 1933–38, a terror system, outside of state control, was developed: the SS organization headed by Himmler. As explained, by the end of 1933 Himmler had achieved control over every German state police force except the Prussian police, which remained a separate agency, as the political police – the Gestapo – organized under Goering (Burleigh and Wippermann 1991: 60). The Gestapo, organized to deal with political opposition, held an estimated 60,000 to 100,000 communists in prisons and concentration camps by the end of 1933 and had virtually destroyed the communist resistance by the mid-1930s. On 20 April 1934, Goering appointed Himmler Inspector of the Gestapo and while Goering remained its Chief, in practice, Himmler was entirely in control of the secret police. The difference between Goering and the Gestapo and Himmler and the SS was that the Gestapo remained part of the state organization. As Frei (1993: 101) explains, 'Goering strove for a political police that would indeed be separate but still organised within the state administration' while 'Himmler's aim from the outset was the radical removal of all competence concerning the political police from the aegis of state power in favour of the SS.'

On 30 June 1934, Himmler was given total responsibility for all concentration camps. By 1937 the small prisons and camps maintained by the SA had been replaced by large concentration camps. Sachsenhausen, near Berlin, was established in 1936 and Buchenwald, at Weimar, was established in 1937. Both were modelled on Dachau, the concentration camp set up near Munich in March 1933 (Broszat 1968: 445; Frei 1993: 103–4). While Dachau held mainly political prisoners, Sachsenhausen and Buchenwald became increasingly filled with 'asocials'. As explained (on p. 134), no comprehensive law on asocials had ever been promulgated and classification as 'asocial', therefore, was arbitrary. The SS had already perfected the practice of taking people off to concentration camps immediately after acquittal at trial or after completion of their sentence (Frei 1993: 104). Before his elevation to Inspector of the Concentration Camps and Führer of the SS Guard Units, the SS Death's Head Units, Eicke had been camp commandant at

Dachau. The SS Death's Head Units guarded and ran the concentration camps and in 1937 there were 5,000 of these guards (ibid.: 101). The Hitler Bodyguard Regiment, recruited from the SS and formed in 1933 (and strengthened in 1938–39) was also under Himmler's control (ibid.: 102). In June 1936, Hitler gave Himmler the new official title of Reichsführer SS and Chief of the German Police in the Reich Ministry of the Interior. From this point the criminal police began to be taken over completely by the SS and the power of the Minister of the Interior, Frick, in practice, passed to Himmler (ibid.).

The second Four Year Plan, introduced in September 1936, had made explicit the requirement for full employment, stating that it 'cannot permit asocial people to evade work and thereby sabotage the Four-Year Plan' (quoted in Frei 1993: 105). Frei argues that, 'Meanwhile, in fact, the key issue had become the recruitment of forced labour for the first SS-owned enterprises' (ibid.). These SS-owned enterprises included brickworks and granite quarries at Flossenbürg and at Mauthausen, and were referred to at the time as the 'Führer's construction projects' (ibid.). Alongside these forced labour enterprises new concentration camps were built. The Flossenbürg concentration camp was established in 1938 followed by the camp at Mauthausen in 1939 (Broszat 1966: 146). In the Basic Decree of December 1937 the function of the SS concentration camps was clear in their specification as 'state correction and labour camps'.

On 26 January 1938, Himmler sent out instructions for a 'single, comprehensive and surprise swoop' on the 'work-shy', arrests to be carried out during the period 4–9 March (instructions cited in Broszat 1968: 450). The local labour offices were instructed to draw up lists of those who were physically fit but had refused work on two or more occasions or had accepted work only to abandon it. In June 1938, after a 'crime prevention campaign' in the newly annexed Austria, instructions went out that 'at least 200 male persons capable of work' (asocials), and in addition 'all male Jews with a previous prison record' were to be arrested in each police area. All of these were to be sent to the Buchenwald concentration camp (Frei 1993: 104). These 'asocials', in addition to those with 'numerous' previous convictions, included anyone without a fixed address and 'gypsies and persons travelling about in the manner of gypsies, if they have shown no willingness for regular work or have rendered themselves liable to legal penalty'. (See Frei 1993: 104.) Thus this 'asocials operation', as it was called, combined racial and economic ends.

The decline of the outward state

As the real power of the SS grew the ostensible power of the state declined. This had begun with the Nazification of the civil service and, most importantly, the growth in influence of administrative departments 'directly responsible to the Führer' which either ran in tandem with the state authorities or acted in direct competition with them. This 'decline and deformation of traditional government', as Frei describes it (1993: 90) had begun in regard to employment and economic policy and had then spread into other areas. For example, after 1936, the Ministry of Economics had to compete with Goering as Commissioner for the Four Year Plan which itself 'went far to supersede the Army Economic Office' (Balfour 1992: 56).

Duplication of offices and multiplication of tasks abounded within the organization of the NSDAP. For example, there was the German Labour Front, DAF, and the Reich Organization Leadership, which itself had five separate sections, and there was also the Reich Labour Service under the Ministry of the Interior. Similarly, the Reich Food Estate duplicated the Reich Office for Agricultural Policy, multiplying tasks and creating confusion. Other dual organizations included: the National Socialist Judges' League and the Reich Law Office; the Head Office for Municipal Policy and the German Municipal Congress; the Head Office for Civil Servants and the Reich League of German Civil Servants; the Head Office for Educators and the National Socialist Teachers' League; the Head Office for War Victims and the National Socialist War Victims' Support Organization; the Head Office for Public Health and the National Socialist German Physicians' League; the Head Office for Public Welfare and the National Socialist German Technical League. Throughout society there were similar carbon copy organizations without either one having the clarity of the master form. For example, as well as the Hitler Youth there was also the German Young Folk and along with the League of German Girls there was also Young Girls in the Hitler Youth. (See Frei 1993: 244–6, Appendix 2.)

The confusion and chaos that epitomizes these arrangements strengthened the power of the leader with each member of the Reich leadership being entirely responsible to the Führer. (See Hiden and Farquharson 1983: 60.) After 1933 the number of times the cabinet, the executive of the outward state, met declined sharply. In 1935, it met just twelve times and its sole function was to pass laws prepared elsewhere. In 1936 it met four times, and, in 1937, six times. The Reich Cabinet met for the last time in February 1938 (Broszat 1981: 280).

The totalitarian regime, 1938–45

During 1938, the Nazi regime transformed from a totalitarian dictatorship to a totalitarian regime. In January and February the army command was changed, which removed resistance to the increase in the armed SS and enabled development of an entirely separate SS domain by October. Both the Foreign Minister and Minister of Economics were also removed. Ribbentrop replaced von Neurath as Reich Foreign Minister and Schacht was removed as Minister of Economics and President of the Reichsbank through the creation of the Organization for the Four Year Plan. (See Broszat 1981: 294–300.) Ribbentrop's appointment opened the way for closer cooperation between the Foreign Office and Himmler, which was later to be important in the movement of the SS into occupied territories and the transportation of Jews. Schacht's removal enabled Goering to press on with rearmament and to push for self-sufficiency through development of synthetic products.

During 1938, Hitler got his way in annexing Austria in March, and taking the German area of Czechoslovakia (the Sudetenland) in the Munich Agreement of September (Kaiser 1992: 183–4). Both Schacht and Fritsch (one of the three dismissed from command of the army) were regarded as political moderates who upheld the rule of law (Broszat 1981: 294). The changed relationship between the army and the Foreign Office released the possibilities for wild schemes in respect of both warfare and movement of peoples. The removal of Schacht, who had introduced the New Plan in 1934, signified the move from substantive rationality, planning anchored to the market, to substantive irrationality, an economy with wild schemes lacking in rational calculation (O'Kane 1996).

The break between totalitarian dictatorship and totalitarian regime was marked by 'Crystal Night', the night of shattered glass, 9–10 November 1938. On that night Jews were beaten and murdered, synagogues were burnt, their shops and homes were destroyed and 25,000 Jews were arrested and sent to concentration camps at Sachsenhausen, Buchenwald and Dachau (Landau 1992: 144).

From plans to wild schemes

Under the totalitarian regime, the wild schemes competed against each other for resources and even had quite contradictory goals. Hitler's wishes to take Austria and Czechoslovakia and then conquer further living space (*Lebensraum*) to the east, which was revealed at the Hossbach Conference of 5 November 1937, had been opposed by the leaders of both the army and the navy and by the Foreign Office (Kaiser 1992: 183). The goal of moving Germans into the newly conquered territories conflicted with military transport needs. This conflict was accentuated by the invasion of Poland in 1939, which began the Second World War. The competing goals of Lebensraum, labour and material, and winning the war, additionally conflicted with the racial goal. The conflicts between these goals were to go far beyond competing demands for transport and resources. Policies on foreign workers, under which 'Jews of all nationalities' (including those from Germany) fell, clashed over the competing demands for labour and the extermination of Jews. As Homze (1967) comments, by 1940:

> Someone had to determine which was more important, be it the resettlement programme, the SS racial programme, Frank's occupational programme, or the foreign labour programme. To allow each individual and organization to run its own programmes in its own way without considering other factors was tantamount to chaos.
>
> (Homze 1967: 44)

Germany's economy, with its crisis of shortages by 1937, had survived as well as it had only because of the booty brought by the annexation of Austria in March 1938 and gaining of the Sudetenland in the Munich Agreement of 30 September through diplomacy. In 1939 Hitler adopted different tactics, he manipulated a means to destroy the remainder of Czechoslovakia, occupying Prague in March and annexing Bohemia-Moravia and Memel from Lithuania. In 1939 resources and production levels in Germany had reached their limits. Foreign exchange had run out and labour shortages had reached 1 million. (See Kaiser 1992: 188.) After signing the Nazi-Soviet pact Germany then invaded Poland in September 1939; so began the Second World War.[6]

In May 1939, in a meeting with Goering and representatives of the military forces, Hitler made it clear that he intended to attack Poland at the first opportunity, arguing, 'We shall be able to rely upon record harvests, even more in time of war than in peace, the population of non-German areas will perform no military service and will be available as a source of labour.' (Minutes quoted in Homze 1967: 16–17.) The serious shortages of labour in Germany by the end of 1938, particularly in agriculture, were added to by army conscription; between May 1939 to May 1940, 4.4 million workers were drafted into the army (Homze 1967: 19). The 'emergency solution' was foreign labour.

Forced labour and foreign workers: racial thinking in practice

Foreign labour was to be exploited in accordance with Nazi racialist views of superior and inferior peoples. In their view, inferior peoples (*Untermensch* meaning literally 'sub human') (Homze 1967: 39) were intended, by nature, to be the slaves of the superior, German 'master race' (the *Herrenmenschen*). These German masters, of course, included only those in mental and physical good health, with no proven record of 'asocial' behaviour such as criminality, homosexuality, communism, being Jehovah's Witnesses, being work-shy, or being without fixed abode. Furthermore, foreigners too could be graded in a scale of superior and inferior races. Jews and gypsies were 'foreigners', irrespective of the number of generations during which their families had been living in Germany. The particular attraction of Polish workers was that as East Europeans they were considered racially inferior to Northern Europeans. In the Nazi philosophy of Untermensch Poles were almost at the bottom of the racial scale with only Jews and gypsies lower. According to Hitler the Poles were 'especially born for low labour' (Homze 1967: 39, from the Nuremberg Trials 1948, Vol. VII: 224–6).

In their attack on Poland, in September 1939, the German forces adopted '*blitzkrieg*' tactics, short sharp attacks by armoured army divisions with close air support from the airforce. Poland surrendered within the month. As the German Army swept across Poland, even before Warsaw surrendered, indeed within days of first crossing the border, Poles began to be recruited for work in Germany. With close cooperation between the German Army and labour offices, newly set up in the Polish towns, 110,000 civilian Polish workers were in the Reich by October 1939. The nearly 1 million captive Polish soldiers became part of the 'vast labour pool' (Homze 1967: 23–4).

In Nazi minds, the speed with which Poland was taken confirmed the superiority of the German race and the inferiority of Poles. In October 1939, Hitler made it clear, to General Keitel, that the living standard of the Polish people was to be reduced to a low level and Poland was to be a work state (*Arbeitsreich*) for the German master people (*Herrenvolk*) (Homze 1967: 26). The western section of Poland became part of the German Reich. Poles were evacuated out of the western area for Germans to move in. The remainder of Poland came under the General-Government headed by Frank, to be turned into what Hitler termed a 'great Polish work camp' (Browning 1992: 21).

On German occupation of Poland, all Polish trade unions were immediately banned and new decrees were issued on wages and work conditions. One of the first of these decrees was the *Arbeitsflicht* which introduced compulsory public labour for all Poles aged 18 to 60, later becoming 14 to 60. Importantly, the Arbeitsflicht excluded Jews stating that 'a special decree will be issued with regard to Jews' (quoted from the decree, Homze 1967: 29). The special regulations for Jews stipulated forced labour (*Arbeitszwang*) (ibid.). By October 1940, there were 880,000 Poles working in Germany and by the spring of 1942 there were 1,080,000, and this out of a population under the General-Government of approximately 16 million (ibid.: 37).

By June 1940 Hitler's blitzkrieg tactics had taken Denmark, Norway, the Netherlands, Belgium, Luxembourg and France, conquests that brought new sources of raw materials and also new pools of labour. With Western Europeans higher up the Nazi racial scale, in these countries selection concentrated on skilled workers. Western foreign labour brought into the Reich was on a voluntary basis until 1942 when force was applied (Homze 1967: 46–7). Prisoners of war, in any case, provided a ready source of captive new labour. By October 1940 there were 1 million western POWs working in Germany, mostly in agriculture. Jews and officers were sent to special camps (ibid.). In addition to workers from these western occupied countries, workers were also recruited from Germany's allies, the bulk from Italy. By May 1941 there were 3,020,000 foreign workers in Germany, an increase of over 263 per cent on a year earlier, the largest increase being in occupations related to the war industries (ibid.: 68).

The attack on Russia

Flouting the Nazi-Soviet pact signed in 1939, in December 1940, Hitler ordered preparations for the war against Russia whose 'natives' he classed 'of inferior race' and whose fate according to Himmler was to become 'a people of leaderless slave labourers' (Jacobsen 1968: 509). The attack on Russia began in June 1941, 'Operation Barbarossa'. Again the blitzkrieg strategy was employed, the war intended to be concluded within three to five months (ibid.: 508). This time, however, the tactics failed, the operation was not to be swiftly concluded. By the spring of 1942, 3,900,000 Soviet prisoners of war had been taken by the German Army. Through a combination of starvation, through genuine shortages and deliberate policy, forced marches, disease and general abuse, by the spring of 1942 only 1,100,000 Soviet POWs were left alive (Homze 1967: 81).[7] On 29–30 September, the massacre at Baby Yar occurred in which 34,000 Jews were killed (Browning 1992: 80–1).

Also by the spring of 1942, very nearly 1 million German soldiers had been lost through death, wounding or going missing (Goebbel's Diaries and Army Reports, see Homze 1967: 131). Between 1 million and 1.6 million foreign workers had to be found to replace the German workers now needed as soldiers. One million of these were to come from the East. The recruitment of Russian civilian workers had begun in September 1941. Coercion was to be used if necessary in the East, though not, at first at least, in the West.

Concentration camps: labour and extermination

In the winter of 1941/42 the concentration camps were developed as an 'SS-owned arsenal of compulsory labour' (Broszat 1968: 483). This occurred at the same time as the policy of extermination of 'undesirables' (a category that was especially applied to Jews) was put into operation. In 1941–42, extermination camps were set up in Poland: Auschwitz II (Birkenau), Belzec, Kulmhof, Majdanek (Lublin), Sobibor, Trawniki and

Treblinka (Broszat 1966: 153). From the summer of 1941, German and European Jews under German occupation were deported to the East and exterminated in the camps. Because Himmler wished to make increasing use of concentration camp labour in the war industry some of these Jews were kept from extermination, at least for the short term. (See Broszat 1968: 483). The use of Jewish concentration camp labour was essentially restricted to Auschwitz.[8] Auschwitz was, however, by far the largest camp which became a huge source of forced labour and, with its large gas chambers, also became one of the biggest centres for extermination (ibid.: 485).

The final solution

On 20 January 1942, the Wannsee Conference was held in Berlin to decide the 'Final Solution' to the 'Jewish Question'. Head of the department that dealt with the 'Jewish Question' within the Reich Security Head Office, RSHA, was Adolf Eichmann, his role at the Conference to make preparations for the meeting and to write the minutes. On page 7 of the minutes he records Heydrich's comments as follows:

> In pursuance of the Final Solution, conscript Jews should now be used in an appropriate fashion, and under appropriate leadership, for labour duties in the East. Jews capable of work will be escorted in large labour columns, separated by sex, on road-building duties in these areas, whereby, no doubt, a large number will drop out as a result of natural decline.
>
> (Eichmann's Minutes of the Wannsee Conference, January 1942, in Frei 1993: 190–1, Document 9)

In his pre-Nuremburg trial interrogation in 1961, Eichmann explains that 'natural decline' is 'a technical term for normal death'. On being referred to page 8 where he had recorded 'those who might possibly still remain . . . will have to be treated accordingly', Eichmann explains that 'will have to be treated accordingly', meant 'killed, killed, certainly'. (See Frei 1993: 190–1, Document 9.) In a telegram of 26 January 1942, Himmler instructed that provision be made for the arrival within a month of '100,000 Jews and up to 50,000 Jewesses in the concentration camps' (Broszat 1968: 483). Reflecting this change of policy to concentration camp labour, the liquidation of the Lódz and Warsaw ghettos in Poland began in July 1942.

At the Nuremburg trials, General Jodl described the plan to eliminate Jews, 'the final solution' to the Jewish Question, as 'a masterpiece of secrecy' (Fleming 1986: 2, quoted in Steinberg 1991: 201). Codes were employed to refer to the Final Solution and Martin Bormann gave strict instructions that 'the Führer's Chancellory must under no circumstances be seen to be active in the matter' (Fleming 1986: 22). Coupled with this, while many documents relating to the 'final solution' survived, many were lost or deliberately destroyed. For example, little is known about the Führer Chancellory and virtually all the records of Auschwitz and Birkenau were destroyed (Breitman 1992: 200). In any case, in general, records for the Nazi era were better kept at the lower and middle level bureaucracies than the top (ibid.: 201). As a consequence of this secrecy and insufficiency of evidence, controversy remains over the exact nature of Hitler's role in the decision to eliminate Jews. Controversy also remains over the date on which the plan was first conceived and over the importance of the Nazi scheme to eliminate Jews, in relation to other goals. (See Kershaw 1989: 82–106; Browning 1992: 86–121.) These controversies highlight the chaos, irrationality and secrecy at the heart of the Nazi regime.

Behind the state façade: the antithesis of government

The lack of records at the top reflected the nature of decision-making in Nazi Germany; the totalitarian regime did not act within a normal decision-making framework. Browning (1992) explains the way the system worked:

> Hitler would give signals in the form of relatively vague statements that established the priorities, goals, prophecies, and even 'wishes' of the Führer. Others, especially Heinrich Himmler responded to these signals with extraordinary alacrity and sensitivity, bringing to Hitler more specific guidelines for his approval.
>
> (Browning 1992: 120–1)

Up to the point at which Hitler's will 'decided', in practice this system gave considerable scope for local control over policy. The wild schemes (the racial policy, Lebensraum, supplies of labour and material for consumers and producers, and winning the war) each competed for scarce resources, such as transport, even contradicted each other, and so added to the confusion and chaos. For example, the Oldenburg Plan for the seizure of captured materials, such as oil and iron ore, issued by General Thomas in the spring of 1941, had a stated aim of maintaining the structure of Russian industry. In May, however, a secret set of directions, 'The Green File', came from Goering's Four Year Plan office which completely contradicted the Oldenburg Plan. It sought to destroy both Russian industry and society totally (Homze 1967: 71).[9]

The duplication of offices and multiplication of tasks of the outward state served the secrecy of the real power of the SS, so centrally concerned with forced labour. Firms involved in the armaments industry, or mines or other war-related industries made requests for prisoners to the Inspector of Armaments in Berlin who passed on the request through the SS Economic and Administrative Office, the WVHA (ibid.: 487–9). Though arrangements had been made between the SS and Speer's Munitions Ministry for the supply of Waffen-SS divisions, unknown to the German economic leaders, the SS was developing its own economic base for the Waffen-SS divisions (Homze 1967: 255). Ostensibly there to police absenteeism among foreign workers, the SS was actually exacerbating the problem. Instead of returning workers to their employers the SS was sending them to SS-run concentration camp factories. From mid-1943 to mid-1944, for certain, the SS were engaging in mass arrests, mostly of foreign workers, in order to expand their concentration camp production.[10]

Along with these workers captured from within Germany, Jews were being brought in from outside under a cloak of secrecy. In line with 'the final solution' on arrival at Auschwitz-Birkenau SS doctors and officers selected those Jews who were to be sent straight for extermination and those who were to be exploited for labour and sent to the neighbouring camp. The relative sizes of the groups assigned to labour or extermination were dependent on current needs and the particular levels of debilitation caused by the journey (Broszat 1968: 484). In line with Eichmann's account, of those selected for labour, Höss, Commander of Auschwitz 1940–43 and WVHA top administrator 1943–45, records that SS doctors in Auschwitz regularly selected 'for extermination . . . in Auschwitz and Birkenau and in the labour camps, Jews no longer able to work and who were unlikely to be fit again within four weeks' (quoted by Broszat 1968: 501).

Adding to the duplication of offices, the multiplication of tasks, and the conflict of goals, in March 1942 Hitler appointed Sauckel to the newly created post of special Plenipotentiary General for the Utilization of Labour. Sauckel stated his position: 'I have received my mandate from Adolf Hitler and I will bring millions of eastern workers into Germany without considering whether they want to or not' (quoted in Homze 1967: 134). At the same time, in April 1942, Speer, Reich Minister of Munitions, got Hitler's permission to set up the Central Planning Board (*Zentrale Planung*) and Speer endeavoured to introduce rationalization. (See Milward 1965: 72–99 for a full account of Speer's policies; see also Homze 1967: 204–29.) Behind the state, however, the economy continued to become ever more reliant on forced labour and the outward state was woven with ever greater overlap and entanglement to conceal reality.

Sauckel's post in charge of foreign labour, Plenipotentiary General for the Utilization of Labour, added greatly to the chaos of the system. Strictly under the authority of Goering's Four Year Plan, the foreign labour section which Sauckel headed was made up from three sections of the Labour Ministry which was headed by Seldte, not Goering. Sauckel's new post added to the confusion by making him responsible for domestic as well as foreign labour. This meant that there were now four ministers of labour, the Minister of Labour, the Reich Labour Leader, the Chief of the German Labour Front and the Special Plenipotentiary of Labour (Homze 1967: 104).

While Speer's actions took place within the outward state (at the Nuremberg Trials, Speer was acquitted of complicity in the organization of slave labour and received a prison sentence of twenty years, not death) (Milward 1965: 190), Sauckel's actions were in the shadowy half world between ostensible and real power. By June 1942 Sauckel had 'recruited' around 800,000 workers from the East, some voluntary, some by force but the SS estimated a need for 2 million foreign workers. By July, Sauckel claimed to have 'recruited 1,639,794 foreign workers, 1,300,993 of these from the East'. If the figures are to be believed, at this point 30 per cent of all foreign labour in the Reich was from Russia. (See Homze 1967: 136–9.)

With Russia still undefeated and Hitler wedded to the view of forced labour as crucial to Germany's war effort, at the end of September 1942 Sauckel's powers were broadened to incorporate the handling of the POWs in the prison camps, the *Stalags*. By December, Sauckel also had control over the allocation of these workers to each individual factory, to accord with the requirements of the armament economy. Again this confirmed that Sauckel was not under the authority of the Central Plan for officially this was Goering's job.[11] By the end of 1942 there were nearly 6 million foreign workers and POWs in the Reich (Homze 1967: 144). In January 1943, the German Army surrendered at Stalingrad. On 15 March 1943, Hitler issued a decree giving Sauckel total control over the departments of the Ministry of Labour (ibid.: 213).

Speer, originally supportive of Sauckel's outward policy for the recruitment of foreign labour, began to perceive the use of foreign labour as a 'crutch' that distorted the economy (Homze 1967: 214–15). He therefore worked to address the crisis with a rationally calculated plan for total war which aimed to release German factories for armament production and so reduce the numbers of foreign workers to be recruited to work inside the Reich. On 4 January 1944, Hitler approved Speer's plan but Sauckel never produced workers on the scale required (ibid.: 224). Speer blamed Sauckel for the difficulties in recruiting workers from the occupied territories and Sauckel blamed Speer's plan. In June 1944, the Allied invasion began into France. In July 1944, Goebbels was appointed as Plenipotentiary for Total War, the position coveted by Sauckel and Speer's plans were never put into action. Sauckel sent out instructions that the army and police were to seize workers from wherever they could (ibid.: 151).

Foreign workers and the toll of innocents

At the end of May 1939, before the outbreak of war, less than 1 per cent of the total workforce were 'foreigners', a term defined to include 'Jews of all nationalities', 'all nationalities' to also include those from Germany (see Homze 1967: Tables I, II, VI). By the end of 1944, 35 per cent of all those employed in armament and armament-related industries were foreign workers, including, therefore, 'Jews of all nationalities' and prisoners of war (ibid.: Table XVII), and as a percentage of all industry, 29.2 per cent were such 'foreign workers' (ibid.: 236). These firms included the massive giant of the chemical industry, I.G. Farben (headed by Krauch), which supplied Zyklon B for the concentration camp gas chambers. By October 1944, 46.1 per cent of all those employed by I.G. Farben were 'foreign workers'. Farben's new synthetic gasoline plant was Auschwitz (Homze 1967: 237–8). The other huge employer of foreign workers was the Herman Goering plant at Regensburg, where by June 1944 fully 58.7 per cent of all workers were 'foreign workers'. Even as early as December 1941, the score had already reached 42.4 per cent (ibid.: 238).

Based on the estimate produced by Speer's statistical office, there were, in total, some 8,102,000 foreign workers and POWs at work in the Reich at the end of 1944 (Homze 1967: 151). Taking account of expiring contracts, deaths and so on the total number of foreign workers brought into Germany was probably 10 million, possibly 12 million (ibid.: 153). All these figures on 'foreign workers' included, of course, 'Jews of all nationalities'.

By August 1943, the total of concentration camp prisoners had risen from 88,000 at the end of 1942, to 224,000. Roughly a third of these (74,000) were in the three Auschwitz camp units – Auschwitz (I), Birkenau (II) and Morowitz (III). Birkenau was the main extermination camp with gas chambers, Auschwitz I was the main administrative camp with labour there used to produce armaments, and at Morowitz the labour camp produced synthetic rubber and petrol. The second largest camp, Sachsenhausen had 26,000 inmates, Dachau and Buchenwald 17,000 each (Broszat 1968: 503). By 5 April 1944, there were twenty concentration camps with, an additional 165 labour camps attached.

In May 1944, Hitler instructed that the Jews were to be deported from Hungary (ibid.). During 1944, 458,000 Hungarian Jews were deported to Auschwitz, of whom 350,000 were gassed and 108,000 were condemned to the concentration camps as slave labour (Herbert 1994: 256–7). In a WVHA report of 15 August 1944 the total number of concentration camp inmates was recorded as 379,167 men and 145,119 women. By 15 January 1945, there were 714,211 inmates controlled by 40,000 SS guards. In February 1945, Germany's defeat in the Second World War imminent, around a third of these prisoners lost their lives in the suffering following Hitler's directive to evacuate camps and to transfer prisoners to camps further from Allied invasions (Broszat 1968: 504).

In May 1945, Germany signed the unconditional surrender. At the end of the war German society was in turmoil, the political system destroyed, the economy wrecked and real earnings based on the weekly wage were lower than in 1939 (see Frei 1993: 79, Table 3). By the end of Nazi rule, a total of 5,978,000 Jews had been killed; 2,800,000 Soviet prisoners of war had been allowed to die by the spring of 1942; large numbers of Poles and Russian workers (Slavs) and other foreign workers had been worked to death or died in transit to Germany; and, in addition, large numbers of communists, gypsies, the mentally ill, the incurably sick, homosexuals, Jehovah's Witnesses and 'asocials' had also been killed.[12]

8 Totalitarian regime

Stalin's Soviet Union

The early days

In the Soviet Union, Stalin, unlike Hitler in Germany, had no need to form a political party and to seek election in order to gain a position of sufficient power to install single party rule. As explained in Chapter 5, following the Bolshevik Revolution the Constituent Assembly was dissolved in January 1918. Left, though not right opposition parties remained and though mostly suppressed by the summer of 1918, throughout the civil war some, mainly Left SRs, remained in the Congress of Soviets. At the end of the civil war, at the Tenth Party Congress, in March 1921, Lenin erected a single party state. All political parties other than the Communist Party were banned and independent trade unions were made illegal. Strong party discipline was made compulsory; opposition within the Communist Party, permitted by the statute of 1919, was banned (Carr 1966, Vol. 2: 208). In October 1921, nearly 25 per cent of party members were expelled from the Communist Party (Carr 1966, Vol. 1: 211–13). From mid-1921, the party organization (Politburo and Central Committee) began to displace the importance of Sovnarkom which had been the centre of the emergency government during the civil war (Rigby 1979: 191–213).

Stalin, again unlike Hitler, had no need to establish a secret police. The *Cheka*, the All-Russian Extraordinary Commission for Combating Counter-revolution and Sabotage, the secret police system that had been set up in December 1917, had been replaced in February 1922 by the new political police, the State Political Administration, the GPU. With the formation of the USSR in 1923 the GPU became the OGPU, the Unified State Political Administration, though the shorter 'GPU' was soon restored to common usage. Concentration camps had also existed in the Soviet Union (the then RSFSR) during the civil war but these were reformed in 1923 and mostly abolished (Dallin and Nicolaevsky 1948: 157). Prisoners worked as correction for their crimes but, before 1926, their work was entirely directed towards the running of the camp; work was not exacted in order to produce goods for consumption outside the prison camp (ibid.: 181).[1]

Though both the political system and the coercive organizations of the Soviet Union afforded Stalin the opportunity for establishing a totalitarian regime, there was much in the economy that remained in the way. At the Tenth Party Conference, at the same time as tightening political discipline Lenin had relaxed economic control. 'War communism', which aimed at central control over both distribution and production (Malle 1985: 373) was replaced with a new economic policy. This New Economic Policy (NEP) went some way towards reintroducing the market to the Soviet economy. Under the NEP, the 'tax in kind', the distinguishing feature of war communism that took all surplus from peasants above that judged necessary for subsistence, was abolished and replaced by a new fixed tax calculated as a percentage of the crop produced (Carr 1966, Vol. 2: 282). By March 1922, this fixed tax was down to 10 per cent of crop production, which left peasants free to sell their surplus on the market (ibid.: 294).

In industry, the NEP had also reintroduced commercialism through the development of leases, for non-profitable nationalized industries and small rural industries, and trusts, for gathering together small enterprises producing the same goods. These leases and trusts could purchase supplies on the market as well as from the state, and their operation was based on proper accounting. The fuel industry became fully commercial in March 1922 (Carr 1966, Vol. 2: 298–309). A free labour market was also reintroduced, compulsory labour gradually abandoned. A money wage system returned, with wages related to productivity, and wage-fixing was replaced by a minimum wage (ibid.: 318–22). Under the NEP cooperatives became viewed as the key to increased production in agriculture (Lewin 1967: 94). Not only was the reintroduction of these market mechanisms in the economy a hindrance to total control, Stalin also had to establish himself as Lenin's successor.

On 3 April 1922, shortly before Lenin's first stroke, Stalin was appointed General Secretary of the Central Committee of the Communist Party of the Soviet Union (CPSU); he was already a member of the Politburo. After Lenin's death, in January 1924, being unlike Hitler in that he lacked the undisputed leadership of his party, Stalin needed to defeat contenders for the supreme position previously held by Lenin. In the autumn of 1924, Stalin first developed his ideas on 'socialism in one country' which stood in direct opposition to Trotsky's internationalist theory of 'permanent revolution'. The novel aspect of Stalin's idea was that it asserted Russia's self-sufficiency (ibid.: 289).

Stalin's 'theory of socialism in one country', which derived from a quotation from Lenin, taken out of context and spun by Stalin's own words, set the pattern for bending Marxism-Leninism to his own purpose

(Daniels 1993: 86). Through this method of exploiting Marxist-Leninist ideas, Stalin conjured his image of infallibility. Any ad hoc decision taken by Stalin was first legitimized by the use of some Marxist doctrine conveniently lifted from anywhere and given only one interpretation. Anyone later questioning the interpretation, attempting to restore the earlier context would be accused of 'petty-bourgeois deviation' and eventually 'counter-revolutionary wrecking'.[2] As Daniels (1993: 86–7) comments, 'no longer did doctrine set the direction of policy; the immediate needs of policy determined the meaning that would be imputed to doctrine'.

Economic crisis

As with Hitler, the background against which Stalin succeeded in establishing himself in supreme leadership was economic crisis, it served as the means for defeating his contenders. To begin with, the New Economic Policy was a success; the harvest of 1922 was the best since the start of the revolution (Lewin 1967: 107). The economic reconstruction needed after devastation of war, revolution and civil war was completed between the years 1925 to 1927. By then, both industrial and agricultural production were back to the real values of pre-war levels. By 1927 workers' wage levels were 11 per cent above what they had been in 1913, both their diets and their education had improved substantially, and 9 million trade union members had the benefit of social insurance (Siegelbaum 1992: 205). By 1927, however, heavy and medium industry had declined as a proportion of the national economy. Levels of efficiency and productivity remained below the levels reached before 1914. In November 1927, industrial production was 18 per cent below its projected level and by December had fallen to 21.4 per cent below. This coincided with a cut in foreign trade, designed to reduce the large trade deficit. A severe shortage of goods on the market developed, decreasing 15.5 per cent just between December 1927 and January 1928, and together with an increase in the money supply this led to inflation. (See Reiman 1987: 43–4.)

The number of people looking for work was also increasing; by the second half of the 1920s urban levels of unemployment reached nearly 2 million (Reiman 1987: 5). Tensions developed between the newly arrived and the established workers, and these tensions were added to by the wage scale reforms adopted in 1927 which narrowed differentials between levels of skill (Siegelbaum 1992: 207–8). Agriculture, like industry, suffered from the lack of good equipment. New farm machinery, tools and fertilizers were completely dependent on imports. Agricultural production had been restored to levels achieved before 1914 but, importantly, grain production had not been brought back to pre-war levels by 1926/7. (See Reiman 1987: 4.)

In late 1927 the failure to collect the expected levels of grain shocked party officials. Between October and December the levels of grain procured fell to 2.4 million tons, it had been 4.58 million tons in the same period in 1926 (Siegelbaum 1992: 190–2). The economy so heavily dependent on grain exports, in November 1927 the trade deficit grew dramatically, up 8 per cent on October, and it continued to climb (Reiman 1987: 43). Stalin used this shortfall in grain to justify force.

In January 1928, under 'extraordinary measures', the GPU and special party workers were sent to search barns and warehouses. Peasants were prosecuted for hoarding and grain was confiscated from the richer peasants. Tax collections were also made more rigorous and in a few cases attempts were made at forced collectivization. (See Siegelbaum 1992: 193; Reiman 1987: 45.) In early March special surveillance powers were given to the GPU over economic transactions (Reiman 1987: 49). These measures initially obtained large amounts of grain but by March/April the levels procured were falling sharply (ibid.: 53). Widespread disorder broke out in the villages and protest took the form of animals being slaughtered and crops going uncultivated (ibid.). Faced with shortages, disorder also broke out in the cities (ibid.: 54). In reaction, Stalin's thinking moved from cooperatives, central to the NEP, to forced collectives (Siegelbaum 1992: 197). He met resistance not only from peasants but also from the Politburo, with Bukharin dubbing him 'a Ghengis Khan' set on 'military feudal exploitation' (ibid.).

From rational plan to wild schemes

Under the New Economic Policy, economists in the State Planning Commission, Gosplan, engaged in a carefully calculated system of economic planning; they produced the first Five Year Plan in 1927 (Daniels 1993: 90). This plan was not, however, formally adopted until the Sixteenth Party Congress in 1929, and then in a highly revised form. Lewin (1967: 267) has termed the intervening year, 1928, 'the year of drift' and also described it as 'this rudderless year' (Lewin 1985: 100). This was the year in which calculations at each stage, Bukharin's 'objectivity of statistics', Weber's substantive rationality, were abandoned (Siegelbaum 1992: 217). In the course of Stalin's battle against Bukharin and the moderates, 'Stalin tore up the scientific plan and ordered his own wild targets' (Daniels 1993: 90).

The major economic debates in 1928 centred on the problem of 'the wage-goods gap' (Swianiewicz 1965: 239). To achieve industrialization the new industrial workers would need to be fed and incentives would have to be offered to peasants in order to attract them out of the countryside where there was underemployment (ibid.). Bukharin's solution was for the development of light industry to meet demand for consumer goods. Preobrazhensky, aligned with Trotsky, argued, rather, for industrial investment to be stimulated through the adjustment of the system of prices. Essentially, his idea was to increase the prices on relatively inelastic state produced goods in order to create the incentive for more to be produced in the villages in order to purchase these necessities (ibid.: 242–3). Though different, both Bukharin's and Preobrazhensky's solutions were in the spirit of the NEP. Both were based on the use of market mechanisms within a rational planning system.

In this economic debate, Stalin was deliberately vague, evading a clear position and, instead, making contradictory statements which consistently served to destroy Trotsky's credibility as his rival claimant to party leadership (Swianiewicz 1965: 245). As such, Stalin mostly supported the Bukharinist policy which dominated Gosplan thinking until, in late 1927, Stalin succeeded in having Trotsky arrested and exiled (Reiman 1987: 30–6). Then, during 1928/9, Stalin came out clearly against Bukharin's slow route to industrialization based on peasant cooperation.

Prefiguring Hitler's tactic of duplicating functions and multiplying offices, Stalin established a new planning organization. In the second half of 1928, Stalin set the Supreme Economic Council (VSNKh or Vesenkha) to work on economic plans. As Reiman (1987: 87) explains, VSNKh was 'counterposed to the more sober State Planning Commission (Gosplan)'. Plans to increase the rate of industrialization were developed by each agency and both sets of plans were rejected as inadequate. As Reiman (ibid.: 89) dryly comments: 'The planning agencies therefore decided on a not entirely customary measure: to balance the plan by means of resources that the economy did not yet have at its disposal.' As Bukharin expressed the problem in 'Notes of an Economist', published in *Pravda* at the time, Vesenkha was trying 'to build present day factories with future bricks' (Siegelbaum 1992: 201).

Calculations for the 'plan' were even more contrived for agriculture. The whole scheme was based on an 'imaginary harvest' (Reiman 1987: 89). State intervention into agriculture was increased to such a level that all state agencies, at every level, were inundated with work. Administration fell apart as coordination collapsed (Siegelbaum 1992: 197). The result: by the end of 1928 the level of grain procured stood at only 61 per cent of the target for the year, threatening starvation and social unrest (Reiman 1987: 81).

Stalin turned the full weight of his attack against Bukharin at the beginning of 1929; Bukharin was ousted from the Central Committee in July. Stalin moved to all-out heavy industrialization and total collectivization of agriculture. Both projects were wild schemes, not based on rational calculations but on substantive irrationality, 'lacking calculations on a firm basis' (Daniels 1993: 91). In the middle of 1929, going all out for rapid heavy industrialization, Stalin ordered 3,400 million roubles to be appropriated for capital investments, five times more than the Commissar of Finance had budgeted for and four times as much as Stalin had demanded earlier (Deutscher 1968: 321). At the Sixteenth Party Congress, in June 1929, Stalin declared, 'We are on the eve of our transformation from an agrarian to an industrial country' and he announced that industry was to raise output by 50 per cent over the year. As Deutscher (1968: 322) remarks, 'an exertion which really belonged to the realm of super-industrial fantasy'.

Wild ideas had already affected the labour force. In January 1929, 'socialist competition' became the issue of the day, the idea being that competition between firms and between workers would increase production at reduced costs. Workers were enrolled in 'shock brigades', an idea first tried out in the autumn of 1928. In April 1929, the role of trade unions was changed to that of fighting for labour discipline and productivity. A system of bonuses, rewards and honours was introduced. The effects were quick to see: quantity soon outstripped the quality of goods produced; the production figures for factories competing with each other were statistically inflated; workers contrived to be described as 'shock workers' to obtain benefits and resentment built up between those benefiting and those not benefiting. Further misguided changes in work practices were also introduced through the year, such as the three-shift system and the continuous work week. Both underestimated the time needed for machine maintenance and repair and both led to quantities being increased but to falling productivity. Worker-discipline was also undermined with absenteeism increasing and processes thereby disrupted. Anger was especially strong over the introduction of work on Sundays and during traditional celebrations.[3]

Stalin's choice of coercion and severance from the market succeeded in defeating those with equal or grander claims to be Lenin's successor, but what it did not achieve was a solution to the grain crisis, its 'principal motive' (Nove 1993b: 35). By June 1929 (the end of the agricultural year), only 8.3 million tons of grain had been procured, a fall of 2 million tons from 1927/8 (Siegelbaum 1992: 201). Panic developed in the cities and rationing was introduced as the country moved back towards the crisis situation faced in the civil war, before the introduction of the NEP in March 1921.

From the middle of 1929 Stalin pressed on with a vengeance to complete collectivization, sending vast numbers of agents to the countryside to force middle peasants into collective farms and, as Stalin said at the time, 'to liquidate the Kulaks as a class' (Deutscher 1968: 324). The peasants reacted by killing their horses and livestock, destroying crops, and leaving land untended. In Deutscher's (ibid.: 326) view, 'The whole experiment seemed to be a piece of prodigious insanity, in which all rules of logic and principles of economics were turned upside down.' Siegelbaum (1992: 213) concludes that, by 1930, 'the market mechanisms that had mediated if not guided economic decisions throughout the NEP had been sundered, driven underground'.

The totalitarian regime, 1930–53

Stalin's aim 'to liquidate the Kulacs as a class' was put into operation by the decree on de-kulakization, which was formally introduced in early January 1930. De-kulakization involved expropriation of property, and expulsion from the village. In the same month a law was introduced on 'exile combined with corrective labour', the first of its kind (Dallin and Nicolaevsky 1948: 40). During 1928/9, Stalin had made a 'chance discovery' (Swianiewicz 1965: 214), the use in the economy of forced labour. In March 1928, a decree had been issued concerning 'a creative use of penal labour'. An official circular of the Central Executive Committee of the USSR of May 1928 defined the purpose of the use of this forced labour as, 'to bring about the realization of a series of economic projects with great savings in expenditure . . . by means of widespread use of labour of individuals sentenced to measures of social projection'. (See documents quoted in Dallin and Nicolaevsky 1948: 206.) In July the Commissariat of Justice had made prison work for all able-bodied prisoners compulsory; this was reinforced by the government in January 1929 (ibid.). In 1930 the GPU established a new department, the Chief Administration of Forced-Labour Camps, the GULAG.

Forced labour and the GULAG

On 7 April 1930, a decree was issued which made it compulsory that anyone sentenced to more than three years and anyone sentenced by the OGPU for whatever term, had to be sent to a 'corrective labour camp'. As explained above, concentration camps had existed in the Soviet Union during the civil war but were reformed in 1923 and mostly abolished. In prisons the inmates worked as correction for their crimes but their work was entirely directed towards the running of the camp. As also explained, no moves to produce goods for consumption outside prison camps began until 1926 (Bacon 1994: 45–6). An experiment for the wider use of hard labour, for production for use outside the camp began in the Solovetsky Camp, the old Solovetsky Monastery used by the Cheka in the civil war, which became the central concentration camp of the GPU in 1923 (Dallin and Nicolaevsky 1948: 173–81). From 1926, intensive labour was used there for lumbering and timber production, quarrying and for loading and unloading ships (ibid.: 182). The workers at the Solovetsky Camp were kept on a minimal diet (ibid.).

With Stalin's turn to forced collectivization the experiment at Solovky spread. At the Solovky Camp itself there had been around 4,000 prisoners in 1923, in 1928 there were over 20,000 (Dallin and Nicolaevsky 1948: 173). In 1929/30 camps in the region were expanded to cover a vast stretch of land and by the beginning of 1930 these camps contained over 100,000 prisoners (ibid.). Whereas in 1926 14.3 per cent of all convictions were to forced labour, in 1929 it was 48.1 per cent, rising to 56 per cent in 1931 and then 58 per cent in 1932 (ibid.: 207). By 1930 there were also five camps in addition to those on the Solovetsky islands: two on other islands in Onega Bay, one near Murmansk, one near Archangel and one in Turkestan (ibid.: 52).

Forced collectivization and de-kulakization

On Soviet estimates, as many as 600,000 farms were de-kulakized in 1930 and 1931, as many as 1.8 million people exiled to remote regions of the USSR (Bacon 1994: 56). Between 1929 and 1933 the number of farms collectivized is estimated as 1.1 million (Viola 1993: 68) and estimates have ranged far higher.[4] At first, those refusing to hand over their farms to collectives were arrested and their families were deported, in cattle trucks under GPU guards, to the White Sea area where they were billeted with peasants. Under the sheer pressure of numbers new waves of deportees were housed in barns and then even lived in holes in the ground before constructing their own mud huts (Andics 1969: 93).

The term 'kulak' was not based on a precise, legalistic definition, it came to mean any peasant who tried to resist the collection agents (Lewin 1985: 150). Viola (1993: 71) argues that, 'in an attempt to find convenient scapegoats for the country's grain difficulties', at the start of the forced collectivization campaign the state launched an attack on the *byvshie liudi*. These *byvshie liudi* were those 'tied in the popular mind to the political, social or economic system of the ancien regime' (ibid.), and included not only noble landowners and wealthy farmers (kulaks), but owners of land or enterprises of any kind. The term was also applied to Tsarist officers, cossacks, pre-revolutionary officials, church and village elders and, generally, to members of any groups who had opposed the Bolsheviks in either the revolution or the civil war. These groups included not only White Army officers and sometimes soldiers but also past members of political oppositions such as Socialist Revolutionaries (ibid.). As time wore on, and more so after 1932, anyone unable to contribute fully to the collective ran the risk of persecution (ibid.: 97).

From January 1933, mass arrests increased again and purges of party members followed (Viola 1993: 155). This increase in arrests followed the introduction, on 7 August 1932, of the law on 'socialist property', signed personally by Stalin, its full title, the law 'On the defence of the property of state enterprises, collective farms and cooperatives, and the strengthening of social ownership'. Conviction under this law brought the death penalty, or ten years' imprisonment, which meant forced labour (Bacon 1994: 51). The accusation of 'theft', even of small items, could result in extremely harsh punishments. As the USSR entered a severe famine, in 1933, following a disastrous harvest in July 1932, the cruelty of the law struck hard. Before six months were out 55,000 people had been arrested under the law and exile for their families soon followed (ibid.).[5]

The initial makeshift arrangements gave way to a scheme for exiles to Siberia to develop nearly a million acres of land into collectives – 'special settlements' – to provide food for the towns and cities. Andics (1969: 93) comments, 'In practice these Siberian collectives, like the other deportee settlements in thinly populated parts of the country, were simply forced labour camps.' The exact figures on deaths resulting from the journey and labour exploitation can only be roughly estimated. Comparing all the existing figures, Rummel concludes that during the collectivization period, put as 1929–35, around 1,400,000 died as a consequence of deportations and 3,306,000 died in the camps or in transit to them (Rummel 1990: 95).[6] During these years the forced-labour camp system was expanded and established as a durable organization.

Labour shortages and labour control

Heavy industrialization needed large numbers of industrial workers. In October 1930, the Commissariat of Labour ordered, 'in view of the great shortage of labour', a cut in unemployment benefits (Dallin and Nicolaevsky 1948: 194). Under the Five Year Plan, the state was to be responsible for directing all the country's resources, including labour. In November 1930, the Deputy Minister for Labour declared that 'the words "labour exchange" and "labour market" should be finally driven out of our vocabulary' (Nove 1993b: 41). A decree was then issued against workers who deserted their jobs or changed jobs frequently and a series of decrees followed restricting workers' freedom to change jobs.

In December 1932, just over two years before work books were to be introduced in Germany, internal passports were introduced in the Soviet Union in which every job undertaken had to be entered. Through them, as in Germany under Hitler, workers' movements were controlled. Collectivization provided the means for controlling the supply of rural labour into industry. The collectives were put under contracts to supply workers to the Labour Department agents and failure to do so resulted in compulsion at the hands of the GPU (Dallin and Nicolaevsky 1948: 196–8).

Labour shortages were a particular problem in the building and the lumber industries (Dallin and Nicolaevsky 1948: 197). Nove (1993b: 63) describes these shortages as 'endemic'. In 1930, 1,700,000 extra workers were needed in the northern lumber industry and the collectives were required to provide 900,000 of them (Dallin and Nicolaevsky 1948: 198). It could not be done. So Stalin exploited his 'chance discovery' that forced camp labour was ideally suited to his plans. In Dallin and Nicolaevsky's (1948: 199) view, 'the great network of labour camps emerged as a function of industrialization and the Five-Year Plans'. As a solution to the needs of the northern lumber industries the required workers were obtained, a small minority of voluntary labour, the rest made up of peasants forcibly recruited for seasonal work, exiled peasants deported to the north but not living in the prisons, and inmates of corrective labour camps and prisons (ibid.: 202). The work of the Solovetsky camps expanded into mining, coal and minerals, and the workforce then began the construction of canals and railways (ibid.: 212–15). In 1933 gold mining began in the Kolyma region of Siberia where the number of labour camps grew rapidly. It is estimated that by the middle of the 1930s the total number of prisoners in the Solovetsky camps had reached 662,000, the greatest number of whom were peasants (ibid.: 190).

The NKVD

With collectivization effectively completed, in July 1934 the OGPU was replaced by the new People's Commissariat for Internal Affairs, the NKVD. On 27 October, by decree, all 'places of detention' were transferred to the NKVD (Dallin and Nicolaevsky 1948: 249–50). The administration of the 'corrective labour camps' under the Gulag remained and so too the use of forced labour stayed central to the whole system. The exiles' camps, developed under dekulakization, were also brought under the Gulag's control (Bacon 1994: 56).

The NKVD Special Board (or Special Tribunal) was set up in accordance with the laws of 10 July and 5 November 1934 (Conquest 1990: 284). Most of the accused were sentenced by a committee of the Special Board; they only rarely appeared before a court of law. Initially sentences were limited to five years but soon terms of eight or ten years were being imposed. Arbitrariness featured in the nature of the accusations. 'Wrecking', essentially circumstantial, was the accusation most common for workers. A 'non informer' or an eavesdropper to a conversation could also be sent to a labour camp as too could a person for no other reason than being a relation of the accused. Arbitrariness also featured in sentencing; at the end of a Board sentence the prisoner could simply be re-sentenced. Indeed, the Special Board laid down that it was to be given those 'cases for which the evidence was not sufficient for turning the defendant over to a court' and the accused had neither right to defence nor appeal, and cases were either tried in absentia or in groups at a time (ibid.: 284–6; Gregor 1982: 161). Furthermore, though strictly charges were made under article 50 of the criminal code, this code was interpreted in the broadest ways.

Though never formally announced, new 'troikas' were put into operation on 30 July 1937, with Ezhov, the head of the NKVD, and Vyshinsky, the Prosecutor-General, at the centre. The troikas were established all over the Soviet Union with the local NKVD chief as chairman. As with the Special Board, the troikas operated terror under a veneer of legality. Defendants were not necessarily present at the proceedings, 40 per cent of all cases were held in absentia and, of the remaining, the appearance of the accused averaged only three minutes. The troikas could impose the death penalty and they did so on a grand scale. (See Conquest 1990: 286; Bacon 1994: 53.)

The Great Terror, 1936–38

The Great Terror of 1936–38 is also known as the Great Purges, or the 'Ezhovshchina' after Ezhov who replaced Yagoda as head of the NKVD in September 1936. (Ezhov was himself purged, in 1938, along with other members of the NKVD, and replaced with Beria.) Most famously during this time were the show trials of Old Bolsheviks: notably those of Zinoviev and Kamenev in 1936, whose arrest in June 1936 is viewed as signalling the start of the Great Terror; of Piatkov and Radek in January 1937; of Bukharin and Radek in 1938. In mid-1937, the Red Army was purged.

Though the mass arrests in the summer of 1936 were directed at Left Oppositionists and their present and past associates the purges changed after Ezhov's appointment. Under Ezhov, the terror expanded increasingly to include industrial managers, engineers and administrators at both the provincial and district level and the main accusation changed from conspiracy to kill Soviet leaders to economic sabotage, 'wrecking'. (See Manning 1993: 117.) As Zaleski (1980: 248–9) comments when summarizing the accusations levelled at the trials, 'the chronic defects of the Stalinist planning system were simply presented as sabotage'.[7] He concludes that 'The accusations of sabotage and the language of repression, however, make it impossible to discuss true responsibility.'

In Rittersporn's (1993: 99) assessment, the entire Soviet system in the 1930s was gripped by a feeling of 'omnipresent conspiracy'. Stalin's political system, like Hitler's in Germany, was a chaotic system cloaked in secrecy based on terror and under the whim of the leader. As Gill (1990) summarizes:

Institutional boundaries, prerogatives, sensitivities and traditions, including the established web of relationships between institutions, became of little account as Stalin's leadership style became more idiosyncratic and less regularised. He could search out and accept information and advice from wherever he chose, unconstrained by bureaucratic norms or regulations. His personal position of supremacy, supported by the uncertainty created by the Terror, meant that he shaped institutional contours and processes rather than his working style being shaped by their patterns.

(Gill 1990: 305)

In spite of the release of statistics from the Soviet archives on the Great Terror, controversy remains over the figures. For example, Conquest (1990: 484–9), has reaffirmed his original 'approximations' for 1937/8 as 7 million arrests, 1 million executions (mostly shot), 2 million camp deaths; giving about 8 million in the camps at the end of 1938. Nove gives far lower estimates, recording the number of shootings following the trials and special tribunals as 353,074 in 1937 and 328,618 in 1938. The total for inmates in 1939 he puts at 3,593,000 in NKVD prisons, camps and colonies with 1,360,000 of these in Gulag camps themselves. (See Nove 1993a: 270–1.) Thurston (1993: 155) confirms that sentencing for 'counter revolutionary crimes' (under Article 58) reached a peak in 1938.[8] Though the figures may differ, there is no dispute that the number of deaths reached its peak in the years 1937 and 1938. Nove's figures on deaths added together for 1937 and 1938 amount to more than the entire score for the remaining years 1931–53 (ibid.).

While deaths were at their highest during the Great Terror the archive evidence suggests, however, that the number of people detained within the Gulag camps was at its peak, not during the Great Terror but in the early 1950s (see Nove 1993a: 270, Table 13.2; Wheatcroft 1993: 277; Bacon 1994: 24). The fact that the highest number of inmates in the NKVD system was at the end of Stalin's years points away from interpretation of his behaviour in terms of the aim of defeating political opposition in order to achieve supremacy. It points, rather, towards the importance of chronic economic crisis and the centrality of forced labour to Stalin's wild scheme solution.[9]

The depth of economic crisis

Though impressive achievements in industrial production occurred in 1934 and 1935, in mid to late 1936, the high economic growth rates turned into what Jasny has termed a 'snail-like crawl, stagnation and even declines' (Jasny 1961: 177, quoted in Manning 1993: 116).[10] By the end of 1936 the effects of shortages, especially in essential fuel and construction materials for the wider economy were evident (Manning 1993: 125–7).

Not only were there shortages in fuels and construction materials, which were blamed on wreckers, but there was also a harvest failure in 1936. Though as poor as the 1932 harvest that had led to the famine of 1932/3, the failure of the 1936 harvest was kept secret. Only in retrospect was the harvest discussed in the press, which, at the time, was full of reports of achievements in areas such as the Ukraine, where there were no crop failures (Manning 1993: 121). The secrecy was achieved by the reports of shortages in 1936 being kept back for a year and then combined with the reports of the 1937 harvest, which was exceptionally high (ibid.: 123, fn 25). Meanwhile, animal deaths from malnutrition and disease were blamed on provincial and district party leaders, on local and national agricultural administrators and on specialists within the Commissariat of Agriculture who were reported as having 'wrecked' the collective farms by deliberately infecting the animals with diseases (ibid.: 124).

In 1936, in addition to production shortages, a disastrous harvest and a slowdown in economic growth, Russia's economic crisis was added to, as in Nazi Germany, by the pressure of increasing military expenditure. From 1924 to March 1934, the armed forces stood at 562,000. At 1 January 1935, the number had jumped to 940,000. By 1 January 1937, it was 1.433 million (Manning 1993: 146–7, Table 5.9). As a percentage of the total government budget, at 11.1 per cent in 1935, in 1936 it jumped to 16.1 per cent, reaching 18.7 per cent in 1938 and leaping as war broke out, to 32.5 per cent in 1940; the armed forces reached 4.2 million by 1 January 1941 (ibid.). This was not expenditure according to plan. In the official second Five Year Plan defence expenditure planned for 1936 was 4.3 billion roubles, changed to 14.9 billion when listed at the beginning of 1936; actual expenditure was 20.2 billion roubles. (See Manning 1993: 135, fn 58.)

As in Germany, the effects on the economy of the slow-down in output of essential materials for industrial output, which hit Russia at the end of 1935, were exacerbated once the armed forces and armaments industries took prior claim over civilian industries. Military needs also took priority over the already overstretched transport system (Manning 1993: 135). With too many people chasing too few goods, inflation escalated. Declining terms of trade on the world market also reduced the quantity of imports that the Soviet Union could trade for exports in 1936 and 1937 (ibid.: 129). The growth in military expenditure was a reaction to international developments. War threatened on both the Asian and European borders, from Japan in Manchuria and from Germany and Italy respectively (ibid.: 136–7). The fear of foreign enemies added to the general feeling of conspiracy already present at home.

The growth of labour camps

With the replacement of Ezhov by Beria, in 1938, the number of executions fell sharply; regulations on worker absenteeism, lateness and so on, however, soon became more punitive and a new kind of camp appeared especially for workers who broke labour regulations. These new camps were set up in places all over the Soviet Union rather than concentrated in the remoter areas where the original forced labour camps were located, a total of thirty-five such camps by the end of 1937 (Dallin and Nicolaevsky 1948: 58–9). In June 1940, a decree introduced the seven-day working week and along with it harsh new laws on worker absenteeism and indiscipline. Under this decree arrival at work more than 20 minutes late became a criminal offence. By the beginning of January 1941, under this decree alone, 28,995 people had been sent to forced-labour camps (Bacon 1994: 51).

By 1940, the NKVD was fulfilling 13 per cent of the volume of capital work, with 2 million forced labourers involved in construction (Bacon 1994: 40). By 1940, fully 8 million names had been entered in the Gulag record of prisoners (ibid.: 111). From 1940 non-Russians formed an increasingly large proportion of the labour camp inmates, at first mainly Poles, Balts and Bessarabians. With the outbreak of war with Germany in 1941, Germans, Italians, Rumanians, Hungarians and Japanese were added. Ukrainians, Tartars and other non-Russian Soviet citizens also formed a growing proportion (Dallin and Nicolaevsky 1948: 263). Members of nationalities viewed as a threat to national security were arrested under the NKVD decree of June 1941 (Bacon 1994: 145). Deportations began, first with Poles, in 1940.

In ways similar to the behaviour of the SS in Germany, people were grabbed from the streets by agents of the NKVD. These people were loaded on to trains and lorries and taken to north and east Russia; around 25 per cent of them were sentenced to labour camps, the rest to special settlements (Dallin and Nicolaevsky 1948: 263). Dallin and Nicolaevsky (ibid.: 277) comment that with the outbreak of war with Germany in 1941, these 'deportations' became 'a repetition of the mass deportation of kulaks in the early thirties with all the ominous consequences'. As these new prisoners were added to the camps, existing prisoners were being 'released' into the army. Bacon (1994: 103) estimates that during the first three years of the war an additional 1.8 million people entered the camps and colonies while 2.9 million were removed. Of those removed around 1 million was as a consequence of death in the camps and a further million due to transfer into the army and some nationalities, notably Poles, Czechs and Slovaks, were released while some prisoners managed to escape, under the cloak of war.

During the war years, industrial labour camps were moved into the production of armaments with the NKVD producing between 10 and 15 per cent of all ammunition. A whole range of goods for the war effort, from timber to gas masks and uniforms, was also produced within the Gulag system. (See Bacon 1994: 134–7.) In the agricultural camps, essential foodstuffs were produced and essential construction work was undertaken (ibid.: 137–40). During the war, outside of agriculture, forced labour constituted 10 per cent of the workforce (ibid.: 143). The increase in the use of forced labour during the war years was part of the trend that had begun before the war with Stalin's move to forced collectivization and heavy industrialization.

1945–53

At the end of the war, in 1945, the Soviet Union was, in contrast to Germany, a victor. Rather than the camp system being broken up, as in Germany, large numbers of new forced labourers were sentenced to the labour camps, including large numbers of German and Japanese prisoners of war. They were sent to a variety of work, including the rebuilding of factories and other buildings destroyed in the war (Dallin and Nicolaevsky 1948: 278). The Russian workers and prisoners of war returning from Germany were 'screened' by the NKVD in verification and filtration camps. Nearly 80 per cent of these were sent to forced labour, some given fifteen to twenty-five years of 'corrective labour', others sent off to hard labour; all were categorized as 'socially dangerous' (Dallin and Nicolaevsky 1948: 283; Bacon 1994: 94–5). In August 1946, Soviet officials were purged.

Wild targets were again produced in the Five Year Plan for 1946–50, designed for economic reconstruction. As Dallin and Nicolaevsky (1948: 298) concluded at the time, 'The fulfilment of this great plan is, under present Soviet conditions, contingent upon the existence and expansion of the system of forced labour.' The number of camps in the Soviet Union continued to expand. By the end of Stalin's rule there were fifty-three camp groupings under direct central NKVD control and seventy-eight under local NKVD control (Bacon 1994: 84–5). In addition, there were also 475 colonies and a further 667 labour camps which were subdivisions not included in the 131 camp groupings (ibid.).

Based on evidence only available since the fall of communism in the Soviet Union, crucially, Bacon does not simply reinforce the importance of Stalin's scheme for all-out industrialization for the expansion of the Gulag system, but actually reverses the usual direction of causation. Bacon (1994: 50) argues that even in the 1930s, 'the economic tasks assigned to the NKVD influenced the number of inmates in the camps to a greater extent than the size of the camp population influenced the setting of plan targets.' The parallels with Germany and the role of Himmler and the SS are evident.

The toll

As a victor in the Second World War, the totalitarian regime continued through to Stalin's death, the number of inmates within the Gulag system reaching its peak in the years shortly before his death. Examining both the inflow and outflow of prisoners year by year, Bacon (1994: 24) calculates that while the highest figure for any year in the 1930s is 1,881,570 (1938) and for the 1940s is 1,356,685 (1949), in 1950 the figure was 2,561,351 falling to 2,468,524 in 1953. These figures are in line with both Nove (1993a: 270, Table 13.2) at 2,561,300 for 1950 and Wheatcroft (1993: 277) at 2,526,402 for 1953. For the years 1934–52, Bacon calculates the total number of prisoners entering the Gulag camps and colonies to have been more than 18 million (Bacon 1994: 37).

Equating camp labour with slave labour throughout history, Swianiewicz (1965: 93) stresses the importance of the lowest expenditure on each worker: 'The economic prerequisite of slavery is the ability of a man to produce more than the minimum he requires for living.' Poignantly, Conquest (1971: 485) observes, 'A man killed by squeezing a year or two's effort out of him is of more use than a man kept in prison.' As Chapter 7 has shown, such thinking had been exactly paralleled in Hitler's Germany, where, through its combination with racial policy, suffering had been exacted so harshly on Poles and Russians, among others, and on Jews, most cruelly.

In sum, deaths as a direct consequence of the process of de-kulakization (the result of people being transported in unheated cattle trucks and the harsh conditions of the deportation areas in particular) were, on conservative estimate, 4.7 million (Rummel 1990: 95). Conquest (1990: 484–9) calculates that by the end of 1938, there had been 1 million executions, 2 million camp deaths and 8 million people in the camps. Bacon (1994: 37) calculates that over 18 million people entered the camps and colonies between the beginning of 1934 and the end of 1952. Nove calculates that by the end of Stalin's rule a total of 11.8 million people had passed through the camps, colonies and prisons with official figures on deaths in the labour camps at 900,000 between 1930 and 1953 of whom 681,692 were executed at the peak of the purges, 1937–38.[11] Even at the lowest these estimates involve millions of innocent victims.

Part IV
Democracy as synthesis

9 Federal Germany

Re-tracing a path to democracy

In 1945, following defeat in the Second World War and unconditional surrender, the Allied victors – America, Britain, France and the Soviet Union – engaged in the occupation of the whole of Germany. In contrast to the pattern after defeat in the First World War, when Ebert was handed power and a new German government was quickly established under a new constitution, the totally defeated Nazi government was replaced not by a new German government but by a government of occupying forces, the Control Council, situated in Berlin.[1] In this, post-Nazi Germany differed not only from Germany after the First World War but also from France after the Second World War. After the German invasion of France in 1940, the Communist Party together with the socialist parties, the SFIO, the radical-socialists and others, had formed the Resistance. Outside France, the occupation was opposed by the Free French Movement, headed by de Gaulle and based first in London and then in Algiers. In 1943, the Free French Movement and the Resistance together formed a provisional government, the Consultative Assembly, in Algiers, with de Gaulle as its head. In June 1944, the Resistance fighters and the French Army joined forces; the liberation of Paris came in August 1944.[2] In Germany there was nothing resembling a government-in-waiting to step into the vacuum left by the collapse of the Third Reich (Ginsberg 1996: 100; Roseman 2000: 148).

The Nazi totalitarian regime, as explained in Chapter 7, had not simply set out systematically to destroy political opposition nor even to do so along with the destruction of social and economic pluralism. Through terror they had sought also to destroy spontaneity, that essential ingredient of collective action, of group formation, without which there can be no civil society. In post-Nazi Germany, though there were brave individuals who had engaged in skeletal underground resistance, such as members of the SPD and KPD, and those who had supported Weimar democracy and had resisted Nazism in their behaviour towards others, there was no organized and networked anti-Nazi group in a position to speak on behalf of the German people, no group, therefore, ready and able to act as an interim German government, with whom the Allied forces might negotiate. Instead there were merely 'scores of political and intellectual leaders and thousands of faithful followers of the democratic groups of the Weimar period who had somehow weathered the totalitarian storm' (Merkl 1963: 20). Conjuring images of Nazi atrocities and destruction, Merkl comments that these leaders 'rose from the catacombs of concentration camps and other hiding places' or from the ' "inner emigration" of resignation or retirement from politics' (ibid.).

As after defeat in the First World War, after defeat in the Second World War the left acted quickly to set up workers' committees in many towns but these were out of line with the Allies' ideas and were swiftly suppressed (Roseman 2000: 148). As Roseman comments, the churches aside, 'it was two years before German institutions emerged that could operate at a level high enough to supply a leadership role' and he adds, 'and they operated in circumstances very much dictated by the Allies' (ibid.).

The Control Council

The four members of the Control Council each took control over their own 'Zone' of Germany with control over the capital, Berlin (situated in the Soviet Zone), itself divided into four 'Sectors', controlled separately by the four powers. The operation of the Control Council was based on unanimous agreement for any policy-decision (see Document, Schweitzer *et al.* 1995: 9). At the Potsdam Conference, which opened in July 1945, there was, unsurprisingly, unanimous agreement for the elimination of National Socialism. This entailed the annulment of all Nazi laws relating to the establishment of the Nazi regime itself and all racial laws and discriminatory laws of all kinds. It also entailed the removal of members of the Nazi Party from their posts, with those holding positions of power interned and war criminals to be put on trial. Similarly, there was unanimous agreement over the ending of Germany's future military potential. Germany was to be totally disarmed and to remain so, the armed forces to be completely disbanded and military equipment and material destroyed.[3] This, again, was a notable contrast with the situation in Germany after defeat in the First World War. More surprisingly, unanimous agreement was also reached within the Allied Control Council that Germany must be 'democratic'. Not fully appreciated at the time, the interpretation of what German 'democracy' would look like differed between the western liberal-democratic powers and the Soviet Union. Nevertheless, preparations began for a future German government to be based on democratic principles and, crucially, one ruling within a democratic society.

Given the support given to the Third Reich by the German people, the country's history of militarism, the perception of the authoritarianism of its society and people, and the total destruction of democratic structures and institutions by the Nazis, it was also made explicit, at Potsdam, that one of the purposes of the occupation was to make the absolute failure of Nazism serve as a lesson to the German people. The lesson intended was that the German people should accept their responsibility for their situation (Balfour 1992: 100). The idea was that Germans' recognition of their guilt would not simply stop such terrible events ever happening again, but, together with a 'program to "re-educate" the Germans to democracy' (Merritt and Merritt 1980: 7), would provide the foundations on which stable and effective, workable, democracy could be built. To this end, the joint report of the Potsdam Conference specified that 'local self-government' and 'representative . . . principles' were to be introduced 'into regional, provincial and state (Land) administration' (quoted in Merkl 1963: 7). Competitive political parties were to be encouraged and freedom of the press, freedom of speech and freedom of religion were to be permitted. In view of the German people's proven support for National Socialism, the establishment of central government was not a priority. Rather, in response to the need for post-war economic reconstruction, administrative departments covering finance, transport, communications, industry and foreign trade were to be set up to work as part of the Control Council. Along with the decentralized political structure the Potsdam Conference also agreed on the decentralization of industry. The purpose of this decentralization was to convey the Allied Control Council's policies for implementation at lower levels. (See Merkl 1963: 7; Balfour 1992: 88.)

Dislocated society and the economy

The immediate problems to be faced by the Control Council, in ways very similar to Germany after the First World War, were the dangers of a dislocated society and economic crisis. The Potsdam Conference had agreed to the transfer of Germans from the East to within the new boundaries of Germany (Merkl 1963: 7). Movement was occurring in every direction. As Frederick Williams, assigned to the Psychological Warfare Division of Supreme Headquarters, Allied Expeditionary Force recalls:

> Germany in 1945 was a nightmare of dislocated persons. Typically, 90 per cent of the buildings in major population centers were destroyed. Bridges were out. Roads were torn up. People lived under the rubble. Refugees streamed west from Soviet-held territories. Soldiers, released from captured armies, walked home. Wives and children who had been evacuated from the cities returned to start rebuilding.
>
> (Williams 1970: xviii)

Outside Germany, there were 7 million German soldiers, sailors and airmen to return home. Within Germany, prisoners of war and over 3 million of the 6 million or more foreign workers had to be returned to their countries of origin. Around 10 million Germans had evacuated from the cities and wished to return. Germans who had occupied Poland, Czechoslovakia and Hungary under Hitler's policy of Lebensraum were sent back to Germany, including some 3 million Germans living in the Sudetenland before 1938 and, as proven supporters of Germany, now no longer welcome to stay. (See Balfour 1992: 84–5). All in all, Germany faced a population increase of more than 10 million people. Data for the American Zone reveal that in October 1946, 16.2 per cent of the population comprised refugees, mostly from the Russian Zone of occupation, and expellees from Eastern European countries. By 1949, this had risen to 20 per cent (Merritt and Merritt 1970: 18). In Roseman's (2000: 146) assessment, this situation was far more severe than in Weimar and, for emphasis, he argues 'after 1945, the millions of refugees and expellees from lost Eastern territories and West German soil seemed destined to provide a source of revisionist protest and resentment for decades to come'.[4]

In the light of the role played in the rise of totalitarianism by the dislocated societies in both Germany and Russia after the First World War, the potential for democracy to succeed in Germany after the Second World War would depend significantly on the capacity of the Allied Control Council to handle this situation with both sensitivity and practicality. The lessons drawn from the effects of the dislocated societies in Germany and Russia after the First World War, also suggest that the Allies would need to avoid economic crisis and the starvation, disease and civil war which could follow and, if economic crisis could not be avoided, above all to ensure that it would not, subsequently, be renewed.

The Allies developed the view that while, as after the First World War, reparations were to be exacted it was crucial that economic crisis within Germany should be avoided and that sufficient resources should remain to ensure a reasonable standard of living and capacity for the economy to function without the inherent need for foreign aid. While agreeing in principle, there were, however, disagreements over interpretations of decisions taken. In particular the Soviet Union took the view that reparations took precedence over Germans' standard of living and so removed plant from Germany to the Soviet Union. The western powers rejected this view but were not of one voice on the correct balance between the level of reparations and the level of the German standard of living. There was also debate on how the reparations should be generated. (See Balfour 1992: 88–9).

Crucially, though people went hungry and conditions increased susceptibility to diseases, starvation was avoided (Balfour 1992: 101–2).

Sensitivity to the situation was translated into real help. In recognition of the limitations imposed by the zones, in September 1946 the American and British zones established bizonal economic administration for economics, finance, food and agriculture, and transport (Merkl 1963: 13). Between the end of the war and the middle of 1947, the American Government gave 11,300 million dollars to Europe, a substantial proportion of which went to Germany and extra relief came from American private agencies (Balfour 1992: 102). Though Britain's recovery itself drew on aid from America, Britain spent 80 million dollars in the first year in Germany supporting the British Zone and maintained rationing in Britain at wartime levels to do so (ibid.: 98). The achievement in avoiding crisis was made the greater by the harsh winter of 1946/7 which affected production, supplies and jobs all over Western Europe and hit Germany hard.

Sensitive to the danger of economic crisis and the humanitarian catastrophe that such crisis threatened and appreciative of the scale of the reconstruction needed in Germany, in June 1947 the Marshall Plan was outlined. Economic recovery through American government finance was promised if the countries of Europe could agree on a combined plan. Britain and France readily agreed. With free trading part of the conditions, the Russians rejected the offer and made Poland and Czechoslovakia follow suit. The plan proceeded for the western zones only. For the Marshall Plan to work, a central bank was necessary. Again, the Russians objected. The three western zones eventually combined as one within the Organization for European Economic Cooperation (OEEC), set up, in the spring of 1948, to run the European Recovery Programme (Marshall Aid). Against this background of a split with the Russians over the economy, at the Anglo-American-French Conference, held in London in the spring of 1948, the decision was taken to allow the Germans to begin drafting a constitution. In reaction, the Russians withdrew from the Control Council in March and restrictions on travel between the Soviet and western zones were introduced at the start of April. Though the Control Council was not formally ended until over a year later, the division of Germany into two countries under separate governments had begun. (See Balfour 1992: 99–101.)

Economic reform

The Soviet Union's withdrawal from the Allied Control Council opened the way for economic reform within the western zones. In June 1948, the currency was reformed, the Reichsmark replaced by the Deutschmark, and a central bank, the *Bank Deutscher Länder* (which in 1957 became the *Bundesbank*), was set up to control the money supply (Balfour 1992: 105). Through these measures, devaluation took place, which put German exports at a comparative advantage. As in the 1923 devaluation, those with savings were hurt the most, but the compensation was that goods began to return to the shops and the black market ended (ibid.: 106).

There was another advantage over 1923 too. Whereas in Weimar the SPD-led coalition government had been given the blame for the devaluation in 1923, in Germany in 1948, it was the western Allies, not a German government, who were positioned for blame for any consequent economic ills (Ginsberg 1996: 99). Furthermore, it was a German, Ludwig Erhard, the Director of the Economic Administration Office in West Germany, who seized the initiative and, on the day that the new currency was introduced, announced his policy of the 'social market economy' (see Document, Schweitzer *et al.* 1995: 15). The controls on prices, wages and supplies were to be ended in all but a few essential cases (Balfour 1992: 109). While rationing is appropriate at a time of post-war economic reconstruction, as made clear in Chapter 7, controls on prices, wages and supplies had been central to Nazi policies. Reaction against the Nazi system lay behind Erhard's thinking on the 'social market economy'. As he declared, in August 1948, 'We had to abjure all intolerance which, from a spiritual lack of freedom, leads to tyranny and totalitarianism' (see Document, Schweitzer *et al.* 1995: 15).

The German economy began to recover. Industrial production rose by 50 per cent in the second half of 1948 and by 25 per cent in 1949 (Balfour 1992: 109). In 1961, Germany gained the rank of the world's third largest industrial producer; by 1964, the Gross National Product was three times its size in 1950 and, in 1958, Germany overtook Britain, to become the second largest exporter in the world (ibid.: 110). Furthermore, from 1951 to 1961, Germany was in a continuous balance of trade surplus. Congratulations for this remarkable success went to Erhard's policy of the 'social market economy' (ibid.).

In reality, Germany's economic recovery was due to a number of factors; Balfour (1992: 110–16) lists sixteen. Though Erhard's policies are included among the factors, top of the list is the 1,389 million dollars, which were given in Marshall Aid. Marshall Aid began just one month after the currency change and Erhard's announcement of his social market policy (ibid.: 110). Balfour also highlights the economic advantages of the unemployment, which was a result of the currency reform, in producing a ready supply of labour so necessary for economic growth (ibid: 110–11). Unemployment rose to 2 million and remained above half a million until 1955. Though such high unemployment potentially posed a risk to social stability, a twenty-four-hour general strike called in November 1948 failed (ibid.: 112). The monetary policy pursued kept wages low, but also kept inflation down and savings high and, also importantly, the high level of unemployment steadily declined (ibid.: 112–13).

As to which of the many factors contributed most to Germany's 'economic miracle' is open to debate but that economic crisis was avoided and that long-term recovery was achieved is indisputable. Equally indisputable, therefore, is that the economy in post-Second World War Germany presented, from 1949, a better prospect for lasting democracy than that during the lifetime of the Weimar Republic. It does not follow from this, however, that economic conditions have primacy over politics. A strong economy is conducive to political stability but so too a stable political system is conducive to economic stability and growth. Balfour, therefore, also includes in his list that 'the new political system quickly established itself on a firm basis' (ibid.: 112) as an important factor in contributing to the economic confidence necessary for the willingness to invest, so essential for economic recovery.

If democratic values and pluralistic structures are critical factors for the success of a newly constructed democratic system, then that the new political system did 'quickly establish itself on a firm basis' was against the odds.

Values and opinions

In addition to the problems of post-war economic reconstruction, the dislocated society, and the fact that political opposition and civil society had been destroyed by the Nazi regime in their construction of a mass society, not only had the population supported National Socialism in large numbers but the same anti-democratic values that had brought the Nazi party to power remained. In contradiction to Bermeo's (1992: 281) hypothesis, the strong 'Never Again' reaction to the hideous interlude of totalitarianism on which discontinuity democracy could be built, did not occur, at least not straightaway. As measured by the election results of 1932, values after 1945 remained disturbingly similar to what they had been in the lead up to the Third Reich.

Public opinion surveys were regularly carried out after the war by the Office of Military Government, United States (OMGUS).[5] In these surveys of the American Zone between November 1945 and December 1946 an average of 47 per cent held the opinion that 'National Socialism was a good idea badly carried out'; this figure rose to 55 per cent in August 1947 (Merritt and Merritt 1970: 32). The opinion survey in December 1946 revealed 39 per cent of the population to be anti-Semitic (ibid.: 40). Among the remaining opinions, however, there was evidence of support both for democracy and for ideas and values associated with democracy. In Merritt and Merritt's (ibid.: 43) assessment, 'Typically, the more democratic individuals were those living in large cities, respondents with 12 or more years of schooling, professionals rather than workers or employees, adherents of the Social Democratic Party, and middle income groups.' An overall assessment of the opinion polls suggested that Germans were split between those with democratic and those with authoritarian positions (ibid.).

It is questionable, in any case, whether a 'Never Again' reaction could be sufficient to make the necessary change to valuing democracy. A democratic policy shift would also need to be present. As Merritt and Merritt (ibid.) report: 'Social psychologists tell us that the moods of entire publics are slow to change. The concatination of traumatic experiences and official policy shifts, however, can shake all but the most deep-seated aspects of political culture.' Merritt and Merritt (1970: 50) argue that the traumatic experiences required was provided by the total defeat in war: 'For Germans, the physical and psychological destruction of the lost war was such a trauma.' The crucial policy shifts, they argue, were provided by the Allies in combination with 'the resurgence of voices suppressed during the Nazi period' (ibid.). The evidence for this is found (in the American Zone) in Germans' attitudes to the Allies.

OMGUS conducted seventy-two major surveys between 1945 and 1949. The responses showed that the Germans accepted the troops, but not uncritically; that they had little interest in the information programmes but were not hostile to them; that they cooperated with the Allied policies directed at destroying the Nazi past; and, crucially, their questionnaire responses indicated that they found the occupation tolerable (Merritt and Merritt 1970: 51). Perhaps the most telling evidence of a value shift is the Germans' willingness to rely on the Allies. In responses recorded between January 1947 and February 1949, as the split between East and West deepened, around 50 per cent of the population consistently chose the following statement as closest to their opinion: 'The Americans should reconstruct Germany as soon as possible in order to avoid her becoming prey to communism.' A further 15 per cent thought 'Germany should be occupied by the Allies until she is able to form a good democratic government' and around 10 per cent thought 'Germany herself should bear the responsibility for her reconstruction under the supervision of the Allies'. The counter position that 'The reconstruction of the country should be left to the Germans themselves without interference from the Allies' rose to 20 per cent in the second half of 1948 and remained at that level.[6] In sum, four-fifths of those in the American Zone wanted cooperation and democratic government.

Social conditions

These desires for cooperation and democratic government in Germany after 1945 could not contrast more sharply with the Hitler years. Yet, ironically, Dahrendorf (1968) argues that the Nazi totalitarian regime, diametrically opposed to democracy, created material conditions in

German society that were to be conducive to democracy once the Nazis were removed. As explained, in Chapter 5, Dahrendorf argues that the Weimar Republic had failed to end traditional society, leaving the country in 'suspended revolution'. Where the Weimar Republic had failed to end traditional society, however, Dahrendorf (1968: 405) argues that the Nazis succeeded in 'the destruction of the traditional basis of German society in family and religion and all other spheres'. He argues that the National Socialists' legal and institutional 'coordination' was designed to break customs, habits and traditional freedoms. Such coordination of laws and institutions took place first, he argues, in the bureaucracy and legal system and was soon extended to other institutions: the army, industry, trade unions, the press and, eventually, churches, universities and private organizations (ibid.: 405–6). He concludes:

> National Socialism has finally abolished the German past as it was embodied in Imperial Germany. What came after it was free of the mortgage that burdened the Weimar Republic at its beginning, thanks to the suspended revolution. There could be no return from the revolution of National Socialist times.
>
> (Dahrendorf 1968: 418)

Dahrendorf's emphasis on rational coordination, however, contrasts with the emphasis given, in Chapter 7 above, to terror and lawlessness in Nazi Germany, from 1938 especially. In essence, it is the irrationality of the Nazi system that has been stressed, not its centralized rationality. The effect was not simply to replace one kind of state with another but to destroy government and to turn the state into a façade, behind which real power lay with the SS and concentration camps. In a system based on secrecy, its operation reliant on the destruction of spontaneity, on the incapacity of people to join together in action, it is little wonder that after the war the widespread reaction was disbelief and denial about the true nature of Nazism. It follows that while there is no denying the total destruction brought by the Nazis it was defeat in war which had the most immediate effect on Germany in 1945.

The return of the 'wretched ragged remains' of the German Army in 1945 contrasted sharply with the return of the army after the First World War (Roseman 2000: 148). After such utter defeat and unconditional surrender in 1945, the accusations about the 'stab in the back' could not be convincingly made against the post-Second World War supporters of democracy (Ginsberg 1996: 99).[7] Importantly, the utter defeat in 1945 sapped support for nationalism, and the Allies' decision to disband Germany's military forces highlighted the futility of both the nationalism and militarism, which had undermined the Weimar Republic.[8] The demilitaritization programme implemented by the Allies also severed any lingering attachments to the Prussian militaristic tradition (ibid.: 98).

The effect of the Nazi regime, the war and the consequences of defeat in 1945 had, certainly, combined to produce a kind of levelling of society, what Merkl (1963: 27) refers to as 'the *de facto* equality of economic condition among large numbers of the German population'. As explained in Chapter 7, to an extent a levelling of conditions had been a consequence of Nazism but, again, conditions after the war were also crucial. At the end of the war, in addition to the 10 million refugees and expellees living in camps, several million more had lost their property. Hundreds of thousands had also been affected by requisitioning during and after the war. Casualties and deaths had brought great hardships to families. Rationing after the war brought further levelling and those more fortunate than the rest mostly felt constrained to avoid conspicuous consumption; quite a turn around for a country once so status-conscious. (See Merkl 1963: 27–8.) Such equality of social and economic condition fits with de Tocqueville's analysis of democracy. Arguments about the relationship between war and democracy have also been linked to the rise of the welfare state (Titmuss 1963: 75–87).

As post-1945 German history clearly shows, however, liberal democracy was not the only route possible for Germany. In the East the communist route was taken, until 1989, for a period of fully forty years. To explain how Germany took the democratic path after 1945, in West Germany at least, it is necessary to consider political factors.

Politics

As mentioned above, long before a new constitution was drafted the process of democratizing society was begun through the setting up of local self-government, state (*Land*) administration, competitive political parties and freedom of speech, press and religion. Indeed, this 'one step at a time' (Ginsberg 1996: 98) towards the setting up of the new democracy under Allied management is viewed as crucial in the success of the German Federal Democratic Republic in achieving stable and effective workable democracy. It was four years before Germany had its own central government, in 1949, and consolidation continued under Allied occupation until 1955 when occupying troops were withdrawn and the FDR became fully independent. But creating a democratic society meant more than introducing new political structures at the local level and encouraging a free press and religious toleration; it meant engaging fully with de-Nazification, and breaking down anti-democratic conditions of authoritarianism and breaking up its structural supports. As Merritt and Merritt (1980: 13) put it, 'It would require the entrenchment of certain kinds of habits – assuming civic responsibilities, becoming informed, voting, obeying just laws, paying taxes, making occasional short-term sacrifices in the community interest, and the like.'

In respect of de-Nazification, the Nuremberg trials of Nazi war criminals were important in bringing into the open the nature of the terrible deeds committed. De-Nazification hearings were also held to remove from positions of responsibility both former members of the NSDAP and those who had actively helped them. It was to this end that big business cartels and banks, which had given such major support to National Socialism, were broken up. Organizations and publications associated in any way with Nazism were banned. For example, along with the ban on the NSDAP and all its ancilliary bodies, other right-wing organizations, such as the veterans' associations, were also disbanded. (See Merritt and Merritt 1980: 10–12.)

In respect of breaking down authoritarian traditions, most importantly, the Allies re-drew the Länder boundaries. This not only opened up new beginnings with old groups with reinforcing memberships now changed and made to cross-cut with new groups, the consequence was also the disappearance of the Prussian State with its Junker class and history of militarism (Ginsberg 1996: 98). The Allied supervision of the setting up of the new parties and local elections also served as practical 're-education' to democracy (Merrittt and Merritt 1980: 7). The Allies' strong hand on the media also played a very important role in combating authoritarianism. As Ginsberg (1996: 99) comments in respect of the Allies 'insisting on liberalization of the press and the establishment of an independent radio system', these were 'alien ideas to the authoritarian traditions of the German media' (ibid.).

The building of democracy after the collapse of the Third Reich was not, however, simply a case of democratization imposed by occupying forces but also one of re-democratization (see Merkl 1963, passim). As made clear in Chapter 5, in pre-Hitler Germany there were both democratic traditions and past experiences of institutions and structures on which to draw. For example, there had been the federal structure and bicameral parliament of Imperial Germany, the universal suffrage and secret ballots of Weimar and the heritage of party competition. The Frankfurt Constituent Assembly of 1848–49 was accepted by all but the Lower Saxony Land Party (the German Party) as a beacon constitutional tradition and the framers of the new constitution adopted its flag for the German Federal Republic.

Though, as Merkl (1963: 20) comments, 'the vast majority' of the German people was 'stunned by the magnitude of the collapse of Nazi totalitarianism and relatively unconcerned about political reconstruction', a crucial minority were deeply committed to democracy. These were his 'scores of political and intellectual leaders and thousands of faithful followers of the democratic groups of the Weimar period' (ibid.). Under the guidance of the Allies, these Germans, wedded to democratic ideas, played a crucial role in political reconstruction. Ginsberg (1996: 100) explains that these surviving German democrats emerged 'to play key roles in the drafting of the *Länder* constitutions, the evolution of the institutions of local and *Länder* governments, and the reconstituting of political parties – all authorized by the occupation authorities'.

The formation of parties

Following the Allies' directives, parties began to organize in September 1945. As the British Zone's wording had it, political parties were to form 'In order to encourage the development of a democratic spirit in Germany and prepare free elections for a date yet to be appointed' (see Document, Schweitzer *et al.* 1995: 12). Both the benefits of past party organizations and the contemporary lessons available beyond Germany's borders were drawn on in the setting up of the parties. The Social Democrat and Communist parties re-emerged from their 'precarious underground existence during the Third Reich' (Balfour 1992: 96). The SPD, with its history stretching back to 1875, had been the one party that had voted against Hitler's Enabling Act in 1933 (by that point the Communist Party, KPD, had already been outlawed). The head of the SPD, Schumacher, had suffered concentration camp imprisonment for ten years (ibid.: 119).

Following the pattern of some other European countries the Christian Democratic Union, CDU (in Bavaria, Christian Social Union, CSU) was formed, headed by Adenauer. The CDU was a centre coalition based in the tradition of the Weimar Centre Party, Zentrum. The CDU/CSU was anti-Nazism, anti-communism and combined democracy with religion. The CDU/CSU differed from the Catholic Centre Party in combining Catholics and Protestants. The old Centre Party re-emerged, but as a separate and far smaller party. In addition, the Liberal or Free Democratic Party (FDP) formed; on the right of the CDU it was non-religious and supported free trade. The German Party, with its nationalist tinge, first formed as the Lower Saxony Land Party based initially on the claim for Hanover's independence. (See Balfour 1992: 95–6; Merritt and Merritt 1980: 15.)

Crucially, the main three parties in Western Germany, CDU/CSU, SPD and FDP, which in Weimar had had clearly delineated social bases of support, now sought to compete for a wide spectrum of votes, turning themselves into what was to become termed 'catch-all parties' (Kircheimer 1966). (See Spencer 1995: 2–3.) For the SPD, the most strongly ideological of the parties, this process of transformation was affected by events which quickly followed. In the Soviet Zone, in

February 1946, the SPD was forced to merge with the Communist Party to form the new Socialist Unity Party, SED. In the western zones a vote was held on the merger which was overwhelmingly rejected, with 82 per cent against, and there the Social Democrats remained a separate party (Balfour 1992: 97). From that point on Schumacher refused to work with the Soviet communists (Ginsberg 1996: 102).

In Weimar Germany, contemporary Soviet history had placed the Communist Party in competition with the SPD for left votes and hardened the cleft between left and right in German politics. In contrast, in post-Second World War Germany, the cleft was not between the left and right but between the Communists (SED) and the SPD together with other pluralist parties. These divisions were then reinforced by events. The Soviet Union's lack of cooperation over currency changes in Berlin led to a blockade in the city, which then produced further important political outcomes. The blockade led to two governments in Berlin: the one, in the West, elected (in December 1948) with an overwhelming majority for the SPD; the other, in the East, a SED government. Neither government recognized the other (Balfour 1992: 108). The air-lifts to Berlin, which broke the blockade, also tangibly demonstrated the West's support for the German people.[9] Contemporary developments in socialist parties outside Germany also drew the German Social Democrats to the western Allies. Not least the example of Britain, where the Labour Party had been swept to power in the 1945 election, gave reassurance to social democrats that workers' interests would be looked after under alignment with the West. (See Balfour 1992: 105–9.)

The separation of the Soviet Zone, however, had a direct effect on the balance of potential SPD support as compared with that of the CDU. Many of the social democrat strongholds in Weimar Germany were now situated in East Germany. With East Germany covering Protestant areas, West Germany also had a far higher proportion of Catholics, at around half the population, than would have been the case had Germany remained one country (Balfour 1992: 118). In 1945, a government dominated by the SPD and led by Schumacher was considered the most likely outcome of a future election. With the separation of East and West Germany, this outcome was put in the balance.

The Länder

As the parties formed, so too did the federalist structure, evolving through a combination of the logic of the zones and convenience (Balfour 1992: 97–8). Crucially, the Allies paid scant regard to old Länder boundaries; eighteen emerged, five of them in the Soviet Zone (Balfour 1992: 97–8; Spencer 1995: 3). The re-drawing of the boundaries was deliberately 'crafted to weaken historic divisions and create new loyalties'

(Ginsberg 1996: 98). Prussia, which had so dominated Imperial and Weimar Germany, was divided up and incorporated into several Länder and was officially abolished in March 1947 (see Document, Schweitzer *et al.* 1995: 9–10).

As in the writing of the state constitutions in America after the War of Independence, in Germany the drafting of the Länder constitutions took precedence over the drafting of the federal constitution. Though the writing of the German state constitutions differed from the writing of American state constitutions in being supervised by the occupying military government in each zone, Germans within each of the Länder played key roles in drafting their state constitutions. Elections for the Land parliaments (*Landtäge*) were held in the western zones between June 1946 and May 1947 (Balfour 1992: 98).

Drafting the Basic Law

The decision for the drafting of a constitution for a German government was made in the spring of 1948. At the Anglo-American-French Conference, held in London, the decision taken was for a

> Constitutional Assembly [to] draw up a democratic constitution which will establish for the participatory states a governmental structure of federal type which is best adapted to the eventual re-establishment of German unity at present disrupted and which will protect the rights of participating states, provide adequate central authority and contain guarantees of individual rights and freedom.
>
> (Document quoted in Balfour 1992: 122–3)

The task of setting up the Constitutional Assembly was given to the minister-presidents of the Land governments, formed into the Länder Council. In evidence of independence, the minister-presidents chose instead to convene a 'Parliamentary Council' to draw up the 'Basic Law'. With Germany now split into East and West, the preference for 'Basic Law' indicated that it was to be viewed as a provisional document. Once completed, Article 23 referred to the Basic Law applying 'for the time being' to the Länder in West Germany, 'to be put into force in other parts of Germany on their accession' (Merkl 1963: Appendix II). Furthermore, the minister-presidents decided that the Basic Law was to be ratified by the state parliaments and not by referendum as proposed at the London Conference (Balfour 1992: 123). The Parliamentary Council was composed of representatives elected from the Landtäge on the basis of one representative for every 750,000 of the population. The Council consisted of sixty-five members. The results of the elections produced seats in the Council as follows: 27 CDU/CSU; 27 SPD; 5 FDP; 2 German

Party; 2 Centre Party and 2 Communists (ibid.). Adenauer, leader of the CDU, was chosen as President of the Council. Similar to the behaviour of the Founding Fathers in America who ignored their brief and set out, instead, to write a completely new constitution, the Parliamentary Council ignored the draft document drawn up by the minister-presidents.

Three issues dominated debate in the Parliamentary Council (Balfour 1992: 124). Two of the issues had also been concerns of the Framers of the American Constitution. The major debate was over the relative power of the central (Federal) government and the states (Länder). The other was over the number of representatives from each state for the upper house and, in addition, there was a split over whether the state representatives should be elected or be delegated by the state parliaments. The third issue was over the electoral system. The view that proportional representation had led to the downfall of the Weimar Republic led many to favour the British first-past-the-post system of simple majority, single-member constituencies.

The balance of powers

In respect of the relative strengths of central and state governments, the SPD and FDP view won the day to make the central government strong, the reverse of the case in Weimar Germany and, ironically, more similar to the American case. Ironical because the latter-day America, that occupying Germany after the Second World War that is, favoured strong Länder (Balfour 1992: 124). It was laid down, as Article 31, that 'Federal law shall take precedence over *Land* law' and the Federal Government could step in if the Land Government failed to implement the Basic Law or other Federal laws.

With respect to the number of representatives for each state, the SPD happened to favour what had been the outcome in the American case: a Senate to be made up of directly elected representatives for each state, the state representatives equal in number for each state, irrespective of the state's size of population. All other parties, paralleling the losers in the American case, wanted Länder representation to be in proportion to the size of population (Balfour 1992: 124). The German outcome was a compromise (Article 51): Länder over 6 million to have six members; Länder between 6 and 2 million, four members; Länder under 2 million, three members. Large states, therefore, could no longer achieve the power and dominance that Prussia, with its seventeen seats out of fifty-eight had had in the past. Significantly, the Control Council Law, Number 36, February 1947, which abolished the Prussian State opened with 'The Prussian State which from early days has been a bearer of militarism and reaction in Germany has de facto ceased to exist' (see Document, Schweitzer *et al.* 1995: 9).

The SPD also lost out both in their wish for the upper house to be called 'Senate' and for the representatives to be directly elected, views also supported by the CDU in the British Zone, including Adenauer (Balfour 1992: 124). Following the German tradition, the upper house returned to the name of Federal Council (Bundesrat) and was to be made up of delegates chosen by the Land governments with block votes (Article 51). To appease the SPD and the minority of CDU members of the Parliamentary Council, the powers of the Bundesrat were reduced but, in practice, the Bundesrat's powers were stronger than bargained for because of the right to vote in all legislation affecting the Länder (ibid.: 128).

The lower house became the Bundestag (Federal Parliament). Elections to the Bundestag were to be direct and suffrage returned to that in Weimar: men and women with a minimum age of 21. The Bundestag was to be elected every four years. The balance of power between the Bundesrat and Bundestag, on legislation that affected the Länder, was achieved through the Bundesrat being able to vote against such legislation. In turn, the Bundestag could then reject the Bundesrat vote but only if the Bundestag achieved a majority for the legislation at least as high as that obtained in the upper house against the legislation, more than half or more than two-thirds. In practice, a joint committee for consideration sorts out the differences between the two chambers (Article 77).

To ensure a balance of power, the Federal Constitutional Court, in much the same way as the US Supreme Court, was given the task of interpreting the Basic Law and settling differences between the Federation and the Länder. Half of its members are elected by the Bundestag and the other half by the Bundesrat, with none of the judges allowed also to be members of either house (Article 93). The independence of judges is guaranteed, under Article 88.

In respect of the president, direct election, which had existed under the Weimar Constitution, was roundly rejected and, instead, the Federal President was to be elected, indirectly, for five years by a Federal Convention made up of the members of the Bundestag together with an equal number of representatives chosen by the Land parliaments through proportional representation (Article 54). Also adopting a provision from the 1871 Constitution, the president's powers were held in check by the requirement of the counter-signature of the chancellor, or relevant minister, for any act (Balfour 1992: 129). The office of president was to be for five years with re-election permitted only once. In contrast to the strong president in the American political system and, yet more poignantly, in the Weimar Constitution, the German president is weak, 'largely ceremonial' (Roseman 2000: 144). Indeed, the president is so weak that the German system is given the term 'chancellor-democracy', *Kanzlerdemocratie*, and is classified not as a presidential but a parliamentary system with the Federal Chancellor (prime minister) the strong figure (Sartori 1997: 103).[10]

The Federal Chancellor is elected by a majority of the Bundestag. One of the duties of the president is to propose the chancellor. If the candidate fails to gain the Bundestag's support the Bundestag can then propose its own candidate who, if supported by a majority, must be appointed by the president. The Federal government is made up of the chancellor and ministers; the ministers are proposed by the chancellor and appointed by the president. (See Article 63.) Again, with the failure of Weimar in their minds, the Basic Law was designed not simply to institute the procedures for the removal of the Federal Chancellor but to ensure that a new government could form. Under Article 67, the 'constructive vote of no confidence', to remove a chancellor from office, not only must a majority in the Bundestag vote against the chancellor but a successor must be nominated with the majority's support and the nomination be made at least forty-eight hours before the vote of no confidence.

Basic Rights

As with the First Amendments of the American Constitution, together known as the Bill of Rights, the Basic Law also had, in effect, a bill of rights. In the German case, however, rather than being a set of amendments, the 'Basic Rights' were the first nineteen articles of the Basic Law, which together constituted its first chapter. In the light of Nazi Terror, understandably, the first of these basic rights is that of the 'protection of human dignity'. Then follow the rights of liberty, equality before the law (including equality between men and women and between people of different races, languages, origins, religions, parentage and political opinions). Freedom of religion and worship are guaranteed, as is freedom of expression (which includes free press, and the absence of censorship, in research and in teaching, so long as compatible with the democratic constitution). The rights of marriage and family and the rights of illegitimate children are guaranteed, as, too, are the rights of parents to choose schools and religious education for their children.

Reinforcing the freedom of religion, five Articles from the Weimar Constitution were included in the Basic Law, together as Article 140. These Weimar Articles not only set out the freedoms of religious association and worship but also that, 'There shall be no state church' (Basic Law 1991: 89–90). The care and detail over protection of religious freedom in the Weimar Constitution together with the fact that the Weimar Constitution was never removed from the statute books by the

Nazis, serves to contradict the easy view of constitutions as guaranteeing democracy.

The Basic Law also gives the basic right of freedom of association, other than for those 'directed against the constitutional order' (Basic Law 1991: 10) and the right to form associations, including trade unions. The basic rights of petition, privacy of communications, privacy of the home and the freedom of movement are also guaranteed, as too is the right to choose one's occupation. The right to choose ones occupation specifically outlawed forced labour, that immovable economic plank of the Nazi system (O'Kane 1996). The free market for labour, backed by the right 'to form associations to safeguard and improve working and economic conditions' (Basic Law 1991: 11) also contrasted with the contemporary conditions in the Soviet Union and Eastern Europe, including East Germany. Again, in sharp rejection of Nazism, the rights of citizenship were guaranteed. The rights to property and inheritance were also guaranteed, but, in addition, the social democratic right of public ownership, 'for the purpose of socialization' (ibid.: 14) was also included.

In strong emphasis of the democratic intent of these rights, the role of the Federal Constitutional Court for dealing with those who abuse rights such as the freedom of the press and of assembly is made explicit, in Article 18. To balance this, under Article 19, the rights of individuals are provided protection by the courts against public authority. (See Basic Law: 8–16.)[11]

The Basic Law also made a significant change from the Weimar Constitution in excluding referendums and plebiscites as a means for democracy (Kommers 1995: 298). Article 20, paragraph 2 of the Basic Law states, 'All state authority shall emanate from the people. It shall be exercised by the people through elections and voting and by specific organs of the legislature, the executive power, and the judiciary' (Basic Law 1991: 17). The central importance of political parties was also made explicit and their role safeguarded in Article 21, which reads as follows[12]:

Article 21 (Political Parties)

(1) The political parties shall participate in the forming of the political will of the people. They may be freely established. Their internal organization shall conform to democratic principles. They shall publicly account for the sources of their funds.

(2) Parties which, by reason of their aims or the behaviour of their adherents, seek to impair or abolish the free democratic basic order or to endanger the existence of the Federal Republic of Germany shall be unconstitutional. The Federal Constitutional Court shall decide on the question of unconstitutionality.

(3) Details shall be regulated by federal statutes.

Unlike the Weimar Constitution, and in accord with its new position, the Basic Law was not put to a plebiscite but to the ratification of the Land parliaments. In line with the good sense of the American case the agreement of all states was not required, only that of a minimum of two-thirds. This was achieved with all Länder apart from Bavaria in approval. The Basic Law of the Federal Republic of Germany came into force on 23 May 1949.

The electoral system

Voting procedures were not part of the Basic Law but formed a separate document on Electoral Law. They constituted a compromise, a mixed system. The electoral system proposed by the Parliamentary Council in 1949 was provisional, to be used for the first election of the Bundestag only. It was a quite new idea, designed to draw on the benefits of both the British first-past-the-post system and PR schemes. The one chosen was for 60 per cent of the 400 seats to be elected in single-member districts by plurality, the remaining 40 per cent to be elected from party lists and each party's total share of seats to be matched to its share of votes (Bawn 1993: 972–3). To guard against the proliferation of parties that had occurred in Weimar Germany, the rule was introduced that in order to obtain any representatives each party had to win a minimum 5 per cent of the votes cast in any Land.

As set down, the first Bundestag reconsidered the electoral system and changes were made for a new permanent system, in time for the 1953 election. First, the 5 per cent rule was made harsher, the 5 per cent threshold to apply for the whole country, not just within each Land, or at least three constituencies had to be won by the party. Second, voters were each to be given two separate votes. The one vote was for representatives in the single-member constituencies on the basis of first-past-the-post, the other vote for a party with seats allocated in proportion to the votes received within each Land. (See Bawn 1993: 976–7.)

Elections and party fortunes

Under the new constitution, a general election was held in August 1949. The outcome produced twelve parties in the Bundestag with seats distributed as follows: CDU/CSU 139 seats; SPD 131 seats; FDP 52 seats; Bavarian Party 17 seats; German Party 17 seats; Communist Party 15 seats, others 31 seats. The SPD's proposal for a 'Grand Coalition' with the CDU was rejected and, instead, a 'Little Coalition' of CDU/CSU, FDP and the German Party was formed (Balfour 1992: 133). The new government settled in the new capital of the Federal Republic, Bonn, where the Parliamentary Council had met to draft the Basic Law. Elections were again held in early 1953. They took place just a few months after the death of the SDP leader, Schumacher, and the election followed heated debate in parliament over rearmament of the Federal Republic, which the SPD wanted to halt (Merritt and Merritt 1980: 17). In the 1953 elections the CDU/CSU increased their seats to 243 out of the total 487 seats in the Bundestag. Though so close to an outright majority, both the FDP and the German Party were retained in the continued coalition cabinet.

In 1952, the year before the 1953 election, the neo-Nazi Socialist Reich Party, SRP, based in Lower Saxony, had been banned under Article 21 of the Basic Law. The judgment by the Federal Constitutional Court on the Socialist Reich Party in 1952, included the following statement:

> German constitutions following World War I hardly mentioned political parties, although even at that time the democratic constitutional life was to a large extent determined by parties. The reasons for this omission are manifold, but in the last analysis, the *cause lies in a democratic ideology that refused to recognize groups mediating between the free individual and the will of the entire people composed of the sum of individual wills* and represented in parliament by deputies as 'representatives of the entire people'. ... *The Basic Law abandoned this viewpoint and, more realistically, expressly recognizes parties as agents – even if not the only ones – forming the political will of the people.*
>
> (Document, Schweitzer *et al.* 1995: 305,
> italics not in the original)

After the 1953 election, the Communist Party having failed to achieve the required 5 per cent threshold, communists were also not represented in the Bundestag. In 1956, the Communist Party, too, was declared by the Federal Government to contravene Article 21, and outlawed (Balfour 1992: 153).

The general election in 1955, the year in which the occupying troops were withdrawn, was again won by the CDU/CSU. Fearing the role of opposition would become permanent, the SPD made important changes and, in the Godesberg Programme, in 1958, sought to attract more votes, with its new policies of a mixed economy and western integration. The SPD had voted for entry into the (European) Common Market in 1957. The new slogan for the party's economic policies became 'Competition as far as possible – planning as far as necessary' (Balfour 1992: 154).

Following the elections held in September 1961, just one month after the building of the Berlin Wall, dividing East from West Germany, the effect of the 5 per cent threshold clause was to reduce the number of parties in the Bundestag yet further, down to four. Not only were lesser parties excluded but votes for the German Party, which had been a member of the previous coalition governments along with the CDU/CSU and FDP, fell to 2.8 per cent and were swept from federal politics (Balfour 1992: 166). The CDU/CSU lost 28 seats (the CDU down from 215 to 192 and the CSU down from 55 to 50) while the SPD gained 21 seats (up from 169 to 190) and the FDP gained 26 seats (up from 41 to 67). Though the CDU and SPD seats were so close in number, again the SPD was kept out of government with a CDU/CSU/FDP coalition emerging (ibid.). The election in 1965 brought little change; the CDU/CSU/FDP coalition remained in government. This was in spite of the fact that the FDP lost 18 seats and the SPD gained 12 seats, bringing its total to 202 seats as compared with the CDU's 195 seats. The CDU gained 3 and the CSU stayed at 50 seats (Balfour 1992: 173 and 251).

A year after the election, in October 1966, Article 67 of the Basic Law – the constructive vote of no confidence – was invoked to remove the chancellor. In November 1966, a Grand Coalition was formed in which for the first time since Weimar the SPD was included. In the CDU/CSU and SPD coalition government, the SPD held nine of the twenty ministerial posts (Balfour 1992: 176). In the presidential election of 1969, again for the first time since Weimar, the SPD candidate won (ibid.: 187). In the Bundestag election of September 1969, the SPD won 224 seats, the CDU 192 seats, the CSU 50 seats and the FDP only 30 seats, having dropped to 5.8 per cent of the votes. The neo-Nazi National Democratic Party (NDP), which had seats in some Land parliaments and which had been considered for exclusion under Article 21, won 4.5 per cent of the votes and, therefore, under the 5 per cent rule, no seats in the Bundestag (ibid.: 188). After negotiations taking more than three weeks an SPD-FDP coalition was formed (ibid.). For the first time since Weimar, a Socialist Democrat chancellor was appointed. In the election of 1972, the SPD share of the vote again grew, by 3.1 per cent, strengthening the SPD position: the SPD at 229 seats, the CDU/CSU at 176/49 (ibid.: 189).

Assessment: twenty years on

By the end of the 1960s, the Basic Law had demonstrably succeeded where the Weimar Constitution had failed. Within the Bundestag, a strong centre had been produced and retained and extremist, undemocratic, parties had been kept out. Standing at three, and some would rate the CSU as only half, a manageable number of parties had been produced. Crucially, too, an identifiable opposition had emerged; lasting, manageable government coalitions had been maintained; and smooth alteration of government had been achieved. Furthermore, a successful balance of power had been produced between the upper and lower houses. In particular, domination by any one Land, as had been in the case with Prussia in both Imperial and Weimar Germany, had been avoided. Significantly, too, the office of president had not become too strong. Rather, chancellor-centred parliamentary democracy with its all-important control by the executive which takes ministerial responsibility and consequent avoidance of disorderly assemblies had been established.

Kanzlerdemocratie

Political explanations for the stability of the Federal Democratic Republic focus on the establishment, over time, of this chancellor-centred parliamentary government, Kanzlerdemocratie, which approximates the British cabinet system. The British system of government with its strong prime minister and cabinet is the consequence of the first-past-the-post system of single member constituencies which leads to a two-party system, with single-party government and the other major party as the official opposition, the government-in-waiting. In spite of coalition governments and proportional representation being part of the electoral system, Germany produced a three (for some a two-and-a-half) party system. The development of chancellor-democracy has been attributed, therefore, to the mixed electoral system and to the 5 per cent exclusion clause. Sartori (1997), however, rejects these as the primary factors in producing the German premiership system. The 5 per cent rule, he argues, is unlikely to reduce the number of parties in parliament down to just three, as happened in Germany. The mixed PR/majoritarian electoral system, he argues, produces, in practice, 'an almost pure proportional representation' and the outcome in the Bundestag is fully proportional (ibid.: 106).

In Sartori's (1997: 105–6) view, Kanzlerdemokratie developed as a consequence of three things, in order of importance: the outlawing of the anti-democratic parties under Article 21; the 5 per cent threshold clause of exclusion (the 'barrier clause', *Sperrklausel*); and, third, the constructive vote of no confidence, Article 67. In arguing for the major importance of the outlawing of the neo-Nazi Socialist Reich Party and the Communist Party in cutting the number of parties in the Bundestag down to three, Sartori is making the point that it was not the direct effect of the electoral system that was crucial but, rather, specific decisions made within the context of the 1950s. This unique period of history followed not only a world war and the Nazi Holocaust but also featured the build up to the Cold War.

In second place of importance, Sartori accepts that the 5 per cent threshold clause of exclusion contributed to the establishment of chancellor-democracy but he also stresses the importance, in third place, of the constructive vote of no confidence. This device, which ensures that an alternative chancellor must be available with the support of parliament before a chancellor can be removed by a vote of no confidence, he argues to be crucial to the strengthening of the chancellor's importance and authority. The chancellor is not a 'first above equals' as in the British parliamentary system but, at least, a 'first among unequals' (Sartori 1997: 107).[13]

For Sartori, then, the strengths of the FDR as a working democracy, one, that is, which is both effective and stable (Sartori 1997: 108), derives, essentially, from the small number of parties in the Bundestag together with executive control, which have been largely indirect, rather than direct, consequences of the constitution's design. The importance of the specific historical context in which these developments occurred suggests, therefore he argues, that the constitution cannot be taken up and adopted elsewhere with guarantees of success. Furthermore, it follows that a threat to stability could follow if the number of parties were to increase (ibid.: 108).

A break with the past or restoration?

While German chancellor-democracy is viewed by political scientists as a strength this view clashes with the assessment of those who view post-war Germany in terms of 'restoration'.[14] The claim of restoration involves a radical critique of the entire post-1945 system, and in particular of the continuation of German authoritarianism, of the retention of large numbers of ex-Nazis in high positions, and of the restored capitalist system.

The earliest complaints of the continuation of German authoritarianism had concerned the distrust of ordinary citizens evident in the new constitution. For example, as explained, the Basic Law was never put to a plebiscite; the role of referendums and plebiscites, which had featured in the Weimar Constitution, were absent in the Basic Law; and the president was not popularly elected. The domination of the CDU-led coalitions, in power from 1949 to 1966, then added to the concern, especially as for some of this time the SPD had more seats than the CDU and support for the FDP was in clear decline.

The cry of restoration became particularly strong following the SPD/CDU Grand Coalition of 1966 and the apparent absence of opposition, made more glaring to the left by the Communist Party, KPD, having been banned as unconstitutional under Article 21 when the neo-Nazi NDP had not. The harshness of police reactions to demonstrations and terrorist groups, notably the Red Army factions, in the late 1960s and 1970s gave further weight to the claim that German authoritarianism had been restored. Reaction against authoritarianism also highlighted the continuation of large numbers of ex-Nazis in high positions in political, economic and social spheres (Roseman 2000: 144–5); and especially in the judiciary (Ginsberg 1996: 100).

The failure to pursue the complete de-Nazification intended by the Allies had been a practical response to the reality of the situation. With limited resources, there were simply too many people with links to the Nazis to be investigated properly (Ginsberg 1996: 99). There was pragmatism involved too; the 50 per cent of Germans accepting the principle of de-Nazification in late 1945 to early 1946 declined to around 17 per cent by 1949 (Merritt and Merritt 1970: 37). The major reason for this was that the view developed over time that the treatment of higher and lower ex-Nazis was unfairly applied. It was an accusation that had the potential to create a backlash against the Allies and their moves to democracy. Importantly, since the 1960s a more active and public attack on Nazi atrocities has occurred. The Länder set up a central office of ministers of justice for finding Nazi criminals and the trials that followed had an educational effect, particularly on young Germans (Ginsberg 1996: 109–10). Again, experience of the workings of the democratic political system played an important part in inculcating ideas and values that support democracy.

In respect of the accusation of the restoration of the capitalist system, while the accusation had resonance in the politically charged times of the student movements of the 1960s and the terrorism of the 1970s, the differences far outweighed similarities. As explained, the Nazis had destroyed the traditional economic system of Imperial Germany. In turn, the post-war economic policies put in place by the Allies together with the introduction of Erhard's social market system had broken decisively with the economy of Nazi Germany with its forced labour, work books and price-fixing. Importantly, along with the end to labour market controls had also come the right to free association and the crucial legal right, therefore, to be a member of a trade union and to participate in action to further workers' interests. Furthermore, the bourgeoisie, too, had changed. Though still anti-communist they were no longer willing to take to the streets in violent action as they had in Weimar Germany and turned rather to ideas of good behaviour, *'guten ton'*, books on which subject were bestsellers (Roseman 2000: 157). The capitalism of post-Nazi Germany approximated not the highly exploitative capitalism identified by Marx and employed in their justification of terrorism by the radicals, but the kind of rational capitalism theorized by Weber which he bemoaned as too weak in Imperial Germany.

The question remains as to whether German democracy, however carefully crafted by the Allies and German democrats to build on past strengths and to integrate Germany into the democratic capitalist West, could have survived without the economy being set on the path of stable growth. Comparative lessons have demonstrated the importance of the avoidance of a dislocated society through both successful economic policy and generous foreign aid in the early years. The lesson is also there to be drawn that the advantages of economic improvements involve not only material gains. After humiliation in war and the unfurling evidence of German atrocities under the Nazi regime, present economic standing contrasted as something for which Germans could be proud. It is in this context that the significance given to Erhard's 'social market economy' is best understood.

10 Communism and its collapse

East Germany and the Russian Federation

The German Democratic Republic: rise and fall

In the Soviet Zone of post-war Germany, the German Democratic Republic (GDR), was founded in October 1949. The republic was based on the Soviet model of a centrally directed economy, society and polity, under a single party, the German Communist Party, now SED. Never simply following Soviet orders the German communists sought to outguess or outdo the Soviet line (Weitz 1997: 367). A centrally planned system was quickly put in place. In 1950, the Ministry for State Security, 'Stasi', was set up along with its ever-expanding system of informants (ibid.: 361). By 1950, 76 per cent of industrial output was produced by nationalized or Soviet-run firms and the banks and insurance firms were entirely nationalized (ibid.: 359). The first Five Year Plan was introduced in 1951 (ibid.). Labour, wages and production levels were centrally controlled; no independent trade unions were permitted (ibid.: 360). Changes were initially more slow in agriculture. By 1959, only 40 per cent of agriculture was in state hands, but in 1960, within the space of three months, the whole of agriculture became collectivized (ibid.: 367). In 1972, virtually everything that remained of a private sector was taken under state control (ibid.: 359).

In November/December 1989, following mass demonstrations, Communist Party rule collapsed. The collapse was completely bloodless. In the first free elections held in the German Democratic Republic, in March 1990, the Communist Party was dealt a resounding defeat. The elected Christian Democrat coalition government negotiated a transition to a united Germany, as envisaged in the Basic Law, under Article 23. In July 1990, monetary union with the Federal Republic of Germany was established, then the two parliaments were unified under the Treaty of Unity. The treaty having been ratified by both parliaments, reunification was proclaimed on 3 October 1990. In December 1990, elections were held throughout the united Germany. (See Schweitzer 1995: 83–4.) In the 1990 election, the Communist Party, SED, under its new name the

Party of Democratic Socialism (PDS) won only 2.4 per cent of the Federal votes (Nicholls 1995: 209).

The collapse of the German Democratic Republic had not been predicted. No uprising against the communist system had occurred since June 1953, when protests against low wages and increased production rates had grown into calls for free elections and an end to the government (Weitz 1997: 381). The 1953 uprising was brutally put down with the help of Soviet forces and tanks (Schweitzer 1995: 76; Weitz 1997: 360). The suppression by Soviet military force of uprisings in Hungary in 1956, which had been spurred on by Khruschev's de-Stalinization speech of that year, and in Czechoslovakia in 1968 reasserted Soviet domination throughout Eastern Europe. East Germany, however, reacted neither to these events nor to those in the 1980s, which began with the Solidarity movement in Poland in 1981.

This lack of spontaneity in the GDR was due, in part, to the experience of Nazi rule, which had destroyed civil society in Germany, both East and West. The short interlude of encouragement of parties and free associations after 1945 had been soon ended in East Germany and the Ministry of State Security ensured that it remained so. In East Germany, a communist totalitarian dictatorship was set up where there had once been a Nazi totalitarian regime. Only the Protestant churches had any existence separate from the state and, even here, in 1978 their declaration of *Kirche im Socialismus*, church within the socialist system, drew them in, ending direct harassment (Schweitzer 1995: 77–80). Furthermore, the state was able to exploit the revolutionary history of the German Communist Party, the KPD, as a heroic, anti-Nazi workers' movement and even the earlier revolutionaries, Liebknecht and Luxemburg, were used in support of SED policies (Weitz 1997: 363). In addition to the GDR's revolutionary communist history and experience under the Third Reich, East Germany was also unlike other East European countries in being only part of a whole. In the GDR the radical objective was not independence but unification with the FDR and as such the one part could not achieve the desired change alone.

Niche society to social movement

Under communist rule, East Germany developed a 'niche society', that is a society of individuals and small groups distanced from the state (Weitz 1997: 388). It took external changes to move the niche society to action. Developments in telecommunications led to East Germans seeing on their television screens the economic advances made in West Germany, advances which they compared unfavourably with their own growing economic discontents (Schweitzer 1995: 79). The success of Solidarity in Poland in the 1980s also signalled a loosening in Soviet domination. Out of the niche society, dissident 'citizens movements' or 'civil rights movements', as they came to be known, began to develop. By 1989 the movements numbered around 150, many of them interconnected through the Protestant churches. (See Schweitzer 1995: 79.) Initially the aims of these social movements were those of peace, justice (essentially human rights) and the protection of the environment (often stressed as 'God's creation'). These were the themes of church organized mass gatherings, which began in 1982 (ibid.). Women's rights and then demands for political liberties and the establishment of democratic institutions were then added (Weitz 1997: 388).

The objectives of these movements had begun with the aim of improvements within the system but, as the lessons of 1953 had shown, to become movements towards replacing the system the Soviet Union itself had to change. From 1985, as will become clear, under Gorbachev's policies of *glasnost* (openness) and *perestroika* (restructuring) the Soviet Union did change and hitherto oppressive policies towards Eastern Europe were replaced with encouragement from Gorbachev for democratic reforms, within the context of socialism. Against this background of changes in the Soviet Union, in Germany, police behaviour in searching out dissidents in late 1987 and carrying out widespread arrests following counter-demonstrations in early 1988 politicized opposition. This opposition was then intensified through protests about the irregularities in the local elections in May 1989 (Weitz 1997: 390; Schweitzer 1995: 78). In July, a call was made for the setting up of a Social Democratic Party (see Document, Schweitzer *et al.* 1995: 96). The decision of the Hungarian government, in the summer of 1989, to allow East Germans seeking refuge in the West German embassy to be allowed, together with others taking refuge in the country, to go to West Germany opened the floodgates for other East Germans to leave for West Germany. This exodus demonstrated the reality of the change in Soviet relations.

On 11 September 1989, New Forum was founded as 'a political platform for the whole of the GDR' (see Document, Schweitzer *et al.* 1995: 95). The new organizing platform served to group opposition movements together 'for concerted action' on justice, democracy, peace and the environment (ibid.). Its foundation was a test of the paper freedom of association of the GDR Constitution (Schweitzer 1995: 82–3). The mass movement, consisting of hundreds of thousands of protesters, took to the streets in October, first in Leipzig and Berlin and then in nearly every city, town and village of the GDR, their slogan 'we are the people' turning into 'we are one people' (ibid.: 82). On 17 October, Honecker, First Secretary of SED and Chairman of the State Council of the GDR, was replaced by Egon Krenz. On 9 November, the Berlin Wall was broken through and the Stasi headquarters were stormed. These actions met no resistance. Attempts by the SED government to accept changes within the GDR came to nothing. Krenz, in turn, was forced out of office on 3 December. Before December was out, the Communist Party radically reshaped itself and changed its name; after much debate, it became the Party of Democratic Socialism (PDS) (Weitz 1997: 394–5). Other parties began to form (Schweitzer 1995: 82–3).

By the end of 1989 the majority view in East Germany was the 'we are one people' position for unification with West Germany. Though unification was not without difficulties, not least because of the economic gulf between the two parts, the availability of a constitution, the Basic Law, ready and waiting for East Germany made democratization a quite different case from that of the Soviet Union and other East European post-communist countries (Rakowska-Harmstone 2000: 165).

The Soviet Union

In the Soviet Union, the death of Stalin, in 1953, signalled the end of the totalitarian regime, changes from then on occurring incrementally within the continuing Soviet system. Along with changes to the Stalinist system resistance to reflex obedience began to grow, as evidenced by the growth of a black market. Dissent in the cultural sphere developed and 'other-thinkers', *inakomyslyashchii*, on issues such as human rights and religious freedom became possible (Sakwa 1998: 201–2). Khrushchev's Secret Speech in February 1956, which called for de-Stalinization – an end to arbitrary and terroristic rule, to be replaced by the rule of socialist law – ushered in a more open era. The trend for dissent, however, went into reverse shortly before Khrushchev's removal in 1964, and suppression accelerated after his fall (ibid.: 203). The system settled into a totalitarian dictatorship with intimidation the means of the secret police and bureaucracy grinding down what 'other-thinking' remained.

Until 1985, in a way similar to the 'niche society' in East Germany, the post-Stalin Soviet Union had developed small 'circles' (*kruzhki*) of 'other-thinkers' concerned with peace and human and civil rights (Sakwa 1998: 207). In the Soviet Union, however, these circles had remained mostly connected with culture.

Under Gorbachev: socialist democracy

When Gorbachev became General Secretary of the CPSU (Communist Party of the Soviet Union) Central Committee in 1985, the Soviet Union had been suffering serious economic slowdown for nearly a decade (Gill and Markwick 2000: 17–18). Gorbachev followed two general secretaries – both short term (Andropov, November 1982 to February 1984; Chernenko, February 1984 to March 1985) – who after the long term in office of Brezhnev had sought to bring changes to the system. Perhaps, more accurately, Andropov had sought changes and Chernenko had not sought to reverse them. Andropov's aims were to end corruption and improve good-practice and he encouraged new approaches to economic management through the introduction of incentives (Kotz with Weir 1997: 53). Importantly, too, he was open about the economic problems faced in the Soviet Union and encouraged debate about them. Having tried small adjustments on first coming to office, in February 1986 at the Party Congress, Gorbachev declared 'now the situation is such that it is impossible to simply limit our measures to partial improvements – what is needed is radical reform' (quoted in Kotz with Weir 1997: 55).

Over the following years, Gorbachev criticized the Soviet system for its stifling of innovation and its failure to operate according to true socialist principles (Gorbachev 1988: 29–36). In particular he drew attention to the two flaws in the Soviet system: first, the absence of incentives to work hard (ibid.: 30); second, 'the excessively centralized management system' (ibid: 34), which, he argued, produced inefficiencies and hindered economic growth. Such criticisms are very much in line with Weber's (1964: 211–18) analysis of the problems that follow from the 'substantive rationality' of state planning.

The solutions that Gorbachev offered for this rigid centralism and lack of incentives in the Soviet system were both narrowly economic and also, more broadly, political economic. The straight economic solution was termed 'commodity-money relations' which meant the reintroduction of a market system with competition based on real prices and wages to be related to performance (Kotz with Weir 1997: 57). Not Weber's solution exactly, but at least planning based on rational calculations, not the irrationality of wild schemes, as under Stalin, nor the inefficiencies and falsification of statistics and corruption which persisted after de-Stalinization. (See Harrison 1993.) The political economic solutions involved the replacement of central planning by a more decentralized and more open form of planning together with the replacement of the authoritarian style of management by worker self-management, the intention being to encourage motivation to work. This 'restructuring' of the economy was termed 'perestroika'. (See Gorbachev 1988: 27–44; Kotz with Weir 1997: 56–8.)

Gorbachev's central idea was for the introduction of democracy to the workplace, 'the transition from an excessively centralized management system relying on orders, to a democratic one' (Gorbachev 1988: 34). Democracy for Gorbachev was a combination of openness and participation; though frequently referring to Lenin, his views on politics and society were close to Luxemburg's.[1] Gorbachev wanted the open declaration of problems, expression of needs and of new ideas, and in 1987 he called for the 'broad democratization of all aspects of society' (ibid.: 32). His view of democratization remained that of socialist democracy, not liberal democracy, and not western social democracy either, though there were some similarities (ibid.: 36–8). 'Public ownership' was to be kept important to the economy, as in social democracy. Again, as in both social democracy and liberal democracy, openness – 'glasnost' – was to be inculcated in society at large; criticism of government policies by the public and through the mass media was to be encouraged. But unlike in either western social democracy or liberal democracy, the democratization of political institutions, announced in 1988, was for openness within the Communist Party, not open competition of the CPSU with other political parties (ibid.: 257–70).

Gorbachev's first moves towards open debate were in the public sphere. Glasnost allowed the circles of 'other-thinkers' to blossom into many hundreds of informal groups (*neformaly*). From concerns mostly with art, music and so on, they developed into new social movements taking on concerns with social, environmental and gender issues and then moving into purely political issues (Sakwa 1998: 207–8). A law on associations was introduced in the spring of 1986; though requiring a procedure of registration for the informal groups most ignored the procedure and simply emerged into the open. In August 1987, a conference of 600 left-radical groups organized by the Club of Social Initiatives, was permitted by the authorities; this was a completely unprecedented break with the past (ibid.: 210). By 1989, the informal groups had expanded to a network of around 60,000 organizations including social and sporting clubs (ibid.).

In January 1987, moves began to open the political system to competition. In June 1987, the first experiment was carried out with contested elections in some of the local soviets; competition being between candidates not parties (Kotz with Weir 1997: 99). At the Communist Party Congress in 1988, Gorbachev denounced the bureaucratic centralism of the party and called for its 'democratization' through openness and reform, including competitive elections to all posts up to the Central Committee and complete freedom of expression for all at party meetings. (See Gorbachev 1988: 258–70.) The first opposition party, the Democratic Union, was founded in early May 1988 (Sakwa 1998: 210). The party called for a pluralist democracy with a competitive multi-party system of parliamentarianism. The party's founding congress was disrupted by police.

The political system under Gorbachev

In December 1988, the Supreme Soviet adopted constitutional amendments and a new electoral law, under which the Supreme Soviet, itself, was to be replaced by a new bicameral parliament. The lower house, the Congress of People's Deputies, consisting of 2,250 deputies, was to have 1,500 of the deputies popularly elected, and in elections that could be contested by individuals though not by parties. The remaining 750 deputies were to be chosen by prominent 'public organizations', the Communist Party being one such, though this arrangement for choosing the 750 deputies was soon ended, in 1989, for being undemocratic. The upper house, the new Supreme Soviet, was to consist of 500–550 members chosen by the 2,250 people's deputies from among themselves. The Congress was also to elect a chairman of the Supreme Soviet who would be the head of state. (See Kotz with Weir 1997: 99–100.) Under the proposed constitution there was also to be a new 'Presidential Council', a kind of cabinet appointed by the president. To pacify those opposed to a presidency a new body, the Federation Council, was set up to review policies on inter-republic and inter-ethnic relations. (See Huskey 2001a: 31–3.)

Elections for the new Congress were held in March 1989 with second rounds where no candidate received over 50 per cent of the votes. In spite of there being only one legal party, the Communist Party, and 80 per cent of the candidates being members of that party, three-quarters of the seats were contested and there was an 89.8 per cent turnout at the polls. Many were elected over the official candidate, including Yeltsin in Moscow with a resounding 89 per cent of the vote. In the Baltic republics, nationalist candidates were highly successful. Even in uncontested seats some official candidates were voted out by a majority of 'No' votes. In all, the Communist Party fared well, 80 per cent of the official CPSU candidates won and 87 per cent of the Congress were members of the party. Importantly, however, in the Russian Republic the official party candidates fared noticeably less well than the average. (See Kotz with Weir 1997: 100–1; Gill and Markwick 2000: 64–5.)

Meeting for the first time, in May 1989, the Congress elected Gorbachev as chairman of the Supreme Soviet, termed 'president' by the media (Kotz with Weir 1997: 102). Six months later Gorbachev began the process of changing the constitution, the debate revolving around the advantages of the American presidential system and the semi-presidentialism of the French Fifth Republic (Huskey 2001a: 30).[2] The model favoured was that of semi-presidentialism. The advantage for the president was to lift him above the day-to-day running of government, but other important lessons from the French system were missed. The effect of the large size of the Congress of People's Deputies and its relationship with the president was hardly considered. The relevance of the timing of elections for unifying the executive and ensuring a presidential mandate was also not understood. The issue of the direct popular election of the president as opposed to indirect election by parliament was understood, but the expedient of indirect election for the first election only proved a mistake, denying Gorbachev the popular mandate, which had he gained as he was likely to do, would have strengthened his position *vis-à-vis* Yeltsin (Kotz with Weir 1997: 106).

In March 1990, the Congress voted to amend Article 6 of the Soviet Constitution and so to remove the Communist Party's right to rule and a presidential system was formalized (Kotz with Weir 1997: 106). The first opposition party, the Democratic Union, having been founded in early May 1988, by the end of 1990, following the amendment to Article 6, an astonishing 500 or so parties had been founded, though 'most no more than "couch" parties whose entire membership could fit comfortably on a single divan' (Sakwa 1998: 210).

Not only had Gorbachev's reforms led to the founding of the Democratic Union back in 1988 and large numbers of associations by 1989, his reforms had also opened the way for a workers' movement to develop and for strikes to increase. These strikes had culminated in the miners' strike of 1989, which demonstrated that pressures for reform had now moved out of government's control (Sakwa 1998: 208). In the non-Russian republics, national movements developed too. The largest mass movement of all coalesced around environmental issues (ibid.: 210), given impetus by the Chernobyl nuclear power station disaster of 1986 which had done so much to highlight the inadequacies of the communist system and the special problems that flowed from lack of openness.

In 1990, legislatures for each of the fifteen Union republics were created. In what Huskey (2001a: 33) calls a 'fateful concession' this semi-presidential scheme was copied in the republics. It broke the central control system. Following elections to these legislatures, Yeltsin became chairman of the Russian Republic parliament, elected to the position by the parliament in May 1990; in July he resigned from the Communist Party (Kotz with Weir 1997: 136). In June, the parliament had provocatively passed a law granting itself sovereignty over the Russian Republic. By October, six other republics had followed Russia and passed sovereignty resolutions. Responding to these pressures, Gorbachev held a referendum on the Union, in March 1991, and the result was overwhelming support for preserving Soviet federation. (See Kotz with Weir 1997: 144–7). In 1991, the Russian Republic independently introduced a direct popular election of their president and popular elections for city mayors. Yeltsin became president of the Russian Republic after winning the popular election held in June 1991 (Gill and Markwick 2000: 123–4). With the Russian Republic claiming sovereignty and Yeltsin's stand for a capitalist democratic system pitted against Gorbachev's stand for a socialist democracy, a situation of dual power developed, which led to a military coup in August 1991. The coup failed, but it opened the way for Yeltsin to oust Gorbachev.

The attempted coup in August 1991 was defeated by Yeltsin's and the Russian parliament's stand against it. The coup had been triggered by the imminent signing of the new Union treaty, negotiated by Gorbachev and designed to give more powers to the republics. Other members of his government, those who participated in the coup, wanted to retain a strong central government. Though announcing the intention to maintain a role for 'private enterprise' and making no mention of the Communist Party, their actions were perceived as a move to return to the old ways of the Soviet Union and this was why Yeltsin, who was pro-capitalist, proved the leading opposition to the coup. The event demonstrated the lack of support for the coup but also highlighted the lack of support for Gorbachev. Yeltsin grabbed the advantage and declared the Russian Republic independent. Within days he had forced Gorbachev to resign as head of the CPSU, to dissolve the party Central Committee, to disband the Soviet Congress of People's Deputies and to transfer authority to the presidents of the republics and a legislative council. (See Kotz with Weir 1997: 149–52.)

Within Yeltsin's Russian Republic the Communist Party was banned on 6 November 1991 (Sakwa 1998: 105). As other republics declared their independence, the Union fell apart and the formation of the Commonwealth of Independent States was announced. On 25 December 1991, Gorbachev resigned and on the last day of 1991 the Soviet Union formally passed into history. Within the Commonwealth of Independent States (CIS), Russia (strictly the Russian Federation), which covered three-quarters of the area and 50 per cent of the population of the old Soviet Union, was by far the largest and most dominant of the fifteen states (Kotz with Weir 1997: 157).

Making comparisons

Having loosened the chains on Eastern Europe, the Soviet Union had itself fallen to the chain reaction of ending Communist Party rule that had begun in 1989. The Soviet Union at the end of 1991, however, stood in stark contrast to East Germany at the end of 1989. East Germany had been but part of one nation while the Soviet Union was an empire of nationalities. Crucially, too, under the Weimar Republic Germany had once been a democracy and the Basic Law, operating successfully in West Germany since 1949, had been designed for the event of reunification and was ready and waiting for the return of democracy to East Germany. In contrast the Soviet Union not only lacked a democratic tradition and a blueprint for democracy it also lacked a practised guiding hand.

Lacking a democratic tradition, Gorbachev's recent reforms aside, at the start of 1992 Russians were faced with a situation which may be compared with the situations after the revolutions in France, 1789, and

Russia, February 1917. What the Russian Federation held in common with these cases was, as explained in Chapter 2, what de Tocqueville had identified as the crucial difference between France and America in the late eighteenth and first half of the nineteenth century. In France, de Tocqueville argued, everyone was so used to the state having control that the people did not have the initiative to act in concert to further their interests, always turning to the state to do things. In America, in contrast, they had this capacity to act in concert, to come together in groups to further their common interests. Though Gorbachev's reforms had unleashed informal groups and new social movements and then parties these did not constitute the kind of civil society that de Tocqueville had in mind.

As Sakwa (1998: 209) comments, 'When *perestroika* finally allowed popular re-engagement with the political process, the institutional framework was lacking to structure this activity and to allow it to take system-integrative forms.' This helps to explain the fragmentation that developed so quickly, producing 500 parties by 1990. Crucially, the majority of the new organizations that burst forth under perestroika were not interest groups, as such, but 'ideas' groups (ibid.: 210). In clarification, Sakwa offers Marsh's (1983: 3) contrast between interest and ideological (ideas) groups. Made in respect of economic groups, interest groups, Marsh explains, 'protect and promote the specific economic interests of their members' whereas ideological groups 'promote or defend legislative or administrative change for ideological reasons rather than to forward their members' particular financial interests'. Interest groups not ideas groups were what de Tocqueville had in mind for democracy.

Following Weber's analysis, as explained in Chapter 5, what Russia at the start of 1992 also compared with was Imperial Germany where the dominant state undermined initiative in the economic system. Russia lacked strong independent entrepreneurs and had no real experience and understanding of the market system outside of the black economy (Gustafson 1999: 109–22). The weight of bureaucracy in both economic and political spheres presented obstacles to both western capitalism and liberal democracy. Indeed, the short interlude of perestroika aside, the case to which Russia in 1991 came closest of all in respect of the economy was Germany after the fall of the Third Reich where Nazism, with its controls on prices and labour, had destroyed the market.

While post-Soviet Russia faced these great historical disadvantages for democracy, it had, in theory at least, the enormous advantage of stepping on to the path of democracy and into a capitalist system at a time when the examples of capitalist democracies were plentiful and thriving. Furthermore, the richness of variety in their political institutions and structures potentially offered suitable models for adaptation for the peculiarities of the Russian case. In addition, modern western capitalism had grown from strength to strength and not only indicated practical lessons to apply, but as for democracy, came with a plethora of theoretical analysis. Furthermore, Yeltsin had a clear idea of Russia's objective: the kind of capitalist democracy found in the West (Kotz with Weir 1997: 158; Tolz 2000: 203).

Post-Soviet Russia: under Yeltsin

The economy: shock therapy

The decision taken by Yeltsin, once in power, was to move, at speed, to transform the economy from state control to modern market capitalism. This policy, spearheaded by Gaidar and declared in a speech by Yeltsin in October 1991, was popularly known as 'shock therapy' (Reddaway and Glinski 2001: 233). Shock therapy was not simply the reintroduction of the market through an end to price-fixing and labour control, it also involved the application of monetarist policies, as advocated by rightist western governments and Chicago school economists, such as Milton Friedman, so fashionable in the 1980s. Furthermore, the Harvard professor Jeffrey Sachs had begun advising the Polish government in 1989 along the lines of shock therapy policies, earlier applied to Bolivia. The International Monetary Fund backed these policies for Eastern Europe's transition to capitalism and a series of meetings were held with the IMF in the autumn of 1991 (Kotz with Weir 1997: 166–8).

The objective of shock therapy was to achieve western capitalism as speedily as possible and to achieve this the therapy had five aims: the end of price-fixing; a balanced government budget; 'denationalization'; an end to all state-control through the central allocation of resources; and free trade. The end of price-fixing entailed prices to be determined by a free market, in all commodities other than fuel, and this included the value of the currency, the rouble. The balanced budget was to be achieved through reductions both in the money supply and in government spending, which together were taken to end inflation. Denationalization of state-owned enterprises, including banks, involved their being turned from organizations seeking plan-fulfilment to ones seeking profits and, eventually, full privatization was intended. Ending all state-control through the central allocation of resources amounted to an end to state-planning. Free trade involved the removal of barriers both to trade in goods and in investment in international markets. (See Kotz with Weir 1997: 162–3.)

As a strategy for transforming the Soviet economy, the policies of shock therapy were diametrically opposed to Gorbachev's ideas of restructuring. Perestroika was gradualist and managed by the state. The view taken in post-Soviet Russia was that perestroika had demonstrably failed and this contributed to the mood for speed in dismantling the old system and replacing it with the new one. The naivety was in the assumption that the spirit of free enterprise, never abounding in the Soviet Union, or indeed in Tsarist Russia before it, had lain dormant, waiting for the opportunity to spring into action.

Shock therapy began to be implemented in January 1992 with state controls on prices, both wholesale and retail, removed straightaway in 80 and 90 per cent of cases, respectively. Prices soared immediately, breaking all IMF predictions. In February all the remaining shock therapy policies were put in place. In March a 24-million dollar aid package to Russia was announced by US President Bush and German Chancellor Kohl (Kotz with Weir 1997: 169). By December 1992, 47,000 state companies had been privatized, rising to 90,000 by the end of 1993. By the end of 1994, 78.5 per cent of industrial output was being produced by non-state enterprises and these firms accounted for 69.9 per cent of industrial employment. The overwhelming number of these firms were sold not openly but secretively. (See Kotz with Weir 1997: 168–72; Reddaway and Glinski 2001: 248.) Soon, import restrictions were lifted, completely.

The effect of this therapy on the Russian economy, however, produced an unexpected shock to everyone, including western economic theorists. Instead of the predicted rise in production, production went into severe decline (Kotz with Weir 1997: 173). Based on 1991, by the end of 1995, Gross Domestic Product had fallen by 42 per cent; by the middle of 1995, industrial production had declined by 46 per cent, agricultural output by 32 per cent; by the end of 1994, investment had fallen by 61 per cent (ibid.: 174). These figures clearly compare unfavourably with the performance of the German economy from 1945 to 1949. Not only that, they also represent significantly worse economic conditions than those experienced in America in the four years after the 1929 Great Crash (ibid.).

In the Soviet Union, inflation ran at below 2 per cent per annum, but hit 5–6 per cent for the year in 1990 and continued to rise in 1991. In the Russian Federation, annual inflation for 1993 was 842 per cent (Bank of Finland 2003). In 1995, the figure was down to 131 per cent for the year (ibid.) but by then real earnings had fallen to 48 per cent of what they had been in 1990 (Kotz with Weir 1997: 179). Furthermore, these declines were additionally aggravated by the growing tendency to pay wages late, sometimes months late, and sometimes paying less than the expected sum (ibid.: 180). Those living on pensions suffered even greater declines in their real incomes (ibid.).

Exacerbating the fall in living standards the level of public services also declined. The government subsidy to health care was cut, sharply (Kotz with Weir 1997: 183–4); the consequences were outbreaks of epidemics in diseases such as cholera and diphtheria (ibid.). Between 1991 and 1994, life expectancy fell dramatically (ibid.: 186). Adding to all this, levels of crime escalated and mafia-style organized crime developed (ibid.: 184). At the same time the murder rate doubled, with figures similar to those in South Africa and twice as high as those in the United States (Rutland and Kogan 2001: 141). Along with crime came bribery and corruption. The Interior Ministry estimated that during those years organized crime controlled 30–40 per cent of the Russian economy (ibid.). Four years after the decision for shock therapy, inequality between rich and poor had grown markedly: the ratio between the top 10 per cent and bottom 10 per cent of households at 4.5 to 1 in 1967, the ratio had reached 13.5 to 1 in 1995 (Kotz with Weir 1997: 183).

In short, the chaos and decline of the economy in Russia four years on from the fall of communism could not have differed more markedly from the economy in Germany four years after 1945 where Erhard's 'social market economy' was taking effect.

The political system: toying with liberal democracy

Though, initially, large numbers of political parties arose, in 1992 they grouped around three main policy positions, essentially related to positions on shock therapy: the 'radical reformers'; the 'centrists'; and the 'red-brown' alliance. The 'radical reformers' (or 'democrats' as the media called them) were followers of Yeltsin and the arch free-market capitalist, Gaidar. The grouping of 'centrists' opposed shock therapy and supported gradual transition to a market economy. The 'red-brown' alliance (as their opponents called them) was a coalition grouping of communists and nationalists united in opposition to Yeltsin's policies. (See Kotz with Weir 1997: 206.) The Communist Party, outlawed in the Russian Federation until the ban was lifted in February 1993, was initially a grouping of several different parties, but the revived Communist Party, the Communist Party of the Russian Federation (CPRF), quickly came to dominate and then moved away from the nationalist alliance. The CPRF soon became the party with the largest membership in Russia (ibid.: 207).

Opposition to Yeltsin's shock therapy grew, as its failures became ever more pressing. December 1992 to October 1993 is labelled as a time of *dvoevlastvie*, 'dyarchy' or dual power (Dunlop 2001: 54). In December 1992, the parliament tried, unsuccessfully, to weaken the presidency but the prime minister was replaced and a referendum on constitutional change was promised for April 1993. In March 1993, some of Yeltsin's powers were removed and the parliament came close to impeaching him. Relations between the president and parliament went from bad to worse. The April referendum was turned into a referendum on Yeltsin's popularity (Kotz with Weir 1997: 212–13). The result was equivocal; 58.7 per cent voted 'Yes' to having confidence in Yeltsin but this represented only 37.3 per cent of the electorate (Gill and Markwick 2000: 159).

In September 1993, under presidential decree, Yeltsin dissolved the Russian parliament (both the Congress of People's Deputies and the Supreme Soviet), saying that parliamentary elections would be held on 12 December when a new constitution would also be ratified (Dunlop 2001: 56). On 3–4 October, he ordered tanks against the parliament and arrested deputies who had resisted (Kotz with Weir 1997: 211). Yeltsin then suspended the constitutional court and suspended both local and regional legislatures. He then replaced regional administrators who had shown opposition to him and forced the resignation of the leader of the trade union federation. He then banned some communist and some nationalist organizations and closed down fifteen newspapers (ibid.: 214). Abandoning the consultation process for designing a new constitution, a new constitution was drafted by a small group of Yeltsin's advisers without any public consultation at all. The constitution was to be voted on in the December 1993 election.

The 1993 Constitution

While the semi-presidential structure of Russian government was formally retained (Huskey 2001a: 37) in the new draft constitution, Yeltsin moved in favour of a very strong presidency: 'with powers that far exceed those of any head of state in an established democracy' (Tolz 2000: 192). Indeed, the strong presidency went squarely against the practices of the French Fifth Republic where under the 'cohabitation' of president and prime minister from different parties the French president adopted a less political and more ceremonial role, deferring to the majority in parliament. Huskey (2001a: 36) comments, 'The French case serves as a reminder that institutional arrangements succeed or fail in large measure because of the willingness of elites to forge compromises in the available constitutional space.' In Russia, however, along with the strong president came a very weak, primarily advisory parliament (Federal Assembly), weaker than any found in contemporary democracies (Kotz with Weir 1997: 214; Tolz 2000: 196). The upper house was to be called the Federation Council, the lower house to be called the State Duma. Ominously, Duma was the name of the powerless parliaments under Tsar Nicholas II and of the ineffectual parliament of the Provisional Government of 1917.

In Sartori's classification, Russia, under the 1993 Constitution, though a version of the semi-presidential system, like the Fifth French Republic, is one 'on the extreme edge of the category' (Sartori 1997: 138, fn 9). There is a president and a prime minister, but the president appoints the prime minister. The 1993 Constitution gave the president rights of decree, which were more likely to be used because the passing of laws by the Federal Assembly was made more difficult by the constitutional requirement for the support of a majority of the membership of each house, not just of those present and voting (as in Gorbachev's design) (Kotz with Weir 1997: 215). Crucially, not only does the constitution permit presidential decrees, it does not make clear whether presidential decree or parliamentary law should take precedence where the two contradict; and practice has given preference to presidential decrees (Tolz 2000: 196).

In addition to presidential decrees, under the constitution the president also has strong veto powers. To overturn a presidential veto two-thirds of the total membership of each house is required, again not only of those present and voting (Kotz with Weir 1997: 215). The president appoints the prime minister but if the Duma rejects the nomination three times the president may dissolve parliament and call new elections (Sartori 1997: 138–9, fn 9). A highly unusual additional power given to the president was that if the lower house passes a vote of no confidence in the government twice then the president can dissolve the parliament (Kotz with Weir 1997: 215).

The president was also given direct control of the ministries of security, defence, internal affairs and foreign affairs, leaving the prime minister, therefore, with only partial control over cabinet ministers (Tolz 2000: 197). The one clear role given to the parliament is the passage of the budget (Kotz with Weir 1997: 215), though even here the government's consent is required (Tolz 2000: 197). As Tolz comments,

> Many sweeping powers accorded to the Russian president (the right to appoint leading members of the government, to dominate foreign policy, and to dissolve parliament, for example) are similar to those of the president of the French Fifth Republic, especially as interpreted by Charles de Gaulle.
>
> (Tolz 2000: 197)

But, she adds, 'Yet the French National Assembly retained the essential parliamentary function in a democracy – the right to monitor the activities of the government' (ibid.). Sartori's (1997: 138–9, fn 9) concern with the design is also, as he explains, that 'when a president does not control a majority in the Duma, the executive-parliament relation is left to confrontation'. From observation of practice, Ostrow (2002: 49–50) confirms that the failure of the design of the constitution to build links between the legislature and executive and so to promote compromise and cooperation has led not to conflict management, a purpose of democratic government, but to its opposite, to the promotion of conflict.

The electoral system chosen was 'loosely modelled after the German system' (Moser 2001: 196), a mixed system of plurality and proportional representation with voters casting two ballots. Half of the seats in the State Duma are filled in proportion to votes for parties or electoral blocs on party lists, the other 225 seats filled by first-past-the-post votes cast for single member constituencies. For the proportionate party votes a 5 per cent threshold applied. For the plurality constituency vote, candidates could stand as independents or as party members (Kotz with Weir 1997: 208). Unlike the German case, the system does not use the PR results to compensate for disproportionality produced by the plurality vote (Moser 2001: 196).[3]

Approval of this constitution required a minimum of 50 per cent of those eligible to vote in the December election. Most of the opposition parties, including the Communist Party, were opposed to the constitution on the grounds of its being undemocratic. There was one major exception, the, oddly named, anti-western, nationalist party, the Liberal Democratic Party of Russia (LDPR). In the December election, the constitution won approval with 58.4 per cent of the votes, on a 54.8 per cent turnout. It is questionable, however, whether the turnout actually reached 50 per cent, the official figure of the electorate being revised down after the votes were returned. (See Dunlop 2001: 58–9; Kotz with Weir 1997: 215.)

The constitution in practice

The first parliamentary elections in independent Russia, in December 1993, produced a win for opposition parties. The largest number of seats in the Duma went to the communist grouping but with so many parties standing this represented only just over one-fifth of the seats. In the 1995 elections, the communist grouping increased their share to 41.6 per cent of the seats, remaining by far the largest group, with support for the centrists down from 9.3 per cent of the seats in 1993 (when Democratic Party and Women of Russia) to only 1.8 per cent in 1995 (when Congress of Russian Communities and Women of Russia). Vying with the centrists in opposition to shock therapy but more cautious in criticism of the government was the Yabloko Party, which gained ground over the centrists with 10 per cent of the seats in 1995. The pro-government party, Russia's Choice, won 16.9 per cent of the seats in 1993, falling to 14.2 per cent in 1995 (when Our Home is Russia together with Democratic Choice of Russia). The nationalist LDPR won 14 per cent of the seats in 1993, going down to 11.3 per cent in 1995. (See Kotz with Weir 1997: 207–9.)

Though opposition parties held the overwhelming share of the seats in both the 1993 and 1995 parliaments, parliament, as explained, lacked sufficient constitutional power to change government policies. This was made only too clear following Yeltsin's decision to take military action against the breakaway republic of Chechnya in 1994 (Tolz 2000: 192). In that decision even the prime minister and his cabinet were bypassed in favour of the National Security Council, a presidential body (Kotz with Weir 1997: 216). As the changing names of parties and groupings illustrate they are not organized in a permanent way.

The one exception to the electoral system's failure to develop strong parties has been the Communist Party, CPRF. Furthermore, contrary to Yeltsin's claims, the Communist Party evolved from a party challenging the political system to one working as a party competing within the system. As Brown (2001a: 515) comments, 'Contrary to the pronouncements of Boris Yeltsin, the CPRF became, increasingly, a within-system party – especially in the second half of the 1990s – and a useful safety-valve for the discontent of many millions of Russian citizens.' As the changing alliances also suggest, the parties were incapable of forming lasting coalitions (Rose's (2001) 'floating party system'). It is, however, fair to point out that in both the 1993 and 1995 parliaments the factions were more organized than under Gorbachev; in being more disciplined, the factions also demonstrated a capacity for internal party discipline (Tolz 2000: 200). Lacking incentives, therefore, to form coalitions within the weak parliament, the power of the president went unchecked.

Under Yeltsin, the power of the president rose as his popularity fell and the balance between authoritarianism and democracy, inherent in the constitution, moved in favour of authoritarianism. This was at its most glaring in 1998 when he unconstitutionally dismissed the prime minister and his entire cabinet (Tolz 2000: 196). It was also especially evident during the war in Chechnya, 1994–97 when unconstitutional methods were used to keep in power (Kotz with Weir 1997: 192). Nevertheless, Yeltsin continued to preserve some important aspects of democracy. He did not annul the 1993 elections, which produced such high numbers of opposition members of parliament, and neither did he annul the 1995 elections, as many thought he might. He also showed willingness to compromise with parliamentary opposition (ibid.: 193). Between 1994 and 1997, parliamentary deputies and representatives of the president worked together, several times, on joint commissions to find mutually agreeable solutions, including negotiations for all federal budgets, the Civic Code and the laws on local self-government and the elections to the State Duma, which, importantly, were held (Remington 1998: 206–7; Tolz 2000: 200). Negotiations also played a crucial role in achieving compromises in the drawing up of treaties between the centre and the regions (Tolz 2000: 200). Yeltsin also went ahead with the presidential elections in 1996, which he won (though with some electoral irregularities) and in December 1996 all top regional leaders in

Russia were freely elected and no longer appointed by the president (ibid.: 193–4).

Unfair elections and public opinion

Free and fair elections are an essential part of representative democracy but in Russia, though elections were essentially free they were not always fair. For example, during the 1996 presidential elections, Yeltsin had 75 per cent of the press coverage and 90 per cent of the television coverage (Tolz 2000: 194). There was also evidence that local governors were permitted to introduce electoral laws that disadvantaged their rivals and allegations of falsification of returns at polling stations are made, regularly (ibid.).[4] The heavy financial backing of election campaigns by business interests closely tied to the government through their benefits obtained through shock therapy policies also undermined popular trust (ibid.: 198). As Brown (2001b: 564) remarks, 'Those, whether in Russia or the West, who have insisted on calling post-Soviet Russia a democracy have unwittingly undermined support for democracy, since the attitude of a majority of Russians has been: "If *this* is democracy, we don't want it."'

In an opinion poll carried out in August 1997, in answer to the question 'Who do you believe runs Russia?', 52 per cent selected the answer ' the mafia, organized crime' (Rutland and Kogan 2001: 140). In a survey conducted in February 1999 by the All-Russian Centre for the Study of Public Opinion (VTsIOM), 94 per cent of respondents thought the federal government was doing a bad or a very bad job of 'guaranteeing timely payment of wages, salaries and pensions'. Ninety-three per cent thought the government was doing a bad or very bad job of providing 'social protection of the unemployed, homeless, and needy'; 92 per cent thought the government was doing a bad or very bad job of 'fighting organized crime'; 87 per cent thought the government was doing a bad or very bad job of 'maintaining law and order'. Importantly, when asked if the country was heading in the 'right direction' only 6 per cent thought that it was and 71 per cent said the country was heading in the wrong direction. (See Dunlop 2001: 67.)

Economic collapse

The adverse reaction to Yeltsin's 'democracy' is hardly surprising given the continuing deterioration of economic and social conditions in Russia. In 1998, GNP per capita had declined to almost half what it had been in 1990 and unemployment levels had risen to 12 per cent of the economically active population, six times higher than in 1990 (Smirnov 2001: 520). While, as Smirnov comments, 'the cruel social-economic reforms of the 1990s' brought 'fantastic riches' to 3–4 per cent of the population, more than 70 per cent of Russians had been 'brutally impoverished' (ibid.). As evidence of the drop in living standards, between 1990 and 1997: consumption of meat had fallen by 35 per cent, of milk by 41 per cent, of eggs by 31 per cent (Dunlop 2001: 67). As further evidence of the worsening economic and social conditions, the number of deaths registered for the year 1997 had risen to 2 million as compared with the 1.6 million recorded for 1991 (ibid.). By the summer of 1998, the economy had revealed the 'complete exhaustion' of the monetarist policies that lay at the heart of shock therapy (Simonia 2001: 281).

Rather than producing a vibrant modern money economy with low inflation, as the theory had promised, shock therapy had produced a shadow economy under a barter system. Furthermore, this black market had grown so important that by 1998 even conservative estimates put it as comprising more than half of the economy (Simonia 2001: 282). Furthermore, instead of being pumped back into the Russian economy, profits were largely going into investments abroad. In addition, the budget, rather than being balanced, as the model required, was in increasing deficit (ibid.). Being unable to print money as forbidden by the model, following the shift made in 1995 the government financed the budget through loans (ibid.). In the same year privatization of state property became the order of the day. The outcome for the Russian economy was what the international financier George Soros called a 'system of bandit capitalism' (Smirnov 2001: 520). The greed which propelled the selling and purchase of state property concentrated economic power in the hands of a group of very wealthy 'oligarchs' (Peregudov 2001 passim). Furthermore, these oligarchs sought short-term profit over longer term investments with devastating consequences for the Russian economy. Smirnov (2001: 520) estimates that 'the old-new elite' channelled 'at least $US 300 billion' out of Russia in the years following privatization.

By August 1998, the state was on the edge of bankruptcy (Simonia 2001: 282). In 1998, external debt rose to a high of 158 billion dollars (Bank of Finland 2003). In March 1998, Yeltsin had dismissed the prime minister, Chernomyrdin; Kiriyenko replaced him on 17 August 1998, the government defaulted on its foreign debts and massively devalued the rouble (ibid.: 283). In September, Kiriyenko was dropped and replaced as prime minister by Primakov.

Changing fortunes

Under the new Primakov government, with the rouble devalued, the economy adopted a new strategy, moving from one geared to self-enrichment to one more concerned with 'socially oriented economic reforms' (Simonia 2001: 284). A thorough overhaul of the banking system occurred, new laws on investments were introduced to help stem the flow of money abroad, and the 'development' budget at 21.6 billion roubles was five times larger than in recent years (ibid.: 285). Crucially, the aim was to support only efficient industries, those increasing exports, those competitive on the domestic market and those of strategic importance (ibid.). In spite of Primakov's popularity in the opinion polls, or rather perhaps because of it, Yeltsin replaced the prime minister yet again; in May 1999, Stepashin was installed in Primakov's place. Only three months later, in August, Yeltsin dismissed Stepashin and Putin became prime minister of the Russian government.

Elections

Parliamentary elections went ahead as scheduled in December 1999. The outcome was that the CPRF, the Communist Party, continued to hold the largest number of seats in the Duma. Holding 127 seats this was, nevertheless, a loss of 31 seats from the 1995 election. It was the centrists, a grouping of parties, who took the largest share of seats. Of these the Unity Party gained 81 seats and the Fatherland-All Russia Bloc, OVR, led by Luzhkov and Primakov, gained 71 seats. Importantly, the Unity Party, which was newly formed, had links with Putin (Huskey 2001b: 86) whereas Fatherland-All Russia had been set up in 1998 as a consequence of a split from Yeltsin and his supporters (Brudny 2001: 159). At the same time, support for the Nationalists fell; the Liberal Democratic Party of Russia (LDPR) won only 18 seats, down from 51 seats in 1995. Support for the grouping of Liberals remained similar overall but Yabloko's seats fell from 45 in 1995 to 21 in 1999 and the Union of Rightist Forces, SPS, gained 31 seats, for the first time. The numbers of seats held by independents increased from 77 in 1995 to 85 in 2000. (See Brudny 2001: 170.)

Following the parliamentary elections, Yeltsin announced his decision to retire on 31 December 1999, six months before the presidential elections were due (Huskey 2001b: 85). Putin, as prime minister of the Russian government became the acting president. In a shortened election campaign, the constitution requiring the elections to be held within three months of the resignation, Putin won the presidential election, in March 2000 (ibid.). What is more, he won the election with 52.9 per cent of the votes, thereby avoiding the run-off; the CPRF candidate, Zyuganov, came second with 21 per cent of the votes (Brudny 2001: 173).[5]

Post-Soviet Russia: under Putin

The economy

Once in office, Putin sought quickly to restore the economy. Benefiting from the massive devaluation of August 1998 and the move to 'more socially oriented economic reforms' the economy began to turn around. In respect of the balance of trade, while imports remained similar in 2000 and 2001 to those in the Yeltsin years (48.8 billion and 59.7 billion euros respectively as compared with a range between 33.1 billion and 63.7 billion euros for the years 1992–99), exports have soared. In a range of between 41.2 billion and 78.8 billion euros between 1992 and 1999, in 2000 and 2001 exports were at 114.8 and 114.7 respectively. Similar dramatic improvements are also to be found in the rate of growth of Gross Domestic Product. In negative growth for all but one of the years 1992–98 and in 1999 at +5.4 per cent, in 2000 the score was +9 per cent and in 2001 +5 per cent. (In 1992 GDP had been –14.5 per cent.) These figures were reflected in industrial production (at its lowest in 1994 at –20.9 per cent, but at +11.9 and +4.9 in 2000 and 2001) and in fixed investments (at its lowest in 1992 at –40 per cent and at +17.4 per cent and +8.7 per cent in 2000 and 2001, respectively). The balance of federal government revenues and expenditures also improved, moving into the black in 2000 for the first time and improving further in 2001. (See Bank of Finland 2003.)

While levels of unemployment did not change much, ranging from 4.9 to 11.8 per cent from 1992 to 1999 and being at 9 per cent in 2001, inflation returned to manageable levels. At its highest in 1993, at 842 per cent, and down to 11 per cent in 1997 but rising again to 84 per cent in 1998 and at 37 per cent in 1999, in 2000 the rate stood at 20 per cent, down slightly to 19 per cent in 2001. (See Bank of Finland 2003.) The evidence of continuing improvements has been added to by the fall of the importance of the black market (Sapir 2002: 11). At the same time, Russia's foreign debt remains high, at 144 billion dollars in 2000, down to 133 billion dollars in 2001. This compares with a high of 158 billion dollars in 1998. Crucially too, as Sapir (2002: 8) comments, 'even in 2001, Russia still is a tremendously impoverished country by comparison with its 1991 situation' and questions also remain over possible future threats to the Russian economy.[6]

Putin also addressed the problems created by the 'oligarchs', the business tycoons who had profited so handsomely from the shock therapy policies through buying state enterprises at give-away prices. These oligarchs had undermined the state through their failure to reinvest their profit back into Russia, preferring instead to make lucrative foreign investments. They had also compounded their undermining of the state through their tax evasions, their control of 'key media outlets' and their corruption (Huskey 2001b: 91). In May 2001, the leading oligarch, Gusinsky, was arrested and charged with embezzlement. Gusinsky was the head of Media-Most, which owned newspapers and the NTV television network. Arrest warrants were also issued against oligarchs of other top companies. These high-profile attacks, while selective, had the effect of reassuring the public that Putin was tackling crime and corruption and instituting the rule of law (ibid.: 92). As Brown (2001b: 566) comments, however, 'selective application of the law is very different from the rule of law'.[7]

A federal system

As well as tackling the economy Putin also sought to restore political order. Immediately on gaining office, he set about creating a new federal structure, dividing the country into seven entirely new federal administrative districts, *okrugs*, and appointing new presidential representatives (or commissioners, *polpred*) to each. Putin's presidential decree on 'The Status of the Plenipotentiary Representative of the President in a Federal District', was issued only days after his coming to office (Kahn 2001: 381). These seven presidential representatives were given seats on the Security Council, the existing twenty-four-seat presidential body, and were given the role of ensuring the observance of federal laws and the conformity of regional laws to the federal constitution (Huskey 2001b: 91).

Under Yeltsin, the regions had been given considerable autonomy over their affairs and had been allowed to write their own constitutions and charters (Kahn 2001: 381). This was consistent with a spirit of democracy, quite in line with the examples of eighteenth-century America and Germany after the Second World War, but as the Founding Fathers recognized and Article 31 of the Basic Law made so explicit in its abrupt 'Federal law overrides *Land* law' it is essential that contradictory decisions are not placed on central and state statute books. The result of Yeltsin's failure to establish this elementary rule was that by the mid-1990s the number of laws and constitutional clauses that were in contradiction of the federal constitution and the federal law ran into thousands. In 1996, it was announced by the Ministry of Justice that nineteen of the twenty-one republican constitutions violated the federal constitution. Somewhat belatedly, at the end of July 1999, a new federal law had come into force, which had gone some way to address the problem, but the regions were given three years before they had to comply. (See Kahn 2001: 381.)

Further decrees soon followed to strengthen the presidential representatives' hands, five of whom were generals (Kahn 2001: 382). Putin's aims were to establish a proper federal structure with, as he explained, 'an effective vertical chain of command' (Putin quoted by Huskey 2001b: 89). As Putin said at the time, 'It's a scandalous thing – just think about the figures – a fifth of the legal acts adopted in the regions contradict the country's basic law' (ibid.). The cosy relationships that had developed between presidential representatives and the provincial authorities were to be broken up (ibid.: 88).

In many ways, the effect of achieving a fresh start and breaking down traditional allegiances was similar to the Allies re-drawing the boundaries of the German Länder in 1945. In Russia, with its nationalities, there was an additional effect, ethnic cleavages were cross-cut. Crucially, Putin's new federal structure enabled the strengthening of the central state over the regions. But, while the aims may have been in line with Hamilton's after the American War of Independence, the Founding Fathers in their careful construction of checks and balances of power would never have entertained Putin's system which gave the president the means to undermine opposition to his policies through the removal of elected officials, who could be suspended under investigations, which were subject to long delays (Huskey 2001b: 90).

While presidents of the republics and the regional governors were given greater control over their areas through increased powers to dismiss mayors and heads of district governments who failed to abide by provincial or federal legislation, the President of the Russian Federation (Putin) was given powers to dismiss the republican presidents and regional governors. Furthermore, the Russian President was also given power to regulate, directly, 'the details of the structures of local government' in cities of more than 50,000 (Huskey 2001b: 90). Yet more significantly, Putin introduced a bill to change the composition of the upper house under which the ex officio members, the eighty-nine republican presidents and regional governors and the ninety-three provincial politicians were to be removed from the Federation Council (ibid.). As Huskey (ibid.: 91) comments, 'One need only imagine the consequences for American federalism if the framers had made the governors of the states members of the US Senate.' The consequences, of course, would have been to undermine the benefits that flowed from the balance and separation of powers. After debate and a conciliation committee meeting, the law came into effect in January 2002 (ibid.: fn 28).

Parties

Putin also sought to restore political order through a reduction in the number of political parties: 139 parties had stood in the 1999 elections to the Duma (Smirnov 2001: 527). A bill on political parties came into effect in June 2001. Its aim was to cut the number of registered parties, at that point standing at 197, down to between twenty and thirty, and the law therefore established the requirement that parties must be nationwide (*Keesing's Record* 2001: 44237). In February 2002, following plans made in April 2001, the Unity Party, the All Russia movement and the Fatherland Party voted at their congresses to dissolve their own organizations and to merge to become the new United Russia party.[8] In March the Unified Socialist Party was newly established. It merged a number of small parties and groups, including the Socialist Party and the Spiritual Heritage movement. Gorbachev had set up a new party in November 2001, the Social Democratic Party of Russia. Both the Socialist Party and the Spiritual Heritage movement had decided against joining forces with Gorbachev's new party. (See *Keesing's Record* 2002: 44468.) In March 2002, the Union of Rightist Forces, SPS, became the seventh party to register under the June 2001 law on political parties (ibid.: 44688).

Luzhkov, the leader of the Fatherland Party and mayor of Moscow, stated at the time of the setting up of the United Russia party that the new party would be the 'largest and most influential in the country' (*Keesing's Record* 2002: 44631). The combined parliamentary seats of the groups that made up the new United Russia party amounted to 240 out of the total 450 seats in the State Duma. The pro-Putin party then had more than half of the seats (ibid.: 44631). A president with majority support in the representative house has a basis for stable and effective democratic government, though the condition provides no guarantees. The major oppositions were: the liberal opposition; the Yabloko Party together with the SPS; and the communist opposition, made up of the CPRF (which had eighty-four seats) together with the Agro-Industrial Union (which held forty-three seats) (ibid.: 4631). Significantly, following United Russia's majority, Duma committee leaderships were taken away from the CPRF (ibid.).

The removal of communists from committee leaderships may indicate the beginnings of the institutionalization of conflict management. Hitherto, in the Duma all leaders of factions have had seats in the coordinating council for the legislatures and all factions have had both leadership positions and chair posts of committees (Ostrow 2002: 51). In Russia, ideas of democracy remain attached to the kinds of revolutionary ideals of mass democracy, with everyone's participation counting for something. As a consequence, however, there continues to be neither consistent party control nor the incentive for retaining a majority on the floor of the house, the condition that led to the Duma being 'plagued by chronic internal breakdown and deadlock' (ibid.: 51, and passim). As the histories of France in the nineteenth century and Germany in the twentieth century have shown, unstable parliaments are vulnerable to dictatorships.

Assessing post-Soviet Russia

Many adjectives have been applied to post-Soviet Russia's political system. For example, Dunlop (2001: 67) describes Russia as a 'proto-democracy', Diamond (1999: 10) as an 'electoral democracy' (in a class with Guatemala, Mozambique and Paraguay). Smirnov (2001: 529) has described it as 'the fledgling Russian democracy'. Chirikova and Lipina (2001: 396) conclude on the basis of examining the power structure in the regions that Russia constitutes a 'guided democracy', a 'manipulated democracy', a 'quasi-democracy' in which both authoritarian and democratic aspects are combined. Robinson (2003: 149) describes Russia as a 'partial democracy'. All of these adjectives are used to convey that Russia is not a western-type liberal democracy and that this is so because though the political system has some of the institutions of western-type liberal democracy, such as elections, the political system is also authoritarian. Simonia (2001) captures the argument particularly well:

> There is a myth that after the unsuccessful August 1991 coup democracy was established in Russia. This myth is supported by the simplistic idea that the presence of such attributes as regular parliamentary and presidential elections, numerous political parties, and a press and other media representing different points of view means the existence of democracy itself.
>
> (Simonia 2001: 268)

Evaluating post-Soviet Russia's democratization, to December 2000, Brown (2001b) concludes that Russia fulfils neither the necessary institutional guarantees of Dahl's polyarchy (the freedom to form and join organizations, freedom of expression and access to alternative sources of information, the right to vote in free and fair elections, and the right to compete for public office) nor the criteria which Brown adds of 'political accountability' and 'the rule of law'. Though impressed by the enormous, if uneven, advances made in the process of democratization since 1988, as compared with the history of the Soviet Union and Tsarist Russia to that point, Brown's assessment of Russia today is that of a 'hybrid political system, or mixed polity, combining elements of democracy, arbitrariness, and kleptocracy' (Brown 2001b: 564).

Like Dahl (1971, 1989) and like Simonia (2001), Brown's (2001b) essential concern is with the authoritarianism of the Russian system. Indeed, Brown (2001b: 568) comments that 'it would be no less misleading to label the contemporary regime "authoritarian" than to regard it as "democratic"'. Furthermore, he keeps open the possibility of either description being appropriate in ten years' time. Not only is the political system viewed as too authoritarian in being too 'top–down' in its decision-making, with its strong presidency, weak parliament, imposed centrally dominated federal system and underdeveloped civil society with insufficient access to independent information. The power of elected politicians is also viewed as undermined by unelected sources of power. In an argument reminiscent of the criticisms of the Soviet Union under communism combined with those found in Mills's (1956) power elite analysis of America, Reddaway (2002) argues that the power of Putin's presidency is undermined by that of the magnates (the oligarchs), the bureaucracy and the *siloviki*, a shadowy group of Russia's special services.

Comparative lessons: Russia and Germany

If post-Soviet Russia today displays too much authoritarianism in its political system to count as an example of a democracy, comparisons made with Germany after the Second World War, nevertheless, suggest some positive lessons. As discussed above, in post-war Germany too, new state boundaries were imposed before democratic government was inaugurated, some four years later. Favourable experiences of democracy at the local level and the promotion of democratic ideas were also imposed within Germany while, importantly too, at the same time extreme, anti-democratic organizations were immediately outlawed and, after 1949, extremist political parties were also judged illegal and banned. Consideration of post-war Germany, with its four years to the setting up of German central government, also draws attention to the importance of immediate needs, more pressing than that of establishing a democratic system. Achieving economic stability as a basis for economic growth is high on the list, as too is tackling the social problems that follow from economic crisis.

Comparisons between post-war Germany and Putin's Russia, however, should not be overdrawn. In Germany these impositions were made by the western Allied occupying forces, America, Britain and France, following the total defeat of the Nazi regime. Not only had Russia not been defeated in war but Stalinist totalitarianism had been changed from within, Gorbachev finally introducing major reforms, before the communist system was overthrown altogether. Rather than the clean slate of a complete absence of a political system, any changes in Russia had had to be made with the constraints of existing institutions and structures and vested interests.

Not only was there no political system in place in Germany in 1945, the Nazi regime had also destroyed the market economic system. The western Allies, therefore, also played a key role in the development of the modern capitalist system. In the special post-war conditions, planned reconstruction and social welfare constituted important considerations in the Allies' minds. In post-war Germany the western Allies, with their long experience of capitalist economies had guided the country out of its Nazi nightmare of wild schemes and central control over labour and commodity markets. Post-Soviet Russia had economic theories and examples of successful capitalist economies to follow, but outside the special circumstances of the post-war era, the fashion of the day had changed. Ideas of social welfare and state-guided capitalism, a mixed economy, could have built on ideas associated with Gorbachev's conception of socialist democracy. Such an approach would have fitted with the experiences and expectations of ordinary Russians used to post-Stalinist communism with equality of social and economic conditions and full employment meaningful principles as guidelines for policies.

At the end of 1991, however, the dominant economic ideas in the West were not Keynesian but monetarist, and had been so for some twenty or more years.[9] Where experience of running markets had existed before in Eastern Europe, as in Hungary, Poland, Bulgaria and Czechoslovakia, such policies might meet with success. In post-Soviet Russia, however, as has become clear, they unleashed not the modern capitalism which Weber saw as the natural basis for liberal democracy but the exploitative capitalism of personal enrichment. It was not the making of money through one's own hard work and the ascetic life of the spirit of capitalism (Weber 1991) but 'the get rich quick' attitude of the speculator, the oligarchs set on personal pleasure. Rather than leading to careful investments within the home economy the oligarchs concentrated their efforts on risky speculation on the international market. The morality of Gorbachev's ideas of socialist democracy, built on beliefs in the values of social equality, cooperation and caring, not the exploitation of the poor, could have served to constrain the activities of entrepreneurs. Though outside of Weber's thought, though not Tawney's (1938), such ideas on ways of behaving could, perhaps, have served, in the absence of a Protestant ethic, to constrain the conduct of entrepreneurs, reigning in the exploitative nature of capitalism and generating a spirit of modern capitalism. In Germany after the Second World War, levelling of living standards and ideas of good behaviour, 'guten ton', had served the country well in respect of both its development of a strong economy and its path to democracy.

Following the then fashionable monetarist theories in Russia under Yeltsin, such ideas of the value of a welfare state for preserving social equality and of the value of behaviour motivated, in significant part, by consideration of others, were relegated. From 1992, and in contradiction of the predictions of monetarist theorizing, the Russian economy, under Yeltsin, went into sharp decline. Investments had left the country and the gap between rich and poor had expanded with devastating consequences for the poor, made not simply financially worse off but now also lacking the welfare infrastructure that the communist system had provided. Under Putin, benefiting in part from the devaluation of 1998 and the turn to more socially oriented policies, the Russian economy, though impoverished as compared with levels in 1991, has seen notable improvements. Comparison with Germany suggests that achievements in improving the economy under Putin may serve positively to the establishment of democracy in Russia, in the longer term, so long, that is, that stable economic growth continues and welfare considerations remain active.

Given the dire economic conditions under Yeltsin, the real question that comparison between Germany and Russia raises, however, is not why Russia has, so far, failed to achieve democracy but how the political system managed to survive at all. There are, of course, no easy answers to this question. One comparative lesson that stands out is that Russia, in 1991, had the advantage over Germany in 1945, in not having a dislocated society, full of movement, with which the economic crisis could combine. The survival of Russia's political system also raises considerations about political climate similar to those raised about economic climate.

While the fashionable economic ideas of the time were monetarist, in politics the fashion in the 1980s and 1990s was for democracy. As Tolz (2000: 203) comments, 'In the late 1990s all political leaders in post-Communist countries have to recognize the compelling power of the idea of democracy.' The fashionable clothes of democracy – competitive elections being absolutely *de rigeur* – provide the right impression for generating the support of other countries and organizations beyond the particular country's border.[10] Designer fashion, as the French political system demonstrated in the nineteenth century, can, however, prove popular when everything else has been tried and tested and been found wanting.

Part V
Conclusion

Lessons for democracy

11 The struggle for modern democracy

This work on paths to democracy began with a method: the comparative historical analysis of the paths to democracy taken by three fertile cases – France, Russia and Germany – guided by hypotheses to include those from the discipline of politics and structured around the major political events of revolution, totalitarianism and democracy. The three fertile cases have each been shown 'wrapped in hypotheses' (Walton 1992) and, therefore, mutually valuable as controls. On the broadest level, Russia has been shown to contrast with France and Germany in respect of democracy; Germany with France and Russia in respect of revolution; and France with the Soviet Union and Germany in respect of totalitarianism. Each path has revealed additional examples of democracy or attempts to achieve democracy which have failed. The cases of Britain, America and Italy have also added to understanding both through providing extra controls and suggesting additional hypotheses.

This work also began with a recognition that the method chosen ruled out claims for general explanation; necessary but not sufficient conditions might be found, understanding of democracy furthered, at best. This followed not only from the smallness of the number of cases, proven in any case far higher than just three because of the fertility of the countries' histories, but also from the recognition that explanation for 'natural' and 'adopted' democracies would differ. In becoming two countries in 1949, the one adopting a democratic political system the other a communist system, Germany has proven a case thickly wrapped in hypotheses. Federal Germany, where democracy rose from the ashes of the Nazi totalitarian regime of a strength, furthermore, sufficient to serve the expansion of democracy to the fallen totalitarian dictatorship in East Germany, has shown that it is possible to achieve democracy in practice even against extraordinary odds. All democratic structures and institutions had been destroyed, both civil society and the spontaneity on which it relied had been crushed, the economy was in crisis, society dislocated and there was no resistance movement with strength to form the basis for a new government. Furthermore, opinion surveys showed that the trauma of the Nazi regime and total defeat in war did not produce values and attitudes for democracy. As such the case has highlighted the futility of searching for any simple theory of democracy but at the same time it has sharpened interest in lessons about democracy.

Social and economic hypotheses

Social and economic hypotheses have, in broad terms, proved valuable in guiding analysis towards understanding of the cases, though the cases have not always proved supportive of the hypotheses. In respect of straightforward claims for direct relationships between variables such as industrialization, urbanization, economic growth, the level and distribution of wealth, and literacy, the cases are too few to draw any firm conclusions. Though modernization occurred over time, industrialization appeared difficult to link, in any clear and systematic way, with either stepping on to or staying on a democratic path. France and Britain in the nineteenth century have been shown so clearly different in terms of levels of industrialization and urbanization and Germany was more similar to Britain than was France. In the twentieth century, in Germany industrialization was also linked to Nazism and as both the Soviet Union and East Germany have shown, in any case, industrialization is also connected to communism. In respect of education, Germany, where democracy failed, had the highest literacy rates in 1870.

In respect of economic crisis, so often blamed for a breakdown in political stability, comparison between France, Germany and Russia has strengthened the claim that it is not economic crisis per se which poses the most serious threat to chances for democracy. Rather, comparative analysis of the cases supports the hypothesis that it is renewed economic crisis, following an earlier experience of economic crisis which combined with a dislocated society, that leads to political collapse. This not only helps to explain why Germany and the Soviet Union but not France became totalitarian regimes but also seems to help to explain why the Russian political system survived the economic crisis brought by shock therapy.

More complex arguments about the significance of commercialization or industrialization in combination with social structural conditions involving the strength of the bourgeoisie and class alignments have been put, somewhat, into question. For example, in France, the acquisition classes in 1848 appeared more important for democracy than class alignments in 1789. In general, the lesson seemed to be that rather than focusing on whether or not a 'bourgeois revolution' had taken place, as in France, England and America but not in Germany and Russia, a more direct concentration on entrepreneurship was more fruitful and not least because it drew attention to the state.

In Weber's argument about the presence of an *Obrigkeitsstaat* in both Imperial Germany and Tsarist Russia, the authoritarian bureaucratic state weakened the capacity of people, in both the economic and political spheres, to take initiative and responsibility. Such entrepreneurship was found lacking in post-communist Russia where people were unpractised in enterprise and where the oligarchs displayed the exploitative behaviour associated with traditional, not modern capitalism. The economic levelling, brought in both cases by the experience of totalitarian regimes and in Russia's case also by communist revolution, had very different effects. In Germany's case the levelling of society turned to democratic advantage whereas in post-Soviet Russia, a new status group of oligarchs developed and social equality deteriorated dramatically.

Comparison of post-Soviet Russia with post-Nazi Germany revealed an additional lesson about the role of state guidance of the economy and the importance of an international condition, the influence and constraints of prevailing economic ideas. Whereas German democracy was built at a time when Keynesian ideas prevailed among the western Allies, post-Soviet Russia faced monetarism as the prevailing western economic thought. The former is compatible with state guidance in the economy and with valuing a welfare state, whereas the latter is opposed to state guidance and is disparaging of welfare.

Values and beliefs

Along with the effect of the state in weakening entrepreneurship and undermining the economy, the dominant role of the state, in line with de Tocqueville's argument, had also incapacitated Russia in the forming of western-type interest groups. Nevertheless, the example of post-Nazi Germany suggests that, in the right circumstances, voluntary, non-exclusionary interest groups can be encouraged through the introduction of democratic ideas. In Germany, this was facilitated by the Allies through local radio stations and through developing local democratic practices. The circumstances in Germany were unique, but the case does draw attention to the importance of the conduciveness of the experiences of government at the time in leading to acceptance of values sympathetic to democracy. As the public opinion surveys showed, the occupying forces were found tolerable.

Of particular note in respect of the role of government in producing feelings of trust and support for democracy was the 'feel good' factor produced by Erhard's 'social market economy'. Experience of the post-war German government produced feelings of satisfaction which, in turn, strengthened support for the democratic political system. In Russia very different experiences produced strongly contrasting views on the value of democracy. Furthermore, reinforcing the view of democratic political values as essentially a consequence not a cause of democracy, disparaging views of democracy – 'if this is democracy, we don't want it' – have not led to the collapse of the Russian political system. Similarly, the continuing anti-democratic views held by the majority of Germans after the Second World War did not make the building of democracy impossible.

On balance, the tentative lesson drawn from the cases on values and beliefs in the wider population, political culture, is that values, such as toleration, develop mainly from experience of the political system rather than toleration being a prerequisite for democracy to take hold. It is significant that in France, after the revolution in 1789, toleration was imposed by government and the state protection afforded Jews played an important part in the differences between the effects of anti-Semitism in France and Germany.

Political ideas

Political ideas are more than beliefs, they include ideas on democracy itself and play a role in the design of constitutions. As the cases have shown, political ideas of democracy and its design may be developed at home, sometimes in reaction against what has gone before, or be brought from abroad, whether as ideas of political philosophers or developed from experience of working political systems elsewhere. For example, in the most recent case covered, the Russian Constitution has drawn on the semi-presidentialism of the Fifth French Republic and the electoral system has been modelled, loosely, on the contemporary German system. In earlier examples, the Frankfurt Constitution was influenced by the American Constitution and the Weimar Constitution drew on American federalism. The history of democracy has been shown to be a history of the interdependence of democracies, no case since England in the seventeenth century has been unaffected by the ideas and models drawn from other political systems. As the cases have also shown, however, ideas brought from abroad may be misinterpreted, be employed selectively, and be applied inappropriately for the particular conditions faced.

Before the War of Independence, America, as the thirteen colonies, had direct connection with English political practices, practices that had built on the events of the Civil War and the 'Glorious Revolution' of 1688. The early settlers in America also carried with them ideas of democracy in sympathy with, some even more radical than, Leveller ideas. As Hill (1969: 168) comments, 'the ideas of the Levellers passed into the radical tradition of the seventeen-sixties, and played their part in preparing the

American and French revolutions'. Unlike structures, rooted in history, ideas travel. In understanding America's path to democracy the decisions made by the Founding Fathers were critical in setting the framework within which modern democracy could grow. In making their decisions when drawing up a constitution the ideas of Locke and Montesquieu and others too were important in shaping the Founding Fathers' thinking. The fact of having had a revolution, the experience of British rule and the pioneering nature of the country were also influences on thought. Ideas travel but arriving in new situations they take on new lives.

In France, not only were social, economic and political conditions less conducive for the success of democratic structures, the presence of competing ideas of democracy compounded the situation. In post-revolutionary France, ideas of government in sympathy with the constitutional monarchy of England or the presidential system in America competed not only with each other but also with ideas based on Rousseau, merged, incompatibly, with the ideas of Montesquieu. In France, the American ideas of the Rights of Man were confused with the unity of nation and the workings of the English constitution were not wholly understood. In addition the calling of elections for the Estates-General had rendered a proto-type political system ill-suited for adaptation. In contrast to America, therefore, in France, political breakdowns occurred frequently through to 1851, the demand for universal male suffrage finally bursting through in the revolution of 1848.

In opposition to the idea of liberal democracy, 'bourgeois democracy', ideas of social democracy, as first expressed in Marx and Engels' Communist Manifesto, came into play. As suffrage widened to include more and more working class men, competition for their vote and ideas of workers' parties developed. From 1870 a social democratic party grew into a major force in German politics. By 1912, the SPD formed the largest party in the Reichstag. In Russia, the Social Democratic Party remained a revolutionary party, communist revolution occurring in 1917. In Britain and America, support for Marxist social democracy, even for what became a reformist social democratic party, never developed.

In both Britain and America their two-party political systems worked against new parties. In France the absence of organized political parties and the existence of socialist ideas prior to 1848 made the French system unconducive to the rise of support for a single social democratic party of the German type. In addition, the wide appeal of mass democracy as promised by socialist democratic parties, was undermined in both America and France by the existence, in 1848, of widespread male suffrage. Furthermore, England, America and France in having had revolutions had not only successfully challenged the power of the aristocracy but also had traditions of mass action for democratic reforms before 1848. In Britain, where suffrage remained highly restrictive even after the 1832 Reform Act, this collective action, the Chartist movement, took the quintessentially democratic form of petitioning of parliament, with non-violent mass meetings, the largest political gatherings in British history.[1]

Germany, where revolution had not succeeded, where the power of the monarchy and aristocracy had not been changed by the events of 1848, where male suffrage was not to be granted until 1870, presented a quite different case for the appeal of reformist Marxist social democracy. Furthermore, in the German system, unlike in France, there were organized political parties, and totalling more than the two found in Britain and America. From the Erfurt Programme of 1891, the German Social Democratic Party ceased to be a party competing for elections as an anti-system party – a disloyal opposition – and became a party seeking election with the aim to become the next government, through the existing political system – a loyal opposition, Sartori's 'within system' party. The SPD played a major role in the writing of the Weimar Constitution and in the running of the Weimar Republic. In contrast, the German Communist Party, the KPD, which split from the USPD in 1918 and refused to stand for elections in 1919, continued to push for violent revolution. After the failure of communist revolution, however, the KPD changed tactic and sought election but remained firmly opposed to joining a government coalition.

Alternatives and democracies

The paths taken to democracy by France, Germany and Russia have confirmed Moore's view of democracy on the path to the modern world as wrestling against the alternatives of dictatorship: in Moore's terms those of fascism and communism, here drawn as the extremes of Nazi and Stalinist totalitarianism. The paths, however, have also revealed that the struggle for democracy is made not only with rival anti-democratic paths to the modern world but also against ideas and institutions of democracy, which are not modern. This contrast between non-modern and modern democracy is the difference between democracy as a means for unity and uniformity and democracy as a means for representing diverse interests and opinions with the system designed as a means for alteration of government not for maintaining consensus in defiance of opposition.

In Sartori's (1987) distinction between ancient and modern democracy, as outlined in Chapter 2, ancient democracy values unity and uniformity and seeks, therefore, to construct institutions to reflect consensus, while modern democracy, which values difference and diversity, dissensus, requires institutions which facilitate pluralism. This is why competing political parties are so important, as too are voluntary associations, freedom of information and so on. This is also why it is crucial that the parties competing are parts of the whole and not against the whole, willing to form loyal oppositions and governments-in-waiting. The difference between ancient and modern democracy is also in Constant's distinction between ancient and modern liberalism, which, as explained in Chapter 4, he made at the time of the Directory in post-revolutionary France. The difference between ancient and modern liberalism is found in the contrasting views of the citizen, the one having a public duty to the state and the other a modern, private citizen, imbued with private opinion, valued in its own right.

The history of liberal democracy, as the cases have shown, has been a movement, over time, though by no means necessarily smoothly, towards the modern pluralist position. Along the route, the fundamentally different positions on democracy, uniformity versus pluralist, are to be found together and, as such, paths to democracy have been a contest. The ancient position, viewing all opposition as disloyal, the path to democracy becomes vulnerable to breakdown, wherever supporters of the ancient position remain strong. Such was clearly the case in France, from 1789 through to 1848, and also in Imperial Germany. In both cases the conflicting ideas of democracy continued to undermine the stability of parliaments. As the cases have shown, the conflict went on to contribute both to the fall of Weimar Germany in 1933 and to the rise and fall of Napoleon III's empire in France, from 1851 to 1870. Furthermore, even once oppositions became viewed as loyal, in the modern way, the institutions of government, erected with ideas of ancient democracy in mind, delayed the arrival of modern, pluralist, democracy, through creating a lag.

In taking a path to modern democracy, a struggle not only against forces opposed to democracy of any kind but also against the ideas and practices of non-modern democracy, the choice of institutions made is itself involved in a kind of Darwinian struggle for the survival of the most fitting. What is set up in practice, though initially designed to serve ideas of democracy in pursuit of unity and uniformity, may turn out to adapt well to modern democracy. Such was the case for America where the system chosen was designed to separate and balance powers; though at first rejecting parties as factions it adapted, quickly and easily, to party competition. In Britain too, though a long time before even near universal male suffrage was achieved, the ideas of 'loyal' opposition and of two houses of parliament were long established. Certainly, both countries benefited in their paths to democracy by having had revolutions, the Civil War in England and the War of Independence in America. France, too, however, had a revolution but there the constitutions chosen were hampered by the model of the Estates-General with its three-tier system. With a conviction of the need for unity, 'the one and indivisible republic', Napoleon's *coup d'état* was viewed as preferable to factions and schisms. In France, instead of adaptation, wholesale changes of the system continued until alternatives became ruled out by negative experiences.

Elections

In pursuit of ancient democracy, as in post-revolutionary France until 1848, elections were viewed as a public duty. This was evident in votes being cast orally. It was also evident in the right to vote being bound up with duties to the state, such as serving in the army, and in the rights given to each vote being related to the paying of taxes, under the three-tier system. The goals of unity and uniformity were also evident in the view of factions as disloyal opposition and, therefore, of political parties as anti-democratic. Though this view of parties was quickly changed in America, the electoral college has remained. In France, ideas of ancient democracy were also shown in the manipulation of electoral results to achieve the desired outcome, agreement that is with those in power, the embodiment of the 'General Will'. The downward adjustment of electoral success for Jacobins during the rule of the Directory are the best examples and Napoleon Bonaparte's plebiscites are also examples. In France, the 'buying' of votes with wine had continued through to the end of the nineteenth century. In Imperial Germany, such examples are found in the two-tier system of votes and in voting being public and therefore under the scrutiny of local landowners.

In the modern view of democracy, the vote is not viewed as a public duty, elections are not viewed as the means to achieve uniformity, consensus with a general will or to achieve the outcome preferred by those in power. In modern democracy elections are the means for alteration in office, that is for changing governments in a peaceful way. This is why parties or coalitions of parties are essential in order to form not only government but also alternative governments. In modern democracy, votes are the means through which private opinions, in reflection of personal interests and judgement of the performance of the present government and the likely performance of another government, are conveyed to be weighed along with the plurality of views found among the electorate. In modern democracy, therefore, elections are the means through which government's actions are held to account. Ever conscious of the need to win the next election, public opinion keeps politicians in check. As Kautsky argued in *The Social Revolution* (1902), 'elections grant the possibility that the opponents will themselves recognize the untenability of many positions'. As Weber saw it, elections in modern democracy are a means to temper politics into the art of the possible.

The essential lesson to be drawn is that the presence of elections in a political system, even competitive elections and even ones with competing political parties, does not constitute proof that the system is a modern democracy, a pluralist democracy, Dahl's polyarchy.[2] Where elections are designed or manipulated for unity and so the preservation of those in power, then it is the struggle for an idea of democracy compatible with that of ancient democracy, not modern democracy, which is dominant. It also follows that because elections may be devised to serve ideas of democracy that are not modern, the presence of elections in a political system does not even signal that the country is on the path to modern democracy.

Universal suffrage

As the cases have made clear, prominent among the devices designed for elections in defence of ancient-type democracy are the open rather than secret ballots and the restriction of suffrage to those with interests vested in the existing system: the tax/property restriction. Class analysis enters into this frame, most clearly in respect of suffrage restrictions according to levels of tax payments and landholdings. Such devices are used to assure the unity of interests represented through the political system, economic and political power together. Examples of suffrage restricted to property owners are clearly present in the history of both British and American democracy. These cases, and the American case most strikingly, also demonstrate, however, that the goals of unity and uniformity are not restricted to class interests alone. Unity of interests may, as in America, also take a racial form: hence the devices to restrict suffrage to whites only and then, when granted to black voters, devices such as proof of literacy and its public demonstration are introduced. These are the ideas and the devices not of modern-type democracy but of ancient-type democracy where uniformity is the priority. Suffrage, given to men but denied to women raises similar issues.

With property or tax qualifications for suffrage the denial of property or income rights to women automatically disqualified women from suffrage. In the same logic of ancient citizenship as a public duty which disqualified slaves, women and servants, so the view of contrasting men's roles in society as in the public realm and women's in the private, concerned with family and home, has served to reinforce the lagged ideas of ancient democracy as a device to deny women the vote. In the modern view of democracy, in which votes are the means through which private opinions are conveyed in assessment of government performance and promise as compared with alternatives, the vote is not a public duty but a private choice. The struggle to replace ideas of ancient democracy with those of modern democracy has been a struggle to preserve the interests of those in power and those with suffrage, against the rest, the majority. This is why mass movements in their struggle for democracy have been so crucial and why women's suffrage, the suffrage of an inherent majority, took so long. Without universal suffrage no democracy can count as modern. Without universal suffrage, the full plurality of private opinion cannot be represented and for this the secret ballot is an essential device for without it the value and independence of opinion cannot be guaranteed.

Pluralistic structures in society

In modern democracy the casting of votes in elections is not, of course, the only means for channelling the diversity of opinion and interests. As well as suffrage being universal and the ballot being secret, in order to ensure that the plurality of interests is served, there must also be an absence of restrictions on the right to stand for office and there must be guarantees of access to information through a free press and so on. Where, as in ancient democracy, a unity rather than a diversity of interests is the goal, then the choice, naturally, will be for the right to stand for office to be restricted accordingly and for restrictions on information. Such restrictions, so to reflect and bolster the domination of those in power, will also be reinforced throughout society.

It follows that where a unity of interests is the goal there will be restrictions on the right to form voluntary associations, social, economic and political, including political parties. In a modern democracy, a democracy, that is, which is pluralist, competition between parties and voluntary associations, with rights to form them, are essential guarantees for the representation of freely formed diverse opinion. It also follows that where a unity of interests is the goal, in order to preserve the uniformity of the interests of those in power there will be restrictions put on access to education. This is why, as discussed in Chapter 2, Beetham (1999) argues political equality to be one of the two essential principles of democracy and why economic equality is so bound up with ideas of democracy. In order to serve the other principle of democracy, that of popular control, the designing of institutional guarantees for the removal of governments and the alteration with loyal oppositions that carry this consent is crucial. It follows, however, that while both inclusive direct democracy and representative democracy fit both principles of democracy, ancient democracy, as exclusive direct democracy, does not.

Social democracy, communism and nationalism

The claim that not only political equality but also social and economic equality, to include universal education, is crucial to modern democracy is not, however, to be confused with claims for socialist democracy. Socialist democracy, as comparison of social democratic parties has shown, has taken two forms. One, the reformist, has adapted to modern democracy, to become a within-system party, part of the pluralist system. The other has not, remaining a party that challenged the system, that sought, whether through election or through violent revolution, to overthrow the pluralist system and replace it with a political system designed to preserve uniformity through the end of party competition and voluntary association. This difference is not, however, simply that between social democratic parties and communist parties, and not, therefore, simply another way of separating out a communist route to the modern world.

In the Weimar Republic, in effect, the KPD took on the mantle of ancient democracy, which believes in unity and uniformity, and adapted it for their own ends. As explained, ancient democracy in the practice of government seeks to restrict suffrage and access to office as the preserve of those who share the consensus of those in power. The KPD, as a party of mass democracy committed to universal suffrage, would not contemplate the role of loyal opposition, but only that of a unitary government under the (unlikely) situation of majority support. This was in contrast to the behaviour of the Communist Party in France, which had formed part of the Popular Front that had won the election in 1936 and which, after German occupation in 1940, had joined with the socialist parties, the SFIO and the radical-socialists, and others to form the Resistance. As also explained, the Resistance then went on to join forces with the Free French Movement, headed by de Gaulle, to liberate the country in August 1944. Following the election in 1945, in which for the first time women had the vote, a tripartite coalition government of communists, SFIOs and members of the new Mouvement Républicain Populaire (MRP) party (similar in nature to a Christian Democratic party) was formed.[3]

Not only had Weimar Germany to contend with the Communist Party, as a party unwilling to share government, remaining a party of unity against the system, Germany also had other parties refusing to be 'within-system' parties, equally set on unity and uniformity in opposition to the ideas of modern pluralist democracy. These parties were nationalist. The issue of the German-speaking people becoming one nation had been important in 1848. Debates about the boundaries of Germany focused on areas where languages were spoken in place of or in addition to German. In 1870, unification of Germany left Austria, viewed as backward looking and too closely bound up with Hungarian history, outside the German Empire. In practice, unification brought militarism to the fore and the design of the federal constitution both affirmed Prussia's dominance and located the balance of power in the upper house rather than in the lower.

Certainly, just as Moore (1969) argues, the dominance of the Prussian landlords, the Junkers, in Imperial Germany shows that Germany contrasts with England, France and America in having not a revolution that fought for commercial interests against the non-commercializing lords and king, but a revolution from above. In Germany the king retained power through to 1918 and, as Dahrendorf (1968) makes clear, the landowners continued as a dominant force in Germany throughout the Weimar Republic. Social class analysis is not, however, sufficient to explain the path to democracy taken by Germany, the path on which Weimar democracy became so unworkable, finally to be so utterly destroyed by the Nazi regime. Though it is fair to allow that the polarization of parties towards the end of the Weimar Republic can be characterized in terms of class – the socialist and communist parties representing the working class, the centre parties the middle classes, and the traditional nationalist parties representing the interests of the landowning classes – the Nazi Party, however, drew support from all classes. Furthermore, as Dahrendorf (1968) argues so strongly, once in power the Nazis destroyed the traditional bases of power. As has been shown in Chapter 7, the Nazi regime was not a regime in the mould of traditional authoritarianism and neither was it a fascist regime like that in Italy.

The effects of the constitution

When the Weimar Republic was set up, in 1918, not only were Britain, America and France on their paths to modern democracy, debates over mass democracy had radicalized ideas. The Weimar Republic adopted both of the most radical ideas of democracy: genuine universal suffrage, votes for all women as well as for all men, first introduced in Australia and New Zealand; and proportional representation so strongly advocated by social democratic parties in Europe and also supported by Liberals in Germany. As the cases have shown, proportional representation has a tendency to lead to a proliferation of parties, which, in turn, may lead to problems of unruly parliaments and to difficulties in forming governments that hold and which, therefore, are capable of governing.

As consideration of examples in France and Germany has also shown, however, there are a variety of devices for overcoming the problems of the proliferation of parties, unruly parliaments and unworkable governments that may follow from PR. These include: the 5 per cent threshold; the formation of coalitions before the election rather than after it; the popular election of the president in a bi-polar race; and 'the constructive vote of no confidence', the requirement that governments cannot be voted down within parliament unless an alternative government can be shown to be ready and able to step into its place. Such devices can ensure that proportional representation serves to enhance pluralist democracy and could have been adopted in Weimar Germany, perhaps through amendment to the constitution, with foresight and sympathetic political circumstances. Such devices were later adopted in Germany's Basic Law of 1949.

The most striking lesson to be drawn from comparison between the German political system before and after the Third Reich, Weimar Germany as compared with the Federal Republic, is that of the treatment of parties opposed to modern democracy. Whereas the Weimar Republic was pulled apart by the nationalist and communist extremes, under Article 21 of the Basic Law, first the neo-Nazi party, the Socialist Reich Party, was outlawed in 1952 and then the Communist Party, KPD, was banned in 1956. The possibility for controlling these anti-democratic forces came out of the specific circumstances, both national and international, faced by Germany following total defeat in war and the complete collapse of the Nazi regime in 1945.

Learning from the past and fitting the present

The constitution as a set of devices for putting democracy into practice plays a crucial role but its design alone cannot account for the success, or otherwise, of democracy. As discussed in Chapter 5, the Weimar Constitution may have contributed to political instability in Germany but it did not, of itself, cause the fall of the Weimar Republic and certainly cannot be blamed for the Nazi regime which replaced it. Both economic conditions and the deliberate undermining of the system by the Nazis were crucial. Similarly, in post-Soviet Russia, there is no denying the dangers for democracy that follow from the strength of the presidency. In France, however, with a similar semi-presidential system, co-habitation demonstrated the importance of the role of politicians in making systems work for democratic ends. Constitutions do not operate in separation from the realities of circumstances, both in respect of material conditions and in respect of political agents with all their unpredictability.

In Dahrendorf's argument, the destruction of society by the Nazis opened the way for the 'suspended revolution' of 1918 to be concluded. In this sense the end of a totalitarian regime has equivalence to the event of a revolution as a break with the past. The lesson of Germany, emerging as a stable modern democracy after 1945, however, is that of an occurrence rooted not just in the post-war, post-Nazi, circumstances of the time but also in the split between East and West Germany and in the emerging Cold War. The Allies learnt the lessons of the First World War and guided Germany towards democracy, rooting the new democracy in Germany's past democratic experiences. For example, the Frankfurt

Constitution, the long history of elections and parties in Imperial Germany and the Weimar Republic, together with present democratic forces, each played a part in the new constitution, securing it through roots. The need to protect the new democracy from anti-democratic support for Nazism in the form of a neo-Nazi party followed from the experience of the Third Reich. The need to protect the new democracy from anti-democratic communism – communism, that is, which seeks the suppression of pluralist opinion and organizations and which is built in the image of the Stalinist system, that led to the other totalitarian regime – equally emerged from the specific circumstances of the day, the parallel development of East Germany in the Stalinist camp.

If democracy was in vogue in western countries after the First World War, and again after the Second World War, the fashion was even more widespread by the time Russia emerged from the Soviet Union, in 1991. As a victor in the Second World War, the Soviet Union had adjusted its totalitarian regime through de-Stalinization, returning it to a totalitarian dictatorship of bureaucratic centralization and Communist Party domination. The Communist Party in Russia, unlike the NSDAP in Germany, remained an organized force. Furthermore, nationalism also emerged, communism and nationalism being the two anti-democratic forces that had served to pull the Weimar Republic apart. Added to this, Russia had no significant experience of liberal democracy on which to draw, no organized competitive parties and, perhaps most poignantly, no modern social democratic party. Russia also lacked western-type interest groups and had nothing equivalent to the Allies' guidance.

While lessons on how to construct democracy had proliferated in line with the growth both of practising examples and of recent 'new democracies' adopting new democratic systems, the problems that Russia faced were not confined to lack of experience combined with the responsibilities of choice. After the Second World War, the fashion in Europe had moved from that of liberal democratic structures to forms of social democracy, in which concerns for social welfare and state-led economic reconstruction are added to liberal democratic structures. In the 1980s and 1990s, however, not Keynesian economics but monetarism was viewed as the cure-all not simply for economic problems but as the foundation for democracy.

Russia, having had both a communist revolution and a totalitarian regime, not only lacked experience of liberal democratic institutions and structures but also had no heritage of independent entrepreneurship on which to draw. In this Russia contrasted with Britain, America and France, and also with Germany. Though Weber drew parallels between Russia and Germany in respect of their weak bourgeoisie in imperial times, Germany, where attempted communist revolution had failed, had offered an opportunity, under the Weimar Republic, for entrepreneurship to develop. In spite of all the destruction wrought by Nazi totalitarianism to the economy, society, the political system, the people's morale and the country's reputation, Germany had within its historical make-up some, at least, of the necessary ingredients for modern democracy. These experiences of liberal democratic institutions, a modern social democratic party, interest groups and entrepreneurship are ones that Russia lacked.

In Russia the battle for containment of anti-democratic factions, the communist and the nationalist, is being fought and the Communist Party appears to be transforming into a within-system party. But, in Russia, the struggle for modern democracy to win out over the pressure for unity and uniformity continues. Like France two centuries before, in the Russian Federation, similar examples are found in the manipulation of results in elections. Both arise from the pressure for uniformity which, in Russia's case, follows from non-reformist socialist democratic ideals of mass democracy.

Conclusion

Putting politics back into the comparative historical analysis of paths to democracy has restored democracy to its rightful place as an essentially political phenomenon. This has been shown, however, to signify no simple lesson about the need not only to investigate social and economic conditions together with the role of revolution but also to include consideration of political conditions. The Russian case today confirms the general lesson drawn from the comparative historical analysis of France, Germany and Russia. It is necessary when assessing the reality of democracy and its chances for survival that, within the political sphere, far more than constitutions, institutions and procedures, such as elections, parties and suffrage, be considered. The issue is whether pluralism is the goal, modern democracy the choice that is capable of winning the struggle not only against anti-democratic forces in society but also against those, within parliament, supporting ideas of democracy that are not modern.

Notes

1 On method: comparative historical analysis and politics

1 Applying Sartori's 'ladder of abstraction' for general explanations an empirical universal concept is required. An empirical universal concept is defined through the logic of negation; it complies with the two interrelated criteria of minimal intension and maximal extension. The intension consists of the properties or characteristics relevant to the term; the extension relates to the list of things to which the term correctly refers (Sartori 1970: 1041 and 1984: 22–8).

2 For expansion of the point see the discussion of Sartori's (1991) 'cat-dog' below. For a practical demonstration of the dangers of conceptual stretching see O'Kane (1993).

3 Among the examples of works offered by Skocpol (1984) are: the first approach (the general model), Smelser (1959); the second approach (the interpretive), Bendix (1977); the third approach (causal regularities), Moore (1969) and Skocpol (1979).

4 See Stinchcombe (1978: 7).

5 As Lieberson (1992: 114) also points out, strictly Mill's methods also require the absence of errors in data and that the same pattern would exist for all relevant cases if included.

6 There is a similar worry about Moore's (1969) 'peasant revolutions'. In viewing Russia as a peasant revolution, the role of industrial workers and workers' ideology is downgraded in the explanation but the role played by the industrial workers, especially in Moscow and Petrograd, may suggest classification as a proletarian revolution to be more appropriate. (See Weiner 1975: 321). Russia is treated as if similar to China because of the hypothesis that both are peasant revolutions. The hypothesis that they are different (one proletarian the other not) goes untested because it is not posed.

7 Such an argument is made by Sewell (1994: 171 and 182–7) in criticism of Skocpol's (1979) treatment of the French Revolution.

8 Lowenthal (1968: 265) counts the use of the word 'eventually' being used seven times in the chapter on England, Chapter 1.

9 Fehér (1987: 67), while considering the Jacobin clubs as fitting the structure of an early political party, argues that the Jacobin idea of a general will in practice prevented the structure acting as a political party because it ruled out factions.

10 This also fits with Marx's view of India, with its Asiatic mode of production, being turned by colonialism from the direct route to communism taken by China onto the western route which must pass through the capitalist stage (see Melotti 1977).

11 An additional contender is the development of the European Community but it differs from these others in respect of its incremental nature.

2 Democracy and empirical political theory: from the present to the past

1 O'Donnell and Schmitter (1989: 8); Diamond, Linz and Lipset (1989: xvi); Di Palma (1990: 16); Linz (1978: 5).
2 Dahl offers an impressionistic view that the use of coercion in such regimes is a significant contrast with polyarchies (1971: 27–8).
3 I have argued elsewhere (O'Kane 1991, 1995) that having a revolutionary reign of terror, Dahl's regression to hegemony, is primarily dependent on whether civil war precedes the revolutionary overthrow or breaks out after it, with permanent state construction being unable to begin until after the civil war is over. In either situation, therefore, at the end of the civil war the opposition at home will have been defeated but only in the case where civil war preceded the revolutionary overthrow (as in America) could the chosen path to democracy proceed. It follows, therefore, that, notwithstanding the need later to defeat the Southern plantation owners as a force for reaction, America's path to democracy does, as Dahl argues, begin with the American Revolution.
4 Drawing on examples, Dahl (1989: 248–9) suggests four possible ways, separately or in combination, of 'taming violent coercion': greatly reducing the size and capabilities of military and police forces; achieving 'local control' over militias; ensuring that military forces are 'civilians in uniform' (that is, made up of mostly temporary rather than permanent recruits); and 'indoctrination of professional soldiers' to ensure feelings of loyalty and obedience to the elected government. While not claiming that any one of these conditions will necessarily achieve the required effect of civilian control of coercion, Dahl is convinced that civilian control is the necessary condition of polyarchy.
5 For detailed discussion of Weber on democracy, freedom, economy and society see Beetham (1985: 215–49).
6 For expansion see Beetham (1985: 95–118; 1987: 57–71).
7 For expansion see Beetham (1987: 57–67).
8 Dahl (1989: 255–60) recognizes that consociational arrangements, in which subcultural groups retain autonomy and leaders representing these groups come together to reach political accommodation at government level, have had some successes in moderating cleavages, though he stresses the importance of leaders' beliefs in achieving accommodation and observes the importance of such beliefs in other polyarchical solutions which have not involved consociationalism. As an example of a non-consociational solution, he offers the case of the United States, stressing 'the rapid assimilation (both voluntary and coerced) of immigrants and their children into the dominant political and general culture' and argues that African-Americans were first denied access to consociational arrangements and were then too small a minority to institute them, operating, rather within the 'loose' two-party system (ibid.: 259–60).
9 Almond and Verba (1965: 12) define political culture in the following way: 'The term "political culture" thus refers to the specifically political orientations – attitudes towards the political system and its various parts, and attitudes towards the role of the self in the system.' They offer three such orientations – 'cognitive', 'affective' and 'evaluational'. The cognitive is concerned with 'knowledge and belief about the political system'; the affective

refers to 'feelings about the political system, its roles, personnel and performance'; and the evaluational relates to 'the judgments and opinions about political objects' (ibid.: 14–15).

10 Inglehart's (1988) tentative argument about pre-adult socialization is brought into question by his evidence which shows West Germany in 1981 closely approximating the score for mass life satisfaction of long-lived democracy, Belgium, and overtaking Belgium's score in the mid-1980s (Belgium recovering a higher score in 1986) (1988: 1206).

11 Inglehart (1988: 1217) admits that De Gaulle was invited to form a government by the last president of the Fourth Republic in 1958, and that 'the suspension of democracy was very brief'. If France, rather, is listed as a democracy from before 1900, then, combined with his evidence of West Germany, Austria, Hungary, and even Argentina, being ahead of France on life satisfaction, together with his evidence that South Africa, Spain and Italy score roughly the same as France, the significance of the finding of difference between the two sets of cases is rather less clear cut.

3 Revolutions and ideas of democracy: from the past towards the present

1 Some Levellers seemed to be in favour of universal male suffrage, certainly the Diggers were (Hill 1969: 119–20).

2 These conditions had been tacitly assumed but never written down at the Restoration of 1660 (Hill 1969: 238).

3 Religious toleration continued to be excluded from many professions and the old universities until the nineteenth century (Hill 1969: 252).

4 The original idea of presidential 'electors' as dispassionate wise men broke down in 1792 since when they have simply agreed with the majority view of voters in each state (Nicholas 1950: 77).

5 For the above see Nicholas (1950: 75–7) and *The Constitution of the United States* (1997: 383–93).

6 For the full text of the Bill of Rights see Appendix in Wilson (1997: 394–5).

7 The Democratic-Republicans became the 'Democrats' in 1828, the Federalists became the Republicans in 1860, having been 'National Republicans' in 1828 and Whigs in 1840 (see Wilson 1997: 10).

8 As quoted by Paine in *The Rights of Man*, Part 1 (1791) (Paine 1989: 115–16).

9 For selections of Marx's work see Feuer (1969).

10 From 'Eine Taaktische Frage', LV, 6 July 1899.

11 Lipset (1963: 86) distinguishes between 'parties of representation' that see their major role as that of winning votes and 'parties of integration', which view themselves as 'in a mighty struggle between divine and historic truth on the one side and fundamental error on the other'.

4 Revolution and the long path to democracy in France

1 Over half of the active citizens qualified as eligibles (Crook 1996: 44).

2 For expansion on the reign of terror see O'Kane (1991: 57–85).

3 A schism was a device by which groups seceded the departmental and national assemblies on the grounds of electoral irregularities, though with the real intent of undermining the legitimacy of the opposition (Crook 1996: 185).

4 Hayward (1991: 121). This famous quotation was written by Constant in 1831 but his views on diversity were consistent throughout and he was politically most active under the Directory (ibid.: 101–2).

5 See Sutherland (1985: 339–40). He adds that 'Until very recently, both contemporaries and historians believed the officially announced results: 3,011,007 yes, 1562 no' (ibid.: 340). Indeed, these are reported as true figures in Harvey (1968: 62).

6 The one exception was Seine where the police was under its own prefect (Sutherland 1985: 344).

7 See Tombs (1996: 98). Each arrondissement had a council made up of 'notable citizens' whose role was advisory only and was essentially concerned with tax allocation to the arrondissements and communes. These notables were also centrally appointed, election a later development. The councils in the communes were elected from the start, but they were similarly constrained to ensure their subordination to the central administration. (See Sutherland 1985: 345.) The mayors in the communes did not become subject to election until 1882 (Tombs 1996: 100).

8 Under the law of 3 frimaire, year VIII (24 November 1799) the collection of direct taxes were given to a special directory within each arrondissement. With financial expertise of a modern kind scarce, local businessmen and financiers were induced to serve, whether on a special directory or as local tax collectors, through permitting them to continue with their private occupations and by paying them a percentage of the taxes collected rather than a salary. (See Sutherland 1985: 345–6.)

9 This later led to upward mobility, with Jews moving into occupations, including the professions, previously barred to them (Eisenberg Vichniac 1998: 180–1).

10 See Tombs (1996: 148–52). As late as 1900, 40 per cent of the industrial workforce were self-employed. In Germany, the figure was 16 per cent, in England only 9 per cent (Tombs 1996: 162).

11 For full discussion of Marx's writings on France between 1848 and 1850 and an argument for the importance of Marx's political analysis see Spencer (1979).

12 In the 1890s, the Lancashire cotton workers in England were paid twice as much as workers in Vosges or Normandy and their productivity was significantly higher (Tombs 1996: 154).

13 For further expansion see Harvey (1968: 113–18). For a detailed account of the Paris Commune see Gould (1995: 153–94).

14 In the first decade of the twentieth century, duration of governments was as follows: 1899–1902 (Waldeck-Rousseau); 1902–5 (Combes); 1906–9 (Clemenceau).

15 See Tombs (1996: 119–20). For example, during the Third Republic an income tax bill was introduced sixteen times without achieving sufficient support to pass.

5 Revolution and the failure of democracy in Russia and Germany

1 Weber stresses, however, that the elections were rigged to exclude some sections and weaken others and that there was also police harassment (Beetham 1985: 195).

2 For a full description of the electoral arrangements see Beetham (1985: 251–74).

3 When VTsIK met in Moscow in July 1918 there were 745 Bolsheviks and 352 Left SRs and 35 other delegates (Carr 1966, Vol. 1: 169–72).
4 Whether this was Lenin's intention or due to his failing health is open to question (Rigby 1979: 191–213).
5 See Harvey (1968: 146). For further examples see Dahrendorf (1968: 36–7).
6 See Beetham (1985: 203–10 and 151–82). As a consequence of late and rapid industrialization, Weber stresses that in Germany, as in Russia, industry was bureaucratic and bound up with the state and in Germany not only were factories large and hierarchical so to were the 'welfare organizations', themselves encouragement for reliance on the state rather than self-reliance. On Weber's analysis too, religion played a similar role in supporting authoritarianism. In its alliance with the state Lutheranism, he argued, came close to the Russian Orthodox Church and was distant from the voluntary organizations of the Puritan sects in America.
7 Convicted criminals, bankrupts, active soldiers and sailors and wards of court were also denied the vote. (See Anderson 2000: 7 and also for what follows in the paragraph.)
8 The parliament had been dissolved in 1861, 1862 and 1863 over finance and consequently, as Bartolini (2000: 345) explains, 'the king decided to rule without deferring to it'.
9 There were fifty-eight members of the Bundesrat; after Prussia, the next largest were Bavaria with six members and Saxony and Württemberg each with four members (Balfour 1992: 13).
10 The Centre Party grew in strength as a consequence of Bismarck's attempt to weaken the Catholic Church's political hold (Arends and Kümmel 2000: 193).
11 Of the remainder of the workforce in 1910, 26.4 per cent were in white collar jobs and 32.9 per cent in agriculture (Bartolini 2000: 133).
12 The Freikorps formed out of the units of regular soldiers disbanded in accordance with the Allies' requirements; the temporary German soldiers simply went home to reclaim their jobs (Balfour 1992: 39).
13 Land policies were included in the government's programme but they benefited the big landowners rather than small ones (see Berger 2000: 107).
14 Ebert became the first president (Balfour 1992: 40).

6 The rise of totalitarian regimes: contrasting France

1 Arendt (1958: 255) argues that loyalty to the state over class loyalties leads to mass society, where isolated individuals, seeking to belong, are ready to be mobilized by a totalitarian leader.
2 See Harvey (1968: 152). A noticeable difference too was that, in spite of a lower level of industrialization, from the turn of the century to the outbreak of war in 1914, real wages in France were relatively high, at around 14 percentage points or more above those in Germany and Britain (ibid.).
3 Dobry (2000: 175–83) argues against the view, popular among historians, that France lacked the right kinds of movements with genuine fascist ideologies, as compared with those in Italy and Germany. In this 'immunization' theory, the events of 1934 are seen as proof that fascist ideology was of the wrong kind. In Dobry's (ibid.: 181) view it was not that the French radical right ideas were quite different from the fascism of Italy and Germany but that the French right's actions took place outside parliament, outside the election arena. In essence Dobry's view is that their tactics were wrong; they should, as had the fascist movements in Germany and Italy, have sought to win support through the electoral system. The argument made here, however, questions the

potential for the success of such tactics and, as will become clear, differentiates the ideas and nature of Nazi Germany from the fascism of Italy.

4 There is a strong tendency in the literature on totalitarianism to view all works as essentially conceptualizing totalitarian government in the same way. Less sweeping comparison confirms a crucial divide between those who view totalitarianism as dictatorship, through the state, and those who see totalitarianism as carried on behind a state façade. For example, in line with Friedrich and Brzezinski's position are Schapiro (1972) and Curtis (1979), who both stress the dictator and leadership, and Aron (1968) and Unger (1974) who stress the party. Alongside Arendt's view of totalitarianism operating behind the state is Buchheim (1968).

5 Arendt (1958: 394–5) notes, for example, that the 1936 Constitution was totally ignored in the Soviet Union and so too was the Weimar Constitution in Germany, which remained in place throughout Nazi rule.

6 Arendt (1958: 349–50) gives the examples of Stalin talking of 'the dying classes' and Hitler of 'the incurably sick' and 'those not fit to live', all of whom prophetically died.

7 See Gregor (1982: 163). Gregor's evidence is in line with Arendt's (1958: 308–9, fn 11) 'proof of the nontotalitarian nature of the fascist dictatorship' in Italy where she notes 'the surprisingly small number and the comparatively mild sentences meted out to political offenders' and that between 1926 and 1932 ('particularly active years') the special tribunals pronounced only seven death sentences and while many were imprisoned (though only 257 to sentences of ten or more years) or exiled, many of the political offenders arrested were found innocent.

7 Totalitarian regime: Nazi Germany

1 The five parties in the coalition were as follows: SPD (German Social Democratic Party), Centre Party (Zentrum), BVP (Bavarian People's Party), DDP (German Democratic Party), DVP (German People's Party) (Arends and Kümmel 2000: 205).

2 In the November 1932 election the Communist Party (KPD) had their best results ever with 17 per cent of the votes and the Social Democrats (SPD) won 20 per cent of the votes, with the centre parties losing heavily (Frei 1993: 32–3).

3 The concentration camps around Berlin were set up in March 1933, and in the city itself 'private prisons' were set up with the SS Columbia prison the most hellish of these torture chambers (Broszat 1968: 408).

4 Both the RNS and the Farm Law infuriated landowners. The one benefit for farmers was the lorry loads of unemployed brought as auxiliary agricultural workers, likened to a 'slave-market' at the time (Frei 1993: 6).

5 With the aim of overcoming the problems of both labour and supply shortages the Plan reversed much of the original policy directed at cutting unemployment. Wives who had been given marriage loans could now obtain work. The forty-hour work week was ignored (becoming a 48 hour week in August 1938). Restrictions on foreign workers were also reduced. (See Frei 1993: 77–80.) Approximately 1.4 million agricultural workers became employed in industry, particularly in armament production, by the outbreak of war (ibid.: 76–7). The high level of unemployment which had won votes for the NSDAP had by the outbreak of war been turned into a labour shortage of half a million workers (Schoenbaum 1967: 96).

6 At the start of the war, in September 1939, shortages of oil and of ferrous-based metals in Germany were acute (Klein 1959: 56–9).

7 Orders went out to kill Russian prisoners of war, the 'General Instructions for the Treatment of Political Commissars', the *Kommissarbefehl* (Jacobsen 1968: 519). In mid-July 1941 Himmler committed two SS brigades (a total of 11,000 men) – the *Eissatzgruppen* – to the operation. By 19 September, 85,000 Russians were dead. Just as the Eissatzgruppen began their operation, however, Hitler, though he had initially ruled against Russian labour being used within Germany, relaxed his position. The army was notified that half a million Russian prisoners of war were needed (Homze 1967: 74).

8 All other camps in the East, with the single exception of Lublin-Majdanek, had been set up solely for liquidation (Broszat 1968: 484).

9 The Green File contained the following statement: 'Many tens of millions of people in the industrial areas will become redundant and will either die or will have to emigrate to Siberia. Any attempts to save the population in these parts from death by starvation through the import of surpluses from the Black Earth Zone would be at the expense of supplies to Europe. It would undermine Germany's and Europe's power to resist the blockade. This must be clearly and absolutely understood.' (Homze 1967: 71).

10 See Homze 1967: 256, fn 57). Complete statistics on SS arrests of foreign workers during the war have never been found but they are available for the first half of 1944. During this time the SS arrested 19,000 Germans (for 'political and religious offences'), a further 13,000 for labour offences and nearly 204,000 foreign workers for similar offences (ibid.).

11 Even so Sauckel never came even close to achieving supremacy over labour. The army controlled drafting policies, the German Labour Front had control over the welfare and training of German workers, the Zentrale Planung had charge of distributing labour to industry, the Food Ministry had charge of agricultural labourers and Himmler, as SS Reichführer, had complete jurisdiction over worker security, concentration camp labour, and racial policies relating to workers (see Homze 1967: 305–6).

12 For expansion see, respectively: Landau (1992: 316); Homze (1967: 81 and passim); Jacobsen (1968); Burleigh and Wippermann (1991).

8 Totalitarian regime: Stalin's Soviet Union

1 For further discussion on the significance of the changes in 1926 see Bacon (1994: 45–6).

2 See Manning (1993: 117). 'Wrecking' was another word for economic sabotage, covering anything from 'incorrect use of equipment, failure to carry out capital repairs, reluctance to introduce new techniques, delays in installations of imported equipment, ordering equipment not corresponding to needs, failure to declare real productive capacities, frequent changing and poor drafting of specifications, dispersion of resources on multiple construction projects, extension of construction schedules, reduction of investment efficiency, disproportions among various workshops and putting into operation blast furnaces not completely finished' (Zaleski 1980, quoted in Manning 1993: 118).

3 See Siegelbaum (1992: 211–13). The three production shift did not survive past 1932 (ibid.: 213).

4 Conquest (1971: 324) estimates that the kulak families affected by collectivization approximated 10 million people. For comparisons of estimates of earlier works see Rummel (1990: 81–108).

5 Figures recently released, based on the 1939 census data, indicate that the death rate rose from an average of around 20 per 1,000 a year in 1925 (it was at 20.5 in 1932) to 37.7 per 1,000 in 1933. This rate represents around 2.75–3.0 million excess deaths for the year and these deaths were also accompanied by a dramatic fall in the birth rate (Wheatcroft 1993: 279–80). The places worst affected were the Ukraine, an area of the Lower Volga, and the North Caucasus, the centre of de-kulakization and the areas of the highest numbers of arrests and deportations.

6 The range of estimates is 985,000 to 2,863,000 deaths as a consequence of deportations and between 1,566,000 and 6,426,000 died in the camps or in transit to them (Rummel 1990: 95).

7 Though workers and managers, particularly those of peasant origin, formed the bulk of the victims, the most recent evidence confirms earlier views (Deutscher 1968; Conquest 1971, 1990) that party members suffered significantly more than non-party members, and especially those who had been members before 1921 (Getty and Chase 1993: 231–6). Vulnerability ran in direct proportion to seniority in the bureaucracy (ibid.: 237). The evidence also shows that while those working in the creative arts and scientific research were relatively safe, those working in the economic administration, the central party and state apparatus (with the exception of foreign affairs) and the military were the most vulnerable (ibid.: 239).

8 Conquest (1971: 708) estimates the number in jail or in the camps by the end of 1938 to be 8 million plus 1 million who were executed and a further 2 million who died in the camps between 1937 and 1938. Rather than the 7–15 million in prisons and the Gulag system by the end of the 1930s (Rummel 1990), Thurston (1993: 155) calculates on more recent data that at the outbreak of the Second World War there were only around 1.5 million people in the labour camps and a further 0.8 million in prisons or exile. By adding the special exiles to the figures, Wheatcroft (1993: 277) approximates Nove's estimate for 1939, giving 4 million people in the entire NKVD system.

9 With the Ezhovshchina taking place from September 1936 to 1938, this sudden change of economic pace has generally been put down to the effects of the Great Purges, aimed as they were at managers, engineers, technicians and administrators at both national and local levels. Based on fresh evidence, however, Manning (1993) has argued that the sharp drop in industrial production was as much a cause of the purges as their consequence.

10 With access to records made available since 1987, Khanin, a soviet economist specializing in finance, has argued that the economic crisis in Stalin's USSR was even worse than western observers suggested, putting the average rate of growth between 1928 and 1941 at only 3.2 per cent, actually below the long-run average for the Soviet Union between 1928 and 1987. This figure contrasts sharply with the official Soviet figures for 1928–41 of 13.9 per cent and even falls below conservative western estimates of 6.1 per cent. (See Harrison 1993: Tables 1 and 2.) Furthermore, on Khanin's analysis the entire economic growth achieved from 1928 to 1941 was actually concentrated on the years of the second Five Year Plan (1933–37). As Harrison (1993: 145) notes, this corresponds with Jasny's 'three "good" years'.

11 See Nove (1993a: 270–3). In the same volume (Getty and Manning 1993), Fitzpatrick (1993: 249) highlights the discovery of mass graves, for example at Kurapaty, and argues that more summary executions of people probably took place between 1936 and 1938 without entering the Gulag system.

9 Federal Germany: re-tracing a path to democracy

1 See Document, Schweitzer *et al.* (1995: 9). The Control Council was made up of the four Commanders-in-Chief of the four Allied countries, each with a political adviser.

2 For expansion see Harvey (1968: 267–83). Germany also contrasts with Italy. For details of the Resistance and the Italian government see Clark (1984: 302–19).

3 See Balfour (1992: 81 and 87–8). These agreements were made official at the Potsdam Conference, 17 July to 2 August 1945.

4 For statistics on resentment in Germany felt towards refugees and expellees see Merritt and Merritt (1970: 19–20).

5 See Merritt and Merritt (1970). These surveys came under the US High Commissioner for Germany, HICOG. HICOG surveys were carried out from 1949 to 1955 (Merritt and Merritt, 1980).

6 See Merritt and Merritt (1970: 53). The remaining 8 per cent declined to choose between these four opinions.

7 Ginsberg (1996: 98–9) also argues that part of the advantage of the presence of the Allies was that it gave the Germans someone other than themselves to blame when problems arose and that this drew opposed groups together such that 'Parliamentary democracy was strengthened in response to, and sometimes in protest against Allied demands' (ibid.: 98).

8 Roseman (2000), comparing the success of democracy after the two world wars argues that the major contrast between Germany after 1918 and after 1945 was the way in which the transition from war to peace was managed. Had events after 1918 been handled in a way similar to after 1945 then, he argues, the Weimar Constitution could have succeeded.

9 Another consequence was that NATO, the North Atlantic Treaty Organization, was set up in the spring of 1949 (Balfour 1992: 109).

10 Arrangements are such that the Federal Government has the potential to run in a way similar to the collective responsibility of the British Cabinet but may also be run more like the Presidential Cabinet of the American system, the actuality much dependent on the particular chancellor (Balfour 1992: 130).

11 Article 19 of the Basic Law makes clear that the basic rights contained within it cannot be amended in 'essence' (Basic Law 1991: 16). Amendment to the Basic Law requires consent of two-thirds of the Bundesrat and two-thirds of the Bundestag (Article 79).

12 For consistency, the wording is taken from Basic Law (1991: 17) but the December 1983 amendment, which adds under section (1) 'and use of their funds and for their assets', is removed. See Merkl (1963: 216) where the original 1949 version of the Basic Law is provided as Appendix II. The statutes promised under section (3) took until 1967 to set up (Nicholls 1995: 201).

13 The important point is that the British prime minister appoints the ministers, decides on the cabinet and can 'shuffle' it how and when he or she chooses. There are more constraints on the German chancellor. The weakest form of parliamentary system is the 'first among equals' (Sartori 1997: 102).

14 See Roseman (2000). The whole question of whether Germany after defeat in the Second World War constituted a break with the past or 'restoration' of traditional sources of economic and political power and traditional authoritarian values has been especially hotly debated by German historians.

10 Communism and its collapse: East Germany and the Russian Federation

1 Smirnov (2001: 518–19) argues that as a value 'democracy' in Soviet ideology and rhetoric goes back to western Marxism and means 'socialist'. There are clear parallels with Luxemburg's 'socialist democracy', outlined in Chapter 2.

2 Following the repercussions of the Algerian Rebellion of 1954, the Suez Crisis and Vietnam, in 1958, the Fourth Republic fell and was replaced by the Fifth Republic in 1958 (Harvey 1968: 308–20).

3 Examining the 1993 and 1995 elections Moser (2001) finds that the system, while weakening parties in general, in allowing independent candidates has brought greater benefits to some parties while undermining others, parties differing as to whether they benefited from PR or plurality, with few, most notably the Communist Party, CPRF, benefiting from both.

4 For examples of the buying of votes and other examples of misuse of political finance in political campaigning and wider corruption see Gelman (2001: 189–90). In addition to elections not always being fair, many important offices also remain appointed posts, particularly at regional level, even though such officials may have wide powers. Of those elected, questions as to whether they are accountable can also be raised in terms of promises made and instantly forgotten after election. (See Tolz 2000: 194–5.)

5 Brudny (2001: 173, fn 28) questions whether Putin did receive 50 per cent of the vote in the first round. Putin had gained advantage from his actions taken in launching a second Chechen war after bombs killed hundreds of people in Moscow shortly after Putin took office as prime minister (Rose 2001: 221–2).

6 Sapir (2002) stresses the need for rapid growth to continue for seven to ten years and argues that to achieve this, investment must increase, property rights must be secured, foreign trade must be developed, particularly with the European Union, and the state must develop a strategic development strategy working with the market.

7 An additional worry is that though there has been a selective crackdown on the oligarchs, an adverse consequence has been that the privately owned media has become far less critical. Furthermore, the price of newspapers has driven down circulation and more respected independent newspapers have been taken over or made financially dependent on oligarchs (Brown 2001b: 552). More positively, in February 2002, at a conference held in Moscow, a council on the freedom of the press was established and it was announced that the Union of Rightist Forces, SPS, had begun moves within the State Duma to limit the level of state control of the media (*Keesing's Record* 2002: 44631).

8 The United Russia party had been formally founded in December 2001 under the name of All-Russian Party of Unity and Fatherland (*Keesing's Record* 2001: 44526).

9 In general on the 'Washington consensus' (Gorbachev 1988: Foreword) see Klein and Pomer (2001) and, in particular, Arbatov (2001) who blames the West for failure to understand the Russian case as so different from Third World countries.

10 For this argument, applied to democracy in Africa, see Joseph 1997.

11 The struggle for modern democracy

1 See Stearns (1974: 171). Though unsuccessful in the 1840s, the ideas led to the wide expansion of male suffrage in 1884 and, eventually, to the Labour Party, a workers' party separate from continental social democracy.

2 For similar conclusions for democracies in Africa see O'Kane (2001).
3 See Harvey (1968: 267–84). The coalition lasted until 1947 when broken by the communists. In 1958, under de Gaulle's new constitution for the Fifth Republic the number of communist deputies fell from 145 to ten as a consequence of the change to single member districts (ibid.). Though the votes also dropped, in the 1962 election votes returned to over 4 million (Blondel and Drexel Godfrey 1968: 88). For the French Constitution of 1958 see Blondel and Drexel Godfrey ibid.: 194–216).

Bibliography

Almond, G. and Verba, S. (1965) *The Civic Culture*, Boston, MA: Little Brown and Co.

Anderson, M. L. (2000) *Practicing Democracy: Elections and Political Culture in Imperial Germany*, Princeton, NJ: Princeton University Press.

Andics, H. (1969) *Rule of Terror*, London: Constable.

Arbatov, G. (2001) 'Origins and Consequences of "Shock Therapy"', in L. R. Klein and M. Pomer (eds) *The New Russia Transition Gone Awry*, Stanford, CA: Stanford University Press.

Arblaster, A. (1994) *Democracy*, Milton Keynes: Open University Press.

Arends, F. and Kümmel, G. (eds) (2000) 'Germany: From Double Crisis to National Socialism', in D. Berg-Schlosser and J. Mitchell (eds) *Conditions of Democracy in Europe, 1919–39: Systematic Case Studies*, Basingstoke: Macmillan.

Arendt, H. (1958) *The Origins of Totalitarianism*, London: George Allen and Unwin.

Arendt, H. (1973) *On Revolution*, Harmondsworth: Penguin.

Aron, R. (1968) *Democracy and Totalitarianism*, London: Weidenfeld and Nicolson.

Bacon, E. (1994) *The Gulag at War: Stalin's Forced Labour System in the Light of the Archives*, London: Macmillan.

Balfour, M. (1992) *Germany: The Tides of Power*, London: Routledge.

Bank of Finland Institute for Economies in Transition (2003) 'Russian Economic Trends, 1992–2002', Sources: Goskomstat, Central Bank of Russia, IMF as reported in the *Russian Economy in Review*, http://www.bof.fi/bofit/eng/4ruec/index.stm

Barry, B. (1970) *Sociologists, Economists and Democracy*, London: Macmillan.

Bartolini, S. (2000) *The Political Mobilization of the European Left, 1860–1980: The Class Cleavage*, New York: Cambridge University Press.

Basic Law for the Federal Republic of Germany (1991) Wolfenbüttel: Roco-Druck GmbH.

Bawn, K. (1993) 'The Logic of Institutional Preferences: German Electoral Law as a Social Choice Outcome', *American Political Science Review* 37, 4: 965–89.

Beetham, D. (1985) *Max Weber and the Theory of Modern Politics*, Cambridge: Polity Press.

Beetham, D. (1987) *Bureaucracy*, Milton Keynes: Open University Press.

Beetham, D. (1999) *Democracy and Human Rights*, Cambridge: Polity Press.

Bendix, R. (1977) *Nation-building and Citizenship*, Berkeley, CA: University of California Press.

Berger, S. (2000) 'The Attempt at Democratization under Weimar', in J. Garrard, V. Tolz and R. White (eds) *European Democratization since 1800*, London: Macmillan.

Berins Collier, R. (1999) *Paths Toward Democracy: The Working Class and Elites in Western Europe and South America*, New York: Cambridge University Press.

Berman, S. (1997) 'Civil Society and the Collapse of the Weimar Republic', *World Politics* 49, 3: 401–29.

Bermeo, N. (1992) 'Democracy and the Lessons of Dictatorship', *Comparative Politics* 24, 3: 273–91.

Black, C. E. (1967) Review of Moore's 'Social Origins', *American Historical Review* 72: 1338.

Blondel, J. and Drexel Godfrey Jr., E. (1968) *The Government of France*, London: Macmillan.

Bollen, Kenneth A. (1991) 'Political Democracy: Conceptual and Measurement Traps', in A. Inkeles (ed.) *On Measuring Democracy: Its Consequences and Concomitants*, New Brunswick, NJ: Transaction Publishers.

Bradley, J. F. N. (1975) *Civil War in Russia 1917–20*, London: B. T. Batsford.

Breitman, R. (1992) 'The Final Solution', in G. Martel (ed.) *Modern Germany Reconsidered*, London: Routledge.

Broszat, M. (1966) *German National Socialism, 1919–1945*, Santa Barbara, CA: Clio Press.

Broszat, M. (1968) 'The Concentration Camps, 1933–45', in H. B. Krausnick, H. Buchheim, M. Broszat, and H-A. Jacobsen (eds) *Anatomy of the SS State*, London: Collins.

Broszat, M. (1981) *The Hitler State: The Foundation and Development of the Internal Structure of the Third Reich*, London: Longman.

Brown, A. (ed.) (2001a) *Contemporary Russian Politics: A Reader*, Oxford: Oxford University Press.

Brown, A. (2001b) 'Evaluating Russia's Democratization', in A. Brown (ed.) *Contemporary Russian Politics: A Reader*, Oxford: Oxford University Press.

Browning, C. R. (1992) *The Path to Genocide: Essays on Launching the Final Solution*, New York: Cambridge University Press.

Brudny, Y. M. (2001) 'Continuity or Change in Russian Electoral Patterns? The December 1999–March 2000 Electoral Cycle', in A. Brown (ed.) *Contemporary Russian Politics: A Reader*, Oxford: Oxford University Press.

Buchheim, H. (1968) *Totalitarian Rule: Its Nature and Characteristics*, Middletown, CN: Wesleyan University Press.

Bullock, A. (1993) *Hitler and Stalin: Parallel Lives*, London: Fontana.

Burawoy, M. (1989) 'Two Methods in Search of Science: Skocpol versus Trotsky', *Theory and Society* 18, 6: 759–805.

Burleigh, M. and Wippermann, W. (1991) *The Racial State: Germany 1933–1945*, Cambridge: Cambridge University Press.

Bury, J. P. T. (1970) *Napoleon III and the Second Empire*, London: English Universities Press.

Carr, E. H. (1966) *The Bolshevik Revolution 1917–23*, Vols. 1 and 2, Harmondsworth: Penguin.

Chirikova, A. and Lipina, N. (2001) 'Political Power and Political Stability in the Russian Regions', in A. Brown (ed.) *Contemporary Russian Politics: A Reader*, Oxford: Oxford University Press.

Clark, M. (1984) *Modern Italy, 1871–1982*, London: Longman.

Cobban, A. (1971) *Aspects of the French Revolution*, St Albans: Paladin.

Collier, D. and Levitsky, S. (1997) 'Democracy with Adjectives: Conceptual Innovation in Comparative Research', *World Politics* 49, 3: 430–51.

Conquest, R. (1971) *The Great Terror: Stalin's Purge of the Thirties*, Harmondsworth: Penguin.

Conquest, R. (1990) *The Great Terror: A Reassessment*, London: Hutchinson.

Conradt, D. P. (1989) *The German Polity*, Fourth Edition, New York: Longman.

Constitution of the United States, The (1997), Appendix in J. O. Wilson *American Government*, Boston, MA: Houghton Mifflin Co.

Crook, M. (1996) *Elections in the French Revolution: An Apprenticeship in Democracy, 1789–1799*, Cambridge: Cambridge University Press.

Curtis, M. (1979) *Totalitarianism*, New Brunswick, NJ: Transaction Books.

Dahl, R. A. (1971) *Polyarchy: Participation and Opposition*, New Haven: Yale University Press.

Dahl, R. A. (1989) *Democracy and its Critics*, New Haven: Yale University Press.

Dahrendorf, R. (1968) *Society and Democracy in Germany*, London: Weidenfeld and Nicolson.

Dallin, D. J. and Nicolaevsky, B. I. (1948) *Forced Labour in Soviet Russia*, London: Hollis and Carter.

Daniels, R. V. (1993) *The End of Communist Revolution*, London: Routledge.

Declaration of Independence (1997) 'In Congress, July 4, 1776: The Unanimous Declaration of the Thirteen United States of America', Appendix in J. O. Wilson *American Government*, Boston, MA: Houghton Mifflin Co.

Deutscher, I. (1968) *Stalin: A Political Biography*, Harmondsworth: Penguin.

Di Palma, G. (1990) *To Craft Democracies: An Essay on Democratic Transitions*, Berkeley, CA: University of California Press.

Diamond, L. (1994) 'Introduction: Political Culture and Democracy', in L. Diamond (ed.) *Political Culture and Democracy in Developing Countries*, Boulder, CO: Lynne Rienner.

Diamond, L. (1999) *Developing Democracy: Toward Consolidation*, Baltimore: Johns Hopkins University Press.

Diamond, L., Linz, J. and Lipset, S. M. (1989) 'Preface' in L. Diamond, J. Linz and S. M. Lipset (eds) *Democracy in Developing Countries: Latin America*, Boulder, CO: Lynne Rienner.

Dobry, M. (2000) 'France: An Ambiguous Survival', in D. Berg-Schlosser and J. Mitchell (eds) *Conditions of Democracy in Europe, 1919–39: Systematic Case Studies*, Basingstoke: Macmillan.

Dunlop, J. B. (2001) 'Sifting Through the Rubble of the Yeltsin Years', in A. Brown (ed.) *Contemporary Russian Politics: A Reader*, Oxford: Oxford University Press.

Eisenberg Vichniac, J. (1998) 'Religious Toleration and Jewish Emancipation in France and Germany', in T. Skocpol (ed.) *Democracy, Revolution and History*, Ithaca, NY: Cornell University Press.

Fehér, F. (1987) *The Frozen Revolution: an Essay on Jacobinism*, Cambridge: Cambridge University Press.

Femia, J. V. (1972) 'Barrington Moore and the Preconditions for Democracy', *British Journal of Political Science* 2: 21–46.

Feuer, L. S. (ed.) (1969) *Marx and Engels: Basic Writings on Politics and Philosophy*, London: Fontana/Collins.

Fischer, M. E. (1996) (ed.) *Establishing Democracies*, Boulder, CO: Westview Press.

Fitzpatrick, S. (1993) 'The Impact of the Great Purges on Soviet Elites: A Case Study from Moscow and Leningrad Telephone Directories of the 1930s', in J. A. Getty and R. T. Manning (eds) *Stalinist Terror: New Perspectives*, Cambridge: Cambridge University Press.

Fleming, G. (1986) *Hitler and the Final Solution*, Oxford: Oxford University Press.

Foord, A. S. (1964) *His Majesty's Opposition 1714–1830*, Oxford: Clarendon.

Frei, N. (1993) *National Socialist Rule in Germany: The Führer State, 1933–1945*, Oxford: Blackwell.

Friedrich, C. J. and Brzezinski, Z. K. (1965) *Totalitarian Dictatorship and Autocracy*, Cambridge, MA: Harvard University Press.

Gallie, W. B. (1956) 'Essentially Contested Concepts', *Proceedings of the Aristotelian Society*, 56, London: Harrison and Sons.

Gasiorowski, M. J. (1991) 'The Political Regimes Project', in A. Inkeles (ed.) *On Measuring Democracy: Its Consequences and Concomitants*, New Brunswick, N J: Transaction Publishers.

Gelman, V. (2001) 'The Iceberg of Russian Political Finance', in A. Brown (ed.) *Contemporary Russian Politics: A Reader*, Oxford: Oxford University Press.

Getty J. A. and Chase, W. (1993) 'Patterns of Repression among the Soviet Elite in the Late 1930s: A Bibliographical Approach' in J. A. Getty and R. T. Manning (eds) *Stalinist Terror: New Perspectives*, Cambridge: Cambridge University Press.

Getty, J. A. and Manning, R. T. (eds) (1993) *Stalinist Terror: New Perspectives*, Cambridge: Cambridge University Press.

Geyer, M. (1984) 'The State in National Socialist Germany', in C. Bright and S. Harding (eds) *Statemaking and Social Movements*, Ann Arbor: University of Michigan Press.

Gill, G. (1990) *The Origins of the Stalinist Political System*, Cambridge: Cambridge University Press.

Gill, G. and Markwick, R. D. (2000) *Russia's Stillborn Democracy? From Gorbachev to Yeltsin*, Oxford: Oxford University Press.

Ginsberg, R. H. (1996) 'Germany: Into the Stream of Democracy', in M. E. Fischer (ed.) *Establishing Democracies*, Boulder, CO: Westview Press.

Gorbachev, M. (1988) *Perestroika: New Thinking for Our Country and the World*, London: Fontana/Collins.

Gould, R. V. (1995) *Insurgent Identities: Class Community and Protest in Paris from 1848 to the Commune*, Chicago: University of Chicago Press.

Gregor, A. J. (1982) 'Fascism's Philosophy of Violence and the Concept of Terror', in D. C. Rapoport and Y. Alexander (eds) *The Morality of Terrorism*, New York: Pergamon Press.

Gustafson, T. (1999) *Capitalism Russian-style*, Cambridge: Cambridge University Press.

Hahn, H. J. (2001) *The 1848 Revolutions in German-speaking Europe*, Harlow: Longman.

Hampson, N. (1986) 'From Regeneration to Terror: the Ideology of the French Revolution', in N. O'Sullivan (ed.) *Terrorism, Ideology and Revolution*, Brighton: Harvester Wheatsheaf.

Harrison, M. (1993) 'Soviet Economic Growth Since 1928: The Alternative Statistics of G I Khanin', *Europe-Asia Studies* 45, 1: 141–67.

Harvey, D. J. (1968) *France since the Revolution*, New York: The Free Press, Macmillan.

Hayward, J. (1991) *After the French Revolution: Six Critics of Democracy and Nationalism*, London: Harvester Wheatsheaf.

Held, D. (1996) *Models of Democracy*, Cambridge: Polity Press.

Herbert, U. (1994) 'Labor as Spoils of Conquest, 1933–1945', in D. F. Crew (ed.) *Nazism and German Society*, London: Routledge.

Hewitt, C. (1977) 'The Effect of Political Democracy and Social Democracy on Equality in Industrial Societies: A Cross National Comparison', *American Political Science Review* 42: 450–64.

Hiden, J. and Farquharson, J. (1983) *Explaining Hitler's Germany: Historians and The Third Reich*, London: Batsford.

Hill, C. (1969) *The Century of Revolution, 1603–1714*, London: Sphere Books.

Homze, E. L. (1967) *Foreign Labor in Nazi Germany*. Princeton, NJ: Princeton University Press.

Huskey, E. (2001a) 'Democracy and Institutional Design in Russia', in A. Brown (ed.) *Contemporary Russian Politics: A Reader*, Oxford: Oxford University Press.

Huskey, E. (2001b) 'Overcoming the Yeltsin Legacy: Vladimir Putin and Russian Political Reform', in A. Brown (ed.) *Contemporary Russian Politics: A Reader*, Oxford: Oxford University Press.

Inglehart, R. (1988) 'The Renaissance of Political Culture', *American Political Science Review* 82, 4: 1203–30.

Jacobsen, H-A. (1968) 'The *Kommissarbefehl* and Mass Executions of Soviet Russian Prisoners of War', in H. B. Krausnick, H. Buchheim, M. Broszat, and H-A. Jacobsen, *Anatomy of the SS State*, London: Collins.

James, H. J. (1987) *The German Slump: Politics and Economics 1924–1936*, Oxford: Clarendon Press.

Jasny, N. (1961) *Soviet Industrialization*, Chicago: Chicago University Press.

Joseph, R. (1997) 'Democratization in Africa after 1989: Comparative and Theoretical Perspectives', *Comparative Politics* 29, 3: 363–82.

Kahn, J. (2001) 'What is the New Russian Federalism?', in A. Brown (ed.) *Contemporary Russian Politics: A Reader*, Oxford: Oxford University Press.

Kaiser, D. E. (1992) 'Hitler and the Coming of War', in G. Martel (ed.) *Modern Germany Reconsidered*, London: Routledge.

Keesing's Record of World Events (2001–2), London and Harlow: Longman.

Kershaw, I. (1989) *The Nazi Dictatorship: Problems and Perspectives of Dictatorship*, London: Edward Arnold.

King, G., Keohane, R. and Verba, S. (1994) *Designing Social Inquiry: Scientific Inference in Qualitative Research*, Princeton, NJ: Princeton University Press.

Kirchheimer, O. (1966) 'The Transformation of the Western European Party System', in J. LaPalombara and M. Weiner (eds) *Political Parties and Political Development*, Princeton, NJ: Princeton University Press.

Klein, B. H. (1959) *Germany's Economic Preparations for War*, Cambridge, MA: Harvard University Press.

Klein, L. R. and Pomer, M. (eds) (2001) *The New Russia Transition Gone Awry*, Stanford, CA: Stanford University Press.

Kommers, D. P. (1995) 'Basic Rights and Constitutional Review', in C-C. Schweitzer, D. Karsten, R. Spencer, R. Taylor Cole, D. Kommers and A. Nicholls (eds) *Politics and Government in Germany, 1944–1994: Basic Documents*, Providence, RI: Berghahn Books.

Kotz, D. M. with Weir, F. (1997) *Revolution from Above: The Demise of the Soviet System*, London: Routledge.

Lakatos, I. (1978) *The Methodology of the Scientific Research Programme*, Cambridge: Cambridge University Press.

Landau, R. S. (1992) *The Nazi Holocaust*, London: I. B. Tauris.

Lepsius, M. R. (1978) 'From Fragmented Party Democracy to Government by Emergency Decree and National Socialist Takeover: Germany', in J. J. Linz and A. Stepan (eds) *The Breakdown of Democratic Regimes: Europe*, Baltimore: Johns Hopkins University Press.

Levytsky, B. (1972) *The Uses of Terror: The Soviet Secret Police 1917–70*, New York: Coward, McCann and Geohegan.

Lewin, M. (1967) *Russian Peasants and Soviet Power: A Study of Collectivization*, London: George Allen and Unwin.

Lewin, M. (1985) *The Making of the Soviet System: Essays in the Social History of Interwar Russia*, New York: Pantheon.

Lieberson, S. (1992) 'Small N's and Big Conclusions: an Examination of the Reasoning in Comparative Studies Based on a Small Number of Cases', in C. C. Ragin and H. S. Becker *What is a Case? Exploring the Foundations of Social Enquiry*, New York: Cambridge University Press.

Lijphart, A. (1971) 'Comparative Politics and the Comparative Method', *American Political Science Review* 65: 682–93.

Lindemann, A. S. (1991) *The Jew Accused: Three Anti-Semitic Affairs (Dreyfus, Beilus, Frank) 1894–1915*, Cambridge: Cambridge University Press.

Lindemann, A. S. (1997) *Esau's Tears: Modern Anti-Semitism and the Rise of the Jews*, Cambridge: Cambridge University Press.

Linz, J. J. (1978) *Breakdown of Democratic Regimes: Crisis, Breakdown, and Reequilibration*, Baltimore: Johns Hopkins University Press.

Lipset, S. M. (1963) *Political Man*, London: Mercury.

Locke, J. (1988) *Two Treatises of Government*, Cambridge: Cambridge University Press.

Lowenthal, D. (1968) Review of Moore's 'Social Origins', *History and Theory* 7: 257–78.

Luxemburg, R. (1967) *The Russian Revolution and Marxism or Leninism?*, Ann Arbor: University of Michigan Press.

Madison, J. (1997a) *The Federalist, No. 10, November 22, 1787*, Appendix in J. O. Wilson *American Government*, Boston, MA: Houghton Mifflin Co.

Madison, J. (1997b) *The Federalist, No. 51, February 6, 1788*, Appendix in J. O. Wilson *American Government*, Boston, MA: Houghton Mifflin Co.

Malle, S. (1985) *The Economic Organisation of War Communism, 1918–21*, Cambridge: Cambridge University Press.

Manning, R. T. (1993) 'The Soviet Economic Crisis of 1936–1940 and the Great Purges', in J. A. Getty and R. T. Manning (eds) *Stalinist Terror: New Perspectives*, Cambridge: Cambridge University Press.

Marsh, D. (1983) *Pressure Politics: Interest Groups in Britain*, London: Junction Books.

Marx, K. (1964) *The Eighteenth Brumaire of Louis Bonaparte*, New York: International Publishers.

Mawdsley, E. (1987) *The Russian Civil War*, Boston: Allen and Unwin.

McKenzie, R. (1963) *British Political Parties: The Distribution of Power within the Conservative and Labour Parties*, London: Mercury Books.

Melotti, U. (1977) *Marx and the Third World*, London: Macmillan.

Merkl, P. H. (1963) *The Origin of the West German Republic*, New York: Oxford University Press.

Merritt, A. J. and Merritt, R. L. (eds) (1970) *Public Opinion in Occupied Germany: The OMGUS Surveys, 1945–1949*, Urbana: University of Illinois Press.

Merritt, A. J. and Merritt, R. L. (eds) (1980) *Public Opinion in Semisovereign Germany: The HICOG Surveys, 1949–1955*, Urbana: University of Illinois Press.

Mill, J. S. (1967) *A System of Logic*, London: Longmans, Green and Co.

Mills, C. W. (1956) *The Power Elite*, New York: Oxford University Press.

Mills, C. W. (1963) *The Marxists*, Harmondsworth: Penguin.

Mills, C. W. (1970) *The Sociological Imagination*, Harmondsworth: Penguin.

Milward, A. S. (1965) *The German Economy at War*, London: The Athlone Press, University of London.

Montesquieu, Baron de (1949) *The Spirit of the Laws*, New York: Hafner Publishing Company.

Moore, B. Jr. (1969) *Social Origins of Dictatorship and Democracy: Lord and Peasant in the Making of the Modern World*, Harmondsworth: Penguin.

Moore, B. Jr. (1978) *Injustice: The Social Bases of Obedience and Revolt*, London: Macmillan.

Moser, R. G. (2001) 'The Impact of Parliamentary Electoral Systems in Russia', in A. Brown (ed.) *Contemporary Russian Politics: A Reader*, Oxford: Oxford University Press.

Nettl, P. (1969) *Rosa Luxemburg*, London: Oxford University Press.

Nicholas, H. G. (1950) *The American Revolution*, Harmondsworth: Penguin.

Nicholls, A. (1995) 'Political Parties', in C-C. Schweitzer, D. Karsten, R. Spencer, R. Taylor Cole, D. Kommers and A. Nicholls (eds) *Politics and Government in Germany, 1944–1994: Basic Documents*, Providence: Berghahn Books.

Noakes, J. (1986) 'The Origins, Structure and Functions of Nazi Terror', in N. O'Sullivan (ed.) *Terrorism, Ideology and Revolution*, Brighton: Harvester Wheatsheaf.

Nove, A. (1993a) 'Victims of Stalinism: How Many?', in J. A. Getty and R. T. Manning (eds) *Stalinist Terror: New Perspectives*, Cambridge: Cambridge University Press.

Nove, A. (1993b) 'Stalin and Stalinism – Some Introductory Thoughts', in A. Nove (ed.) *The Stalin Phenomenon*, London: Weidenfeld and Nicolson.

O'Donnell, G. and Schmitter, P. (1989) *Transitions from Authoritarian Rule: Tentative Conclusions about Uncertain Democracies*, Baltimore: Johns Hopkins University Press.

O'Kane, R. H. T. (1991) *The Revolutionary Reign of Terror: The Role of Violence in Political Change*, Aldershot: Edward Elgar.

O'Kane, R. H. T. (1993) 'The Ladder of Abstraction: The Purpose of Comparison and the Practice of Comparing African Coups d'État', *Journal of Theoretical Politics* 5, 2: 169–93.

O'Kane, R. H. T. (1995) 'The National Causes of State Construction in France, Russia and China', *Political Studies* 43, 1: 2–21.

O'Kane, R. H. T. (1996) *Terror, Force and States: The Path from Modernity*, Cheltenham: Edward Elgar.

O'Kane, R. H. T. (2001) 'Interactive Society and Democracy: Civil Society and Pluralism in Africa Revisited', *Democratization* 8, 3: 129–48.

Ostrow, J. M. (2002) 'Conflict-management in Russia's Federal Institutions', *Post-Soviet Affairs* 18, 1: 49–70.

Paine, T. (1989) *Thomas Paine: Political Writings* (ed. B. Kuklick), Cambridge: Cambridge University Press.

Peregudov, S. (2001) 'The Oligarchical Model of Russian Corporatism', in A. Brown (ed.) *Contemporary Russian Politics: A Reader*, Oxford: Oxford University Press.

Pulzer, P. (1992) *Jews and the German State: The Political History of a Minority, 1848–1933*, Oxford: Blackwell.

Putnam, R. D. (1993) *Making Democracy Work: Civic Traditions in Modern Italy*, Princeton, NJ: Princeton University Press.

Rakowska-Harmstone, T. (2000) 'Post-Communist East-Central Europe: Dilemmas of Democratization', in J. Garrard, V. Tolz and R. White (eds) *European Democratization since 1800*, London: Macmillan.

Reddaway, P. (2002) 'Is Putin's Power More Formal than Real?', *Post-Soviet Affairs* 18, 1: 31–40.

Reddaway, P. and Glinski, D. (2001) *The Tragedy of Russia's Reforms: Market Bolshevism against Democracy*, Washington DC: United States Institute of Peace Press.

Reiman, M. (1987) *The Birth of Stalinism: The USSR on the Eve of the 'Second Revolution'*, London: I. B. Tauris.

Remington, T. F. (1998) 'Political Conflict and Institutional Design: Paths of Party Development in Russia', in J. Löwenhardt (ed.) *Part Politics in Post-Communist Russia*, London: Frank Cass.

Rigby, T. H. (1979) *Lenin's Government: Sovnarkom 1917–22*, Cambridge: Cambridge University Press.

Rittersporn, G. T. (1993) 'The Omnipresent Conspiracy: On Soviet Imagery of Politics and Social Relations in the 1930s', in J. A. Getty and R. T. Manning (eds) *Stalinist Terror: New Perspectives*, Cambridge: Cambridge University Press.

Robinson, N. (2003) 'The Politics of Russia's Partial Democracy', *Political Studies Review* 1, 2: 149–66.

Rose, R. (2001) 'How Floating Parties Frustrate Democratic Accountability: A Supply-side View of Russia's Elections', in A. Brown (ed.) *Contemporary Russian Politics: A Reader*, Oxford: Oxford University Press.

Roseman, M. (2000) 'Restoration and Stability: The Creation of a Stable Democracy in the Federal Republic of Germany', in J. Garrard, V. Tolz and R. White (eds) *European Democratization since 1800*, London: Macmillan.

Rueschemeyer, D., Huber Stephens, E. and Stephens, J. D. (1992) *Capitalist Development and Democracy*, Chicago: Chicago University Press.

Rummel, R. J. (1990) *Lethal Politics: Soviet Genocide and Mass Murder since 1917*, New Brunswick, NJ: Transaction Publishers.

Rutland, P. and Kogan, N. (2001) 'The Russian Mafia: Between Hype and Reality', in A. Brown (ed.) *Contemporary Russian Politics: A Reader*, Oxford: Oxford University Press.

Sakwa, R. (1988) *Soviet Communists in Power: a Study of Moscow During the Civil War, 1918–21*, London: Macmillan.

Sakwa, R. (1998) *Soviet Politics in Perspective*, Second Edition, London: Routledge.

Sapir, J. (2002) 'Russia's Economic Rebound: Lessons and Future Directions', *Post-Soviet Affairs* 18, 1: 1–30.

Sartori, G. (1970) 'Concept Misformation in Comparative Politics', *American Political Science Review* 64: 1033–53.

Sartori, G. (1976) *Parties and Party Systems: A Framework for Analysis*, New York: Cambridge University Press.

Sartori, G. (1984) 'Guidelines for Concept Analysis', in G. Sartori (ed.) *Social Science Concepts: A Systematic Analysis*, Beverly Hills, CA: Sage.

Sartori, G. (1987) *The Theory of Democracy Revisited*, Chatham, NJ: Chatham House.

Sartori, G. (1991) 'Comparing and Miscomparing', *Journal of Theoretical Politics* 3: 243–57.

Sartori, G. (1994a) 'Compare Why and How: Comparing, Miscomparing and The Comparative Method', in M. Dogan and A. Kazancigil *Comparing Nations: Concepts, Strategies, Substance*, Oxford: Basil Blackwell.

Sartori, G. (1994b)'The Background of "Pluralism" ', Paper presented at the International Political Science Association World Conference, Berlin, 1994.

Sartori, G. (1997) *Comparative Constitutional Engineering: An Inquiry into Structures, Incentives and Outcomes*, Basingstoke: Macmillan.

Schapiro, L. (1972) *Totalitarianism*, London: The Pall Mall Press.

Schoenbaum, D. (1967) *Hitler's Social Revolution: Class and Status in Nazi Germany 1933–1939*, London: Weidenfeld and Nicolson.

Schumpeter, J. A. (1952) *Capitalism, Socialism and Democracy*, London: Unwin University Books.

Schweitzer, C-C. (1995) 'Germany Reunited 1989 – Her First Successful Revolution, and a Peaceful One', in C-C. Schweitzer, D. Karsten, R. Spencer, R. Taylor Cole, D. Kommers and A. Nicholls (eds) *Politics and Government in Germany, 1944–1994: Basic Documents*, Providence, RI: Berghahn Books.

Schweitzer, C-C., Karsten, D., Spencer, R., Taylor Cole, R., Kommers, D. and Nicholls, A. (eds) (1995) *Politics and Government in Germany, 1944–1994: Basic Documents*. Providence, RI: Berghahn Books.

Sewell, W. H. (1994) 'Ideologies and Social Revolutions: Reflections on the French Case', in T. Skocpol *Social Revolutions in the Modern World*, New York: Cambridge University Press.

Siegelbaum, L. H. (1992) *Soviet State and Society between Revolutions, 1918–1929*, Cambridge: Cambridge University Press.

Simonia, N. (2001) 'Economic Interests and Political Power in Post-Soviet Russia', in A. Brown (ed.) *Contemporary Russian Politics: A Reader*, Oxford: Oxford University Press.

Skocpol, T. (1979) *States and Social Revolutions: A Comparative Analysis of France, Russia and China*, New York: Cambridge University Press.

Skocpol, T. (1984) 'Emerging Agendas and Recurrent Strategies in Historical Sociology', in T. Skocpol (ed.) *Vision and Method in Historical Sociology*, New York: Cambridge University Press.

Smelser, N. (1959) *Social Change in the Industrial Revolution: An Application of Theory to the British Cotton Industry*, Chicago: University of Chicago Press.

Smirnov, W. V. (2001) 'Democratization in Russia: Achievements and Problems', in A. Brown (ed.) *Contemporary Russian Politics: A Reader*, Oxford: Oxford University Press.

Smith, D. (1983) *Barrington Moore: Violence, Morality and Political Change*, London: Macmillan.

Spencer, M. E. (1979) 'Marx on the State: The Events in France between 1848 and 1850', *Theory and Society* 7, 1 and 2: 167–98.

Spencer, R. (1995) 'The Origins of the Federal Republic of Germany, 1944–1949', in C-C. Schweitzer, D. Karsten, R. Spencer, R. Taylor Cole, D. Kommers and A. Nicholls (eds) *Politics and Government in Germany, 1944–1994: Basic Documents*, Providence, RI: Berghahn Books.

Stearns, P. N. (1974) *The Revolutions of 1848*, London: Weidenfeld and Nicolson.

Steinberg, J. (1991) *All or Nothing: The Axis and the Holocaust 1941–43*, London: Routledge.

Stinchcombe, A. (1978) *Theoretical Methods in Social History*, New York: Academic Press.

Sutherland, D. M. G. (1985) *France 1789–1815: Revolution and Counterrevolution*, London: Fontana Press.

Swianiewicz, S. (1965) *Forced Labour and Economic Development: An Enquiry into the Experience of Soviet Industrialization*, London: Oxford University Press.

Tawney, R. H. (1938) *Religion and the Rise of Capitalism*, Harmondsworth: Penguin.

Thurston, R. (1993) 'The Stakhanovite Movement: The Background to the Great Terror in the Factories, 1935–1938', in J. A. Getty and R. T. Manning (eds) *Stalinist Terror: New Perspectives*, Cambridge: Cambridge University Press.

Titmuss, R. M. (1963) *Essays on 'the Welfare State'*, London: Unwin University Press.

Tocqueville, A. de (1862) *Democracy in America: The Republic of the United States of America, and its Political Institutions, Reviewed and Examined*, New York: A. S. Barnes and Co.

Tocqueville, A. de (1966) *The Ancien Régime and the French Revolution*, Manchester: Fontana/Collins.

Tolz, V. (2000) 'Russia's Democratic Transition and its Challenges', in J. Garrard, V. Tolz and R. White (eds) *European Democratization since 1800*, London: Macmillan.

Tombs, R. (1996) *France 1814–1914*, London: Longman.

Ulam, A. B. (1969) *Lenin and the Bolsheviks: The Intellectual and Political History of the Triumph of Communism in Russia*, London: Fontana/Collins.

Unger, A. L. (1974) *The Totalitarian Party: Party and People in Nazi Germany and Soviet Russia*, Cambridge: Cambridge University Press.

Vanhanen, T. (1997) *Prospects of Democracy: A Study of 172 Countries*, London and New York: Routledge.

Viola, L. (1993) 'The Second Coming: Class Enemies in the Soviet Countryside, 1927–1935', in J. A. Getty and R. T. Manning (eds) *Stalinist Terror: New Perspectives*, Cambridge: Cambridge University Press.

Walton, J. (1992) 'Making the Theoretical Case', in C. C. Ragin and H. S. Becker *What is a Case? Exploring the Foundations of Social Enquiry*, New York: Cambridge University Press.

Weber, M. (1964) *The Theory of Social and Economic Organization* (ed. T. Parsons), New York: The Free Press.

Weber, M. (1991) *The Protestant Ethic and the Spirit of Capitalism*, London: HarperCollins Academic.

Weiner, J. (1975) 'The Barrington Moore Thesis and its Critics', *Theory and Society* 2: 301–30.

Weitz, E. D. (1997) *Creating German Communism, 1890–1990: From Popular Protests to Socialist State*, Princeton, NJ: Princeton University Press.

Wheatcroft, S. G. (1993) 'More Light on the Scale of Repression and Excess Mortality in the Soviet Union in the 1930s', in J. A. Getty and R. T. Manning (eds) *Stalinist Terror: New Perspectives*, Cambridge: Cambridge University Press.

Wick, D. (1996) 'The Court Nobility and the French Revolution: The Example of the Society of Thirty', in P. Jones (ed.) *The French Revolution in Social and Political Perspective*, London: Arnold.

Williams, F. W. (1970) 'Foreword', in A. J. Merritt and R. L. Merritt (eds) *Public Opinion in Occupied Germany: The OMGUS Surveys, 1945–1949*, Urbana: University of Illinois Press.

Wilson, J. O. (1997) *American Government*, Boston, MA: Houghton Mifflin Co.

Wolf, E. R. (1973) *Peasant Wars of the Twentieth Century*, London: Faber and Faber.

Zaleski, E. (1980) *Stalinist Planning for Economic Growth, 1933–1952*, Chapel Hill, NC: University of North Carolina Press and London: Macmillan.

Index

Lightning Source UK Ltd.
Milton Keynes UK
03 November 2010

162324UK00001B/14/P